Once in a while, a book comes along that's truly accessible to a diverse audience in second language education and that moves the field forward by exploring, in-depth, under-investigated actual (and in this case, virtual) classroom-based and theoretically informed effective pedagogies. Julian Chen's book provides deep insights into the use of SL over a decade spanning teaching and research practices, and the chapters collectively take readers on an exciting journey into the world of technology-mediated, meaningful, and fun language teaching and learning. Much needed and highly recommended!

Rashi Jain, *Associate Professor in the Academic English Language Program, Montgomery College, USA*

A solid pedagogical guide to the ins and outs of task-based-oriented learning in Second Life. Julian Chen has managed with an easy-to-follow story-telling approach to outline their experiences working with language students in a virtual world setting – many of which I personally had the pleasure of observing or learning about while Julian was in the process of conducting their research. I can wholeheartedly and especially recommend this book to any and all educators who share a passion for virtual world language learning and teaching. Many of their insights are indispensable and undoubtedly useful as those are based on the first-hand experiences with language students and educators in-world.

Kip Boahn, *Creator of Virtlantis in Second Life, Co-owner of Oxford School for English, Freelance English Teacher*

Julian Chen has produced an excellent account of their experiences with Second Life as an instructional platform and as their research focus. Chen's thorough and pedagogically sound lesson outlines will appeal to educators curious about the platform's potential as an instructional tool. Readers pursuing research in Second Life or other 3D MUVEs will profit from their evidence-based approach and the wealth of resources they provide. Finally, Chen's friendly and approachable writing style make this book a terrific resource for Second Life beginners and experts alike. There is truly something here for everyone interested in Second Life within an educational context.

Jessamine Cooke-Plagwitz, *Associate Professor of German and Applied Linguistics, Northern Illinois University, USA*

This volume provides a unique window into the nature and potential of the virtual world Second Life in foreign language education. Based on the author's wealth of experience as a researcher and language educator, this accessible publication brings together theory-informed insight with sound practical advice. This timely volume will doubtless prove invaluable to a wide range of practitioners and all those with an interest in the field of computer-assisted language learning.

Mark Peterson, *Associate Professor of Foreign Language Acquisition & Education, Kyoto University, Japan*

SECOND LIFE AS A VIRTUAL PLAYGROUND FOR LANGUAGE EDUCATION

This insightful book offers language teachers and teachers in training the opportunity to delve into 3D virtual worlds and see the benefits they provide for immersive language teaching and learning. Based on a decade of experience teaching and researching in Second Life (SL), Chen demystifies the dos and don'ts of SL teaching and research, whilst vividly walking readers through each step of the journey.

Written in an accessible, jargon-free, and personalised tone, the book is divided into three parts. Part I builds the foundation in SL research, task-based language teaching (TBLT), and understanding fundamental skills for SL teaching. Part II showcases the author's SL teaching blog that generously unveils their task-based, SL-enabled lessons, participant observations, critical reflections, and lessons learned from each SL session. Part III is complete with the highlights of the author's SL research and hands-on resources and tips for readers. Each chapter also features a "Checkpoint" section to gauge reader understanding of chapter content, followed by a "Your Task" section to promote learning by doing in SL.

Teachers and curriculum designers will find the well-detailed and guided lesson planning useful when starting their first SL class. Graduate students and novice researchers will also find the systematically recorded data collection helpful for their SL research.

Julian Chen (they/them) is an Associate Professor of Applied Linguistics and TESOL, and the Coordinator of Asian Languages Program at Curtin University, Australia. Their research synergises technology-enhanced language learning, task-based language teaching, 3D virtual learning, netnography, inclusive education, and action research.

SECOND LIFE AS A VIRTUAL PLAYGROUND FOR LANGUAGE EDUCATION

A Practical Guide for Teaching and Research

JULIAN CHEN

LONDON AND NEW YORK

Designed cover image: Getty Images

First published 2023
by Routledge
4 Park Square, Milton Park, Abingdon, Oxon OX14 4RN

and by Routledge
605 Third Avenue, New York, NY 10158

Routledge is an imprint of the Taylor & Francis Group, an informa business

© 2023 Julian Chen

The right of Julian Chen to be identified as author of this work has been asserted in accordance with sections 77 and 78 of the Copyright, Designs and Patents Act 1988.

All rights reserved. No part of this book may be reprinted or reproduced or utilised in any form or by any electronic, mechanical, or other means, now known or hereafter invented, including photocopying and recording, or in any information storage or retrieval system, without permission in writing from the publishers.

Trademark notice: Product or corporate names may be trademarks or registered trademarks, and are used only for identification and explanation without intent to infringe.

British Library Cataloguing-in-Publication Data
A catalogue record for this book is available from the British Library

ISBN: 9780367716172 (hbk)
ISBN: 9780367716189 (pbk)
ISBN: 9781003152958 (ebk)

DOI: 10.4324/9781003152958

Typeset in Trade Gothic
by KnowledgeWorks Global Ltd.

To Jase

CONTENTS

Pxiv   LIST OF TABLES

Pxvi   PREFACE– FLASHBACK TO MY 3D TEACHING AND RESEARCH JOURNEY

P1   PART I   BEFORE WE TAKE OFF

P2   CHAPTER 1
LANGUAGE TEACHING AND LEARNING IN SECOND LIFE

P26   CHAPTER 2
TASK-BASED LANGUAGE TEACHING IN SECOND LIFE

P52   CHAPTER 3
SECOND LIFE FEATURES AND LOGISTICS

P83 **PART II   LET'S GET OUR HANDS DIRTY**

P84 CHAPTER 4
COURSE PREPARATION – A BUMPY ROAD
―

P90 CHAPTER 5
PRETEST: A ROLLERCOASTER RIDE
―

P98 CHAPTER 6
LESSON 1 (GREETINGS)
―

P106 CHAPTER 7
LESSON 2 (FOOD PART 1)
―

P112 CHAPTER 8
LESSON 2 (FOOD PART 2)
―

P120 **CHAPTER 9**
LESSON 2 (FOOD PART 3)
—

P134 **CHAPTER 10**
LESSON 2 (FOOD FINAL)
—

P146 **CHAPTER 11**
LESSON 3 (HOLIDAY/ FESTIVAL/ CLOTHING PART 1)
—

P154 **CHAPTER 12**
LESSON 3 (HOLIDAY/ FESTIVAL/ CLOTHING PART 2)
—

P168 **CHAPTER 13**
LESSON 4 (MUSIC)
—

P176 **CHAPTER 14**
LESSON 5 (SPORTS)

P188 **CHAPTER 15**
LESSON 6 (ARTS PART 1)

P196 **CHAPTER 16**
LESSON 6 (ARTS PART 2)

P206 **CHAPTER 17**
LESSON 7 (JOBS)

P216 **CHAPTER 18**
POSTTEST

P228 **CHAPTER 19**
LESSON 8 (TRAVEL & FAREWELL PARTY)

PART III — WEAVE IT ALL TOGETHER

P247

CHAPTER 20 — SNAPSHOTS OF MY SECOND LIFE RESEARCH

P248

CHAPTER 21 — SECOND LIFE RESOURCES FOR TEACHING AND RESEARCH

P262

INDEX

P278

LIST OF TABLES

2.1	Syllabus considerations across TBLT approaches	37
2.2	Considerations of complexity in task design	38
2.3	Summary of considerations of sources, methods, and questions in needs analysis	41
2.4	An SL-enabled, task-based syllabus co-designed by the teacher and mentor	45
21.1	SL basics and wikis	264
21.2	Conference and social networking	265
21.3	Language teaching islands & demonstrations	267
21.4	Academic publishing	269
21.5	SL researchers and specialists	269

PREFACE

FLASHBACK TO MY 3D TEACHING AND RESEARCH JOURNEY

Let's start by walking down memory lane to see how this book came into being, shall we? In 2008, I was just a PhD student striving to find a potential dissertation topic that would hopefully set myself apart from my counterparts. Given my research home base in technology-mediated TBLT, I started to explore various digital platforms to see how they could make a difference in language learning and teaching. When I first came across Second Life (SL), I was blown away by its immensely pedagogical and research possibilities to transform a mundane language classroom into a three-dimensional (3D) virtual playground. The unique features afforded by SL, be they teleporting, 3D simulation, or multimodal communication, open up viable opportunities for learners to perform real-life tasks that are meaningful and engaging to them rather than rote drilling. Reciprocally, SL stimulates teachers to teach outside the box, engendering creativity, autonomy, engagement, fun, and immersion. The sky is the limit.

Note that I wasn't a diehard geeky gamer (still not one), obsessed with playing online games, or to be exact, massively multiplayer online role-playing games (MMORPGs) such as World of Warcraft (WoW), Fortnite, or Dark Knight. I didn't even know (still don't) how to code or programme, which is way beyond my technical repertoire. Doing research and teaching in SL was as exciting and promising for my dissertation as it was daunting and challenging to a newbie like me. To test out research instruments and gather data in my pilot study, I told myself to "suck it up," hoping to see some silver linings. So I plunged right into this "scary"' and unknown 3D world — I took a series of SL training workshops offered by the SLOAN-Consortium (SLOAN-C) Certificate Programmes, and attended virtual classes to hone my SL skills and understanding of designing SL-enabled tasks for my pilot study. I frequented SL (almost every day) to get a hang of those features, interacted with other SL residents (language teachers and students mostly) from all over the world, and explored various virtual islands that might potentially serve as my teaching/research sites. Gradually, I grew more confident in my SL skill set and was ready to give teaching in SL a crack.

Bearing TBLT principles in mind, I ventured to design interactive, authentic, and culture-oriented tasks supported by SL functions. The 3D form had made task delivery more real-life like and engaging. Still uncertain about how those tasks would play out in practice, I teamed up with another English teacher from Argentina to co-teach my first task-based class in SL. I piloted all the tasks with the students, observed their task performance, kept a teaching blog to reflect on what worked and what didn't, fine-tuned the task design, and fed students' evaluations back in modifications of tasks and instruments. This pilot also paved the way for my official study, thus reinvigorating my sense of agency and identity as a capable SL teacher researcher. Gathering momentum, I presented my task outcomes and preliminary findings at several conferences and symposiums held in SL, such as the 2011 Virtual Worlds Best Practices in Education (VWBPE) Conference.

A decade had almost passed (2012–2022) before I finally come around to share this rollercoaster ride with my fellow teachers and emergent researchers. This resolution, though hibernating, never ceases to arise when the time is right. Having worn both hats of an SL teacher and researcher since my doctoral studies, I have witnessed the optimal potential SL could offer for language education and research. Valuable lessons and implications from my debut 3D virtual teaching were consistently documented in my reflective blogging, and candidly reported in a number of publications. My SL journey epitomises how this 3D approach can empower language teachers to be more well-rounded in the new realm of online teaching, which reciprocally benefits student learning. Whenever presenting my SL research findings in conferences and invited talks, I can see the sparks of genuine excitement and interest flickering in the eyes of those attendees. Questions and comments raised during the Q&A sessions also imply that teacher researchers, especially the novices, would very much like to embark on this SL journey. They just don't know where and how to hit the ground running.

Frankly, research-oriented, theory-driven books on 3D multi-user virtual environments (MUVEs) are already available on the market. For teacher practitioners, novice researchers, and those in between, what they really need is a book that breaks down the steep learning curve, or a practical guide that walks them through each step of teaching and research in SL. Additionally, given our younger generation wired with digital technologies 24/7, ignoring this 3D alternative to conventional language instruction not only does our learners a disservice by overlooking their digital learning styles and interests, but also forfeits taking teacher professional development to the next level. These concerns propel me to pick up where I left off to write a book that is informed by evidence-based, pedagogically sound research, as in the case of my dissertation research. I reckon it is better late than never. Hopefully this book will motivate and inspire other language teacher researchers to give it a shot, and above all, enjoy the challenging but rewarding 3D ride!

IS SECOND LIFE A PASSING FAD?

Those who play devil's advocate may question if SL is a bit too "dated." They would also argue that the life cycles of digital tools are manifested in that the "older" generation, popular in its heyday, is gradually elbowed out to the sidelines by more recent technological advancements. Fair enough. However, my counterargument is that these digital predecessors are not vanishing or retired just because they have been on the market for a long time. Take social media, Facebook, Twitter, WhatsApp, WeChat, for example. They are certainly not new to us and still commonly used worldwide. These tools have also been utilised for teaching or research purposes in tandem with students' personal use for social networking. Similar to the life spans of its 3D counterparts, SL is no longer in its infancy since its 2003 launch by Linden Lab (acquired by Holding Company in 2021). Nevertheless, it has attracted more than 36 million registered SL users worldwide according to the 2013 Report published by Linden Lab. SL hit its peak of 57 million registered accounts and an average growth of 350,000 new registrations monthly, as highlighted in a 2018 infographic to celebrate the 15th-year anniversary of SL.[1] Ebbe Altberg, the late CEO of Linden Lab, also indicated in his 2020 interview with VICE News that the active SL users remain around 900,000 monthly.[2] Just like WoW is still popular on the 3D gaming market, SL also has its loyal residents (i.e., registered SL users) around the world even when it is approaching its 20-year mark. Though not a typical MMORPG (I will talk more about it in Part I), SL would have been wiped out of the market if users no longer found it appealing or contemporary. I rest my case here.

AIM AND OVERVIEW

The aim of this book is straightforward: to provide a reader-friendly, pedagogically driven, and research-informed guide to demonstrate how to design SL-enabled, real-world tasks and conduct a virtual class from scratch. It also intends to portray the book as a light read or a practical guide that is easy for readers to pick up irrespective of their skill set, experience, and background. Each chapter is anchored by a brief blurb that serves as a road map to ease readers into the text. Readers will also find the chapter "Checkpoint" helpful to solidify their understanding, and "Your Task" conducive to putting task planning into SL practice.

The first part of the book orients readers to the synergy of language teaching/learning and 3D MUVEs, builds their foundation in the principles of TBLT, and outlines the key SL functions needed for teaching and research in the 3D world. Because my SL teaching blog was also part of my doctoral research instruments, I documented how I taught the SL class in tandem with gathering research data. Specifically, I depicted how each class progressed and the type of tasks and instruments utilised. I reported with brutal honesty on what actually worked in that day's lesson and what still needed refinement for the next class. Hence, each chapter in the second part of the book embodies a lesson topic of the day, supported by students' reactions to the tasks and verbatim chat logs in SL. Harnessing my personal blog, I replay my teaching trajectory of how I created lessons by tapping into students' needs and interests, devised SL-enabled tasks, and evaluated my delivery of those tasks vis-à-vis students' performances after each virtual class. Novice researchers, graduate students, and academics involved or interested in technology-mediated TBLT will find this blogging particularly relevant to their research or teaching agendas. Readers can also jump to any lesson topic (chapter) that takes their fancy.

The last part of the book highlights my published research, and annotates its implications for readers who are motivated to explore how this 3D approach can generate evidence-based research outputs. The final chapter shares thoughtfully selected resources with readers who consider embarking on their own SL journey. I wrap up the book with my final two cents about what I have gained from the whole experience and future directions in teaching and research in SL.

READERSHIP

This book intends to set itself apart from other theory-laden, research-dense collections, which have already predominated the academic market. With teacher practitioners in mind, I purposefully use accessible language to suit the needs and interests of the readers who are new to SL. Using my teaching blog to restory my SL journey, I hope to transport readers to the ups and downs in this 3D trajectory, and connect to a wider readership through my own story. This personalised style has an edge over abstruse language and complex sentence structure favoured by other academic books. Specifically, this book speaks to readers with various interests and agendas, ranging from language teachers who are curious about teaching beyond the class walls; instructional designers who consider developing curricula in the 3D virtual world; administrators who like to know the potential of integrating SL and TBLT for developing online language programmes; graduate students and novice researchers in the Applied Linguistics, TESOL, and Educational Technology programmes who like to conduct

3D research and gather data remotely; to university academics who like to include technology-mediated TBLT in their lectures and student projects. Above all, it is for everyone who simply enjoys reading an online language teacher's first-hand storytelling.

As this book is free of jargon and presented in narrative form, it is very accessible to readers who are either laymen or pre-service teachers. No SL background is needed. Therefore, this handy guide is suitable to be included as recommended reading for courses related to areas in Computer-Assisted Language Learning, Technology-Enhanced Instruction, Educational Technology, Game-Based Language Learning, Language Teaching, 3D Virtual Learning, Task-Based Language Teaching, Research Methods in Applied Linguistics, Online Teaching and Learning, E-Learning, and Curriculum Design in the Virtual World. It is also versatile enough to be included as a textbook for pedagogy-oriented courses offered at the vocational, post/undergraduate, Open University, and Continuing Education levels.

BEYOND THE CLASSROOM

Whilst I was proposing this monograph in 2020, it was also the beginning of the pandemic that turned the whole world upside down. Who would have thought this unprecedented crisis would paralyse our education sector, forcing the traditional classroom teaching into remote teaching overnight? Even after 2 years of the global pandemic, not all the schools in the world can go back to class but rely on remote teaching or Zooming to counter the formidable COVID mutations. Living in this pandemic world with global border lockdowns and social distancing, we can't immerse ourselves in the target country as we used to, much less communicate with the locals in the target language. So how can language teachers bring the real world to distance learning, recreating authentic, engaging, and interactive learning experience even from afar?

In the midst of every crisis, lies great opportunity. Thanks to the unique 3D affordances that allow for real-world simulation, authentic communication, and virtual community building, SL breaks down the spatiotemporal boundaries, enabling us to teleport anywhere (fly, if you prefer) in the world with simply a mouse click! In this sense, SL creates boundless opportunities for education that transcend the constraints set by a physical classroom, especially during the school shutdown under COVID restrictions. It enables us to not only continue language education amid the pandemic, but also minimise social distancing by bringing us all together at the same time. 3D MUVEs, such as SL, come in the right place, at the right time. (Though it is not my hope to live in a never-ending pandemic world!) In fact, Ebbe Altberg also pinpointed that the global lockdowns have resultantly stimulated an unexpected surge in SL users for business, professional, educational, and recreational purposes. The reason for this is simple: users would rather conduct meetings and classes, or simply reconnect with people in a 3D virtual world that is more immersive, fun, and connected (in avatar form) than in a linear, static space that feels distant and remote from each other (especially when a mic and camera turned off).

Despite the dark cloud of COVID-19, it also sheds light on how we can reinvigorate our future education. This is the time to challenge and rethink whether teaching is better suited following printed worksheets and preloaded PowerPoints in a physical class, or take a step further to explore the immense potential in 3D virtual teaching. The palpable engagement and being in the moment (together) is just priceless — a no-brainer for both the students and teachers alike. That said, it is not my intention to play down classroom teaching, which still plays a pivotal role in the mainstream education sector. Rather, I would like to put forth how SL can be an optimal alternative to classroom teaching and how this exhilarating 3D world can pump our creative juices in language education and research, particularly amid the pandemic and in a post-pandemic world.

Regardless of your background, skill set, and experience, I hope you all will find a cosy spot in this page turner and enjoy your 3D ride with me.

Julian Chen
Perth, Western Australia, 2022

NOTES

1 Source: https://nwn.blogs.com/nwn/2018/04/second-life-15th-anniversary-infographic.html
2 Source: https://www.vice.com/en/article/4aydzg/virtual-reality-is-going-to-change-live-events-culture-forever

PART I

BEFORE WE TAKE OFF

Chapter 1: Language teaching and learning in Second Life   2

Chapter 2: Task-based language teaching in Second Life   26

Chapter 3: Second Life features and logistics   52

CHAPTER 1

LANGUAGE TEACHING AND LEARNING IN SECOND LIFE

OVERVIEW

As the saying goes, "theory without practice is futile; practice without theory is fatal". Before we get down to the nuts and bolts of Second Life (SL) (Chapter 3), it is crucial to engage with 3D MUVE research and understand the praxis it connects to language teaching and learning in SL. Because this book is written for teachers, students, and novices at heart, I deliberately play down over-referencing or embellishment with jargon. Instead, I highlight the key takeaways from 3D MUVE and SL studies related to language education. My goal is to synthesise the relevant literature and make it accessible to my fellow teachers and readers. The rest of the book follows suit.

Today's students are different. They are no longer the people that our teachers were trained to teach. So much of the new instruction the Digital Immigrants develop – even if it has a "computer" component to it – is often essentially old, and doesn't work for a great many of our students ... [I]t 'sucks the fun out.'

If we are smart, the mobile phones and games that our students are so comfortable with will soon become their learning tools.

The most important things to remember are: multi-player, creative, collaborative, challenging, and competitive.

Marc Prensky (2004)

At the turn of the 21st century, Marc Prensky posited that the digital divide[1] cannot go overlooked because it is "the root of a great many educational problems" (Prensky 2001b, p. 1). Ironically, this imbalanced ecology in teaching and learning observed in Prensky's seminal propositions, almost two decades later, still rings true. As a language educator, I often ponder over how we can spice up our teaching and make learning more engaging, authentic, and immersive. I also can't help but wonder how many of us really speak our students' "language" in everyday classroom teaching, or simply run business as usual? Can we teach our language learners sans reliance on prescribed textbooks, PowerPoint slides, and rote drills? How can we upskill our teaching toolkit and instil the fun element in language education? Wouldn't it be exhilarating to see our students genuinely engage and have fun using the target language spontaneously to perform real-life tasks like playing games?

If any of these questions has ever crossed your mind, voilà, my friend, you are in the right place, at the right time! Staying curious and having the willingness to challenge ourselves is a hallmark of the innovation and scholarship of teaching and learning. We can certainly do more than teaching inside a physical class. Teaching in the 3D virtual world, for example, is one of the innovative alternatives to conventional language instruction. To enter the 3D teaching arena, we may want to acquaint ourselves with the literature regarding how our students prefer to learn and operate in the digital age, and how 3D MUVEs and digital game-based learning (DGBL) come into play. Because this book is situated in SL, it is pivotal to understand the nature of this MUVE and why SL has drawn many institutions worldwide to explore its immense potential for education. Language educators may also wonder how we can capitalise on its 3D affordances to benefit language learners and transform language teaching. We will now unravel these burning issues.

GENERATIONS Z AND ALPHA IN THE DIGITAL AGE

The digital information age has drastically changed the current teaching/learning landscape. As language educators, we face challenges of teaching each new generation of students. The teaching materials and methods on which we comfortably relied somehow don't work wonders anymore. Images of learners listening to the music on AirPods; playing online games; constantly texting on their mobile phone; and thumb-liking comments, photos, and videos posted on Instagram and TikTok whilst doing homework or sitting in class couldn't be more vivid. This phenomenon mirrors the Generation Alpha (or Gen Alpha, born in the early 2010s) and Generation Z (or Gen Z, born after 1997) that populates today's student populations in K-12 and college (McCrindle, 2021). Sharing the traits of their predecessors, Millennials (born in the early 1980s to mid-1990s, also known as Gen Y, Net Generation, or Digital Generation; Dimock, 2019), the Gen Zers, and Gen Alphas have grown up with the Internet, smartphones, social media, and digital gadgets around them. If our former teacher training and experience can't seem to suit their digital learning needs and interests, maybe it is time to re-evaluate our teaching practice and even revamp it.

We are probably no stranger to another observation that Gen Zers and Gen Alphas tend to have short attention spans, enact multitasking, and expect immediate feedback (Schukei, 2021). Further, they are *experiential learners*, think in a nonlinear fashion, and tend to focus on personalised learning (Dawley & Dede, 2014). They also like to learn at their own pace, and work collaboratively and creatively to construct knowledge through real-life problem-solving tasks that are meaningful to them (McGlynn, 2005). When these learning styles translate into classroom learning, quick access to information through parallel processing is preferred over listening to lectures only. In other words, their "information-age mindset" is manifested in "Reality No Longer Real", "Multitasking Way of Life", "Typing Rather Than Handwriting", "Staying Connected", and "Zero Tolerance for Delays" (Frand, 2000, p. 16). This digital mindset has seamlessly changed the way they live, think, study, and communicate, which differs strikingly from that of their parents and teachers in the baby boom generation or Gen X. The information explosion in the digital age, therefore, shakes up the way we used to teach and the way younger generations prefer to learn.

Nevertheless, just because digital natives are generally perceived to be tech-savvy, multitaskers, and have split attentions doesn't necessarily mean that every student shares those attributes (Goertler, 2009). For example, they may be savvy about typing on their smartphone or using mobile apps but find it challenging to use the keyboard and work on a computer (Schukei, 2021). Not every student, such as those that are culturally/linguistically marginalised and socioeconomically disadvantaged in particular, has equal access to the Internet or possesses digital devices. The levels of digital literacy and technical skills also vary from individual to individual. Therefore, within-group variance should be taken into account without making over generalisations.

Similarly, the phenomenon of digital mania has reconfigured the ecological balance of language learning and teaching and sparked multimodal ways of delivering curricula. The plurality and diversity of language education in the digital age, nevertheless, is challenging both language teachers and learners. That is, the former may feel intimidated by the technological revolution that shakes up teachers' comfort zones in *old-school* teaching, whereas the latter finds that their learning styles[2] and interests connected to day-to-day digital applications are not accommodated. They are dissatisfied with and disengaged in the static interface of delivering courses, or in Prensky's (2001a) term, have to "power down" in class (p. 3). Even if certain technologies have been widely integrated into the curriculum, such as using PowerPoint to deliver content materials, these types of technology still cannot appeal to our Gen Zers and Gen Alphas, and are disconnected from their actual everyday practice. In Marc Prensky's term, the *language* teachers speak is still outdated and accented.

The digital divide, in this sense, divorces what we generally regard as the best way for language teaching and learning from what our students perceive really works for them.

A red flag, therefore, is raised for language teacher educators: the current language learners, be they in a K-12 setting or at the college level, are not passively receptive to conventional teaching anymore. They are characterised by their multitasking, impatience, and varied learning styles and are driven by multiple digital gadgets and online activities. The substantial time Gen Zers and Gen Alphas spend on online games and the reasons why they are so immersed in 3D MUVEs is worth noting. For instance, popular 3D online games, or massively multiplayer online role-playing games (MMORPGs), have attracted digital natives worldwide, such as the old-time favourite, World of Warcraft (WoW; 2004) and more recent inventions, Fortnite (2017) or the Korean MMORPG, Lost Ark (2019). Another popular MUVE that allows players to create their own virtual world is SL (which will be discussed in detail later). These MUVEs characterise the "immersive mediated interaction" and "augmented realities" that foster situated learning (Dede, 2005, p. 9).

Ironically, we tend to attribute students' disengagement to their short attention spans and impatience. The reality check is that they do engage in extended immersive games and online social networking beyond the class walls. The stereotypical connotation of "game and play" with "unlearning" needs to be redefined in language education. Digital games may hold pedagogical implications for language education, given that DGBL has attracted increasing research attention (Godwin-Jones, 2014; Peterson, 2016a,b; Reinders & Wattana, 2014; Sykes, 2018). Researchers also see the digital divide as a wakeup call for language educators to note its negative washback on the stakeholders (i.e., students, teachers, parents, institutions) (Chen, 2016; Reimers & Chung, 2019; Schrum & Levin, 2009). Using digital games to reinvigorate classroom teaching/learning may potentially bridge the divide, as we will examine below.

DIGITAL GAME-BASED LEARNING (DGBL)

How are today's language educators attuned to the digital mindset and revamping teaching approaches to accommodate digital natives' needs and interests? A recent survey (Ohashi, 2018) on a Japanese university's English as a foreign language (EFL) students' use of devices and games inside and outside of class reveals that smartphones are the most commonly used device (60%), followed by computers (40%) and tablets (18%). Popular online games for recreation (e.g., Pokémon Go, Second Life, Puzzle and Dragons) or language practice (e.g., TOEIC Galaxy, Quizlet, Kahoot) are also indicated in the survey. However, in a traditional and fixed language class setting, the time given to each individual learner to practice their L2 is unfortunately insufficient. The situation is even worse in a big class size or following a scripted textbook that limits interactions with teachers and peers (Chen, 2016; Humphries et al., 2015). Emerging digital technologies, such as simulation gaming or mobile learning apps, make interaction more accessible to them within and outside of the class. These digital tools also match their Gen Z and Gen Alpha mindset, as mirrored in collaboration, engagement, and incidental learning in both online and face-to-face social networking modes (Vaibhav & Gupta, 2014).

Gamification is an innovative approach to pedagogy that transforms traditional instruction through "using game-based mechanics, aesthetics, and game thinking to engage people, motivate action, promote learning, and solve problems" (Kapp, 2012, p. 10). It has proven to be conducive to active learning (Kiryakova et al., 2014; Wood & Reiners, 2012), learner motivation (Glover, 2013; Pirker et al., 2014), and task engagement (Nicholson, 2012; Vaibhav & Gupta, 2014). In his seminal piece, *What Video Games Have to Teach Us About Learning and Literacy*, Gee (2003) justified what good (serious) games can offer for learning supported by 36 DBGL principles. For example, good games are situated in contexts with achievable learning goals to challenge players' problem-solving skills, thereby allowing them to actively involve and create as agents rather than passively receive as consumers. Hence, those serious games enable learners to retain engagement, simulate real-life tasks by taking on new identities, and promote collaborating and sharing knowledge/skills (Gee, 2007, 2008). Research has also shown that games can hold language learners' attention longer and boost their motivation whilst they are embarking on collaborative and problem-solving tasks (Sykes, 2018; Yeh et al., 2017).

Despite the positive claims, we also need to be cautious that not all games are good for all learners nor yield positive learning results. "Serious" games need to be carefully designed and guided by learning theories and research-sound pedagogies. For example, Dede (2005) provided some useful principles that can be linked to digital game design: co-design (instruction personalised to students), co-instruction (capitalise on students' know-how shared among peers), guided learning-by-doing pedagogies (experiential simulation), and assessment beyond tests and papers (student-initiated assessments in nonlinear representations) (p. 11). Following this train of thought, learners' development of thinking skills, mental representations, inductive discovery abilities, and quick responses to stimuli can be enhanced through exposure to online games or multimedia, especially in 3D MUVEs (Chen, 2016; Dawley & Dede, 2014; Peterson, 2016a). Through game play, the whole cognitive process intellectually challenges players to form hypotheses about how to tackle challenging tasks, test their hypotheses, and revise them until missions are successfully accomplished (Wood & Reiners, 2012). This approach further retains their active engagement and long-term memory. No wonder DGBL has been hyped in higher education (e.g., the Serious Games Center housed at Purdue University to discover innovative ways of using digital games in virtual environments; The New Media Consortium, 2012).

Some teachers may feel uncomfortable or even intimidated by applying those "fancy and sophisticated" digital technologies in their language classes. However, teachers do not need to know all technologies to incorporate them in class. They can try to accommodate digital learning styles by incorporating the students' technical skills into the classroom and turn them into learning tools that connect to their real lives and "turn on the lights" for them (Prensky, 2008). Gee (2008) also implicated that learners can retain the newly learned information and knowledge longer and more effectively when engaged in (or playing) goal-oriented learning activities (or games) that are situated in meaningful contexts. This principle also applies to language learning in that second language acquisition (SLA) can take place more effectively if learners can be immersed in environments that are meaningful and engaging. As such, teachers can revamp students' learning experiences with a "fun factor" that is intellectually challenging and motivating (Chen, 2016, 2020; Ohashi, 2018; Yeh et al., 2017). Because a majority of our learners were born in the digital age, they generally have acquired technical skills and knowledge in much the same way that they learned their first language – without realising they were learning it. Hence, it forecasts the potential benefits DGBL can bring to language education (Godwin-Jones, 2014; Sykes, 2018).

As such, we should seek ways to accommodate students' learning styles and needs in the digital age before the divide deepens. MMORPGs or MUVEs may hold the pedagogical potential for language education due to the unique 3D gamified feel. Nevertheless, there are some probing questions that we language teachers need to think about before jumping on the SL bandwagon:

1. How do the affordances in SL realise and augment learners' real-life task learning experience?
2. Do learners perceive their language practices in the 3D virtual world as more engaging and effective than in a traditional class or other Web 2.0 environments?
3. Will learner interaction with other avatars enhance their sense of belonging that further benefits their language production?

These pressing but also intriguing questions propelled me to share my own evidence-based research on learners' language practices and perceptions in this dynamic 3D virtual space in SL.

CHECKPOINT

- Describe with a colleague or in a group the demographic backgrounds and learning characteristics of your current or former class(es). Do your students also share the similar learning traits of Gen Z and Gen Alpha, such as short attention spans, multitasking, preferring typing over writing, eyes on phone, etc.? What are your teaching approaches to retaining their attention and engagement?
- What is your take on aligning your teaching with their digital learning styles? Is the use of technology really necessary in today's language education? Can't printed handouts, PowerPoint slides, and rote drills also deliver the same learning outcomes?
- Have you tried gamification with your students? How did it work? Would you also consider incorporating DGBL in your (language) teaching? Share your experience and thoughts with colleagues and exchange some useful DBGL tools.
- Have you played any MMORPG, such as WoW? Do you think MMORPG has a role to play in education? Discuss your concerns or identify its benefits with your colleagues.

WHAT IS SECOND LIFE?

Second Life, a 3D MUVE, was developed by Linden Lab (a San Francisco-based software company founded by Philip Rosedale) and initially launched in 2003 and acquired by Holding Company in 2021. Whilst SL was a big hit in the mid-2000s, its novelty had dimmed since its launch, typical of any type of digital platform. Unexpectedly, SL has resurged amid the pandemic as customers realised that immersive environments help reconnect people and break through social distancing and global lockdown. As of 2021, SL has attracted over 64.7 million registered users worldwide and still continues to grow in popularity (Second Life Community, 2021). Members can choose to register for a free *basic account*, or upgrade to a *premium account* (US$11.99 monthly), which includes features such as building a private home or virtual commodities. Although SL is an open virtual environment, only adult users are allowed to join SL (Second Life Community, 2011). SL used to provide an age-appropriate version called Teen Second Life,[3] which was intended for users aged 13–17 where mature content was prohibited. On 14 August 2010, Linden Lab decided to close the Teen Grid due to issues with improving both adult and teen versions of SL. However, teenagers over 16 years old can still register for a free account in SL, whereas younger users (aged 13–15) can only access restricted regions in SL affiliated with an organisation such as a school or educational institution.

In SL (*in-world*), every user is called a *resident* and can create an *avatar* to represent one's own virtual identity. In the in-world context, the choice of customising one's avatar does not have to be confined to a fixed persona as in real life (RL). A male user can switch his gender to female or choose to become an animal or even a superhero character. SL offers the flexibility for residents to take on different digital personae. Avatars can meet with millions of other residents from all walks of life in RL and communicate via either *text* or *voice chat*. They can either send public text chat, group chat, or use "IM" to privately text their avatar friends. Another animated feature in SL is that avatars can also perform certain non-verbal gestures as in RL, such as laughing, making faces, shrugging, crossing legs, and clapping. However, those non-verbal cues are not automatically signalled as in a face-to-face context and need to be manually configured by the avatar user. Additionally, avatars can walk, run, fly, teleport (i.e., instantly travelling to a new in-world location), and participate in a myriad of virtual social events held by SL residents. They can also use a built-in camera to take visual snapshots of an instantaneous moment of activity in which he/she/they/it is involved.

Even though SL is a free virtual space, SL residents need to buy Linden dollars (L$) – virtual dollars that can be exchanged for real-world dollars – for recreational or business purposes. The currency exchange rate for one US dollar is approximately equal to 241 L$ as of my writing (see current L$ exchange rate in-world or on LindeX).[4] Residents can buy L$ to pay for products and services of their interest as they normally do in the real world. They can purchase clothing, jewellery, and accessories to customise their avatar appearances, or pay for a cover charge to dance in a club. They can also buy or rent a land or an "island" to build their virtual world or create their own *primitive objects* ("prims"). Only premium account members are allowed to own land, whereas basic account members can rent land by paying different fees, depending on the size of the land.[5] Currently, SL also offers eligible non-profit or educational institutions a 50% discount on the in-world region setup and maintenance fees.[6]

The virtual world has become so popular with our digital natives because SL provides a 3D social platform for players to not only simulate their day-to-day routines and activities, but also take advantage of their imagination and creativity. In SL, residents can go window shopping in a mall, attend a conference, and chitchat with other avatars over coffee as we do in RL, but avatars can also fly or teleport to any in-world location or change their appearances instantly. Anything can happen in this 3D simulation world and avatars do not die in SL (e.g., avatars can breathe under the water for as long as they wish).

Noteworthy is that whilst SL also shares similar features of MMORPGs, they also differ in many ways. SL enables residents to manipulate the virtual environment (i.e., user-generated content) and allows their imagination to run wild. SL residents do not need to follow a storyline or preprogrammed game plan as in WoW to successfully accomplish a task (e.g., steps needed to kill a dragon). Residents have total flexibility to create their own plots and virtual activities, depending on their preferences and creativity. That is why SL is also called "metaverse", an MUVE that "mirror[s] the real world" and is "imagined and created" by residents (Kluge & Riley, 2008, p. 128). In other words, metaverse is a centralised 3D world that is "parallel to the physical world" (Clark, 2021) and juxtaposes the virtual reality (VR) and real-world experience in which users can fully immerse themselves through VR or augmented reality (AR) technology. Hence, SL embodies the real world in a sense that residents can continue their various RL activities or simply socialise in SL. It is also one of the longest lasting metaverse providers and has been around for nearly two decades, followed by the recent rebranded Facebook as Meta(verse).

WHY SECOND LIFE?

The so-what question we may pose is: *Why bother with Second Life in today's education*? According to the *Horizon Report: 2009 K-12 Edition*[7] (Johnson et al., 2009), MUVEs, such as SL, were envisioned as one of the emerging technologies in the 21st century in which "[s]tudents often find these spaces very engaging" through "collaboration within 3D virtual worlds and multiplayer gaming environments" (p. 9). The 2009 report also documented several productive collaborative projects between teachers in K-12 settings and university game design programmes. *Global Kids* (http://www.globalkids.org) was one of the projects that created a simulated MUVE to intellectually challenge kids in grades 5–8 to develop skills across subject matters. The *International Virtual Collaboration Space* project used SL for students both in Finland and Connecticut to collaborate in the 3D virtual space. DeMers (2010), an instructor in the Sloan-C Online Workshop on *Intermediate to Second Life for Educators*, seconded the Horizon Report:

> Second life is a prime opportunity for educators to explore the idea that learning is inherently social, and happens most effectively in a student-centered, social environment where students can share their knowledge with one another…We are disappointed in the proliferation of tools to show PowerPoint-like presentations to students, and the large number of learning spaces that put the teacher front-and-center…The sound learning theories and best practices that formulate our philosophy of teaching and learning have the potential to transform learning, not only in Second Life, but in real life as well.

Since the 2009 Horizon Report, we can't help but wonder if the hype about MUVEs for education over a decade ago has waned by now. (Un)surprisingly, their recent reports on the trends of emerging technologies (Alexander et al., 2019; Brown et al., 2020) rightly coincide with their 2009 findings. Not only has VR kept its 3D momentum and impact on education, more innovative, hybrid technologies that blend and blur the physical and virtual worlds have also come of age. For example, extended reality (XR) is an umbrella term that encompasses VR (which immerses users in a simulated, computer-generated environment), AR (which overlays computer-generated content on real-world objects), and mixed reality (MR; which creates a real-virtual mash-up and both the digital and physical contents/objects can interact with each other).[8] These engendered terms reflect how technological affordances can hybridise and (de)reconstruct real-virtual learning environments, thus reinvigorating student learning experiences.

What if we ask the same so-what question in the context of language learning? Some scholars may argue that other asynchronous and synchronous Web 1.0 or Web 2.0 tools can also prompt language learners to interact with other (non)native speakers in a computer-mediated communication (CMC) environment. For example, they can use Skype or IMs (Web 1.0) to communicate with other interlocutors and practice the target language via text or voice chat, or co-construct a writing project using blog or wiki (Web 2.0). However, when it comes to simulating authentic scenarios in which learners are required to use a target language to perform RL tasks (e.g., dining in a restaurant, visiting an art gallery), those CMC tools operated in a two-dimensional (2D) environment are still virtually remote and less immersive (Pellas, 2014). This view is further validated by Linden Lab (2011) regarding its cutting-edge advantages that set SL apart from other digital platforms:

> Second Life amplifies learning beyond capabilities afforded by teleconference calls and web presentation tools…simulations are also incredibly powerful in Second Life because they simulate complex, processes in the physical world and avatars can take on different roles to enhance learning…it enables deeply immersive, meaningful, and memorable experiences. (p. 2)

Also added to these advantages of SL that can optimise remote work[9] are the following:

- Work safely from the comfort of your home
- Reduce travel time and cost
- Increase creativity and innovation
- Improve collaboration and communication
- Meet in private or public spaces - the choice is yours!
- Communicate with text and spatial voice chat
- Engage your audience with fun avatars and 3D environments
- Replicate a sense of shared presence across distances

These SL affordances lend themselves to educational, business, or recreational benefits. For language learners in particular, using the avatar form to socialise with global citizens using target language(s) in real time without spending a penny on travel is just priceless. For language teachers, imagine taking your students on virtual field trips to in-world islands that simulate real-world sites, and listen to local curators describe famous paintings or artefacts in the Louvre Museum in Paris and Guggenheim Museum in New York City. Also imagine time travelling with your class to Shakespeare's Theatre (the Globe) in the 16th century to interview him about his plays. It is exhilarating to know that SL offers abundant opportunities for teachers to recreate immersive, engaging learning experiences that are not possible in a traditional classroom or 2D setting. These exciting opportunities only await us to unlock our creativity for revamping conventional language teaching and learning. We will soon learn some best practices and research implications from language practitioners and researchers who have been involved in SL.

> **CHECKPOINT**
>
> - Have you heard of or played SL before? How does SL differ from its MMORPG counterparts, such as WoW and Lost Ark?
> - After reading the previous SL affordances, brainstorm with a colleague(s) on how those unique features (e.g., teleporting, changing avatar appearances, etc.) can facilitate your teaching and maximise immersive learning experience. Please give a few concrete lesson examples that can be undertaken in SL.

SECOND LIFE IN LANGUAGE EDUCATION

Although SL was not initially designed for educational purposes, many institutions worldwide have embraced SL and reimagined its multifold benefits for teaching and learning. In its heyday, over 700 universities, such as Harvard University, Stanford University, and Oxford University (Second Life Wiki, 2022), and nonprofits built 3D campuses or offered virtual courses across disciplines such as social work education (Reinsmith-Jones et al., 2015), foreign language education (Kim et al., 2018), research methods (Kawulich & D'Alba, 2019), and medicine (Lorenzo-Alvarez et al., 2020). Down under, the University of Western Australia has recreated a 3D campus in SL to not only invite guests to immerse themselves in beautiful "flora and fauna" indigenous to Australia, but also to conduct lessons across disciplines in law, business, anatomy, and education (UWA in Second Life, 2022). The *Chinese Island*, built by the Chinese Studies programmes at Monash University, allows undergraduate students to simulate authentic RL tasks related to Chinese language and culture (Wang et al., 2021). Rockcliffe University Consortium, one of the nonprofits advancing 3D virtual learning, has also built a virtual island to hold regular workshops, events, festivals, film screenings, and art gallery exhibits, as well as archiving academic resources in a virtual library (Linden Lab, 2022). We also witnessed exciting projects on cutting-edge course modules developed in SL for students at Florida State University to use their learned knowledge in chemistry to solve a mystery case through 3D simulation and game design (CNDG, 2022). The list goes on.

The fact that numerous institutions have jumped onto the SL bandwagon is a no-brainer. As a free, open, and multimodal MUVE, SL enables educators to bring the real world to the class and create experiential learning experiences through immersive simulation (Chen,

2016, 2020; Peterson, 2016b). My fellow language teachers would probably also agree that immersion in a country where the target language is spoken can expedite L2 learners' language learning curve. However, the reality is that not every student can afford the cost of traveling, let alone immersing themselves in the target culture for a long period of time. In some EFL contexts, for example, students switch back to their local language outside of the class. Chances that communicating with native speakers or international visitors in English on a daily basis are apparently slim. Despite the constraints of budget and practicality listed previously, we language teachers should not sacrifice incorporating immersive language learning in ways that are more affordable, personalised, and motivating. SL provides rich resources of 3D *simulators* ("SIMs") that embody real-world tourist attractions to which language learners can teleport instantly and immerse themselves in authentic target-language speaking environments (Sadler, 2017; Swier & Peterson, 2018) without the cost of traveling (Cooke-Plagwitz, 2009). Because teleporting allows users to transverse anywhere in-world, this hands-on feature facilitates teacher planning on field trips to multiple in-world destinations (e.g., museum, gallery, library, theatre, tourist spots) for students to enrich their real-world experience by interacting with the "locals", 3D objects, and exposing themselves to rich input in different target languages (Chen & Kent, 2020; Dawley & Dede, 2014).

Given the unique affordances of SL illustrated earlier, language teacher researchers have started to examine the effects SL has on learners' language production and affective factors. First, the multimodal features of SL enhance the development of writing (via text chat) and speaking (via voice chat) proficiency. Similar to any social encounters in RL, learner avatars can use any chosen language to simultaneously interact with SL residents coming from all walks of life with culturally and linguistically diverse (CaLD) backgrounds, thus fostering cross-cultural competence (Jauregi-Ondarra et al., 2022). Second, language learning can occur incidentally anywhere, anytime in this open and highly social 3D MUVE (Peterson et al., 2019). The embodiment of authentic communication in RL promotes real-time collaboration, which deepens a higher level of spontaneous, authentic interaction (Canto & Jauregi-Ondarra, 2017). Interestingly, research also finds that the interactive and anonymous nature of SL encourages learners to take risks in practising different aspects of a target language, be it the four skills, grammar, or vocabulary, thereby lowering foreign language anxiety (see for example, Melchor-Couto, 2018; Wehner et al., 2011).

Next, being able to interact with and create 3D objects allows learners to personalise and solidify their learning experience in a more concrete form, which also fosters learner engagement and sense of accomplishment (Peterson et al., 2019). Similarly, language teachers can amplify the commonly used activity, role-play, through manipulating Holodecks and SIMs that resemble real-world scenarios in which learners can practice a target language spontaneously in an immersive environment, thus enabling them to transfer skills learned in SL to RL (Chen, 2016; Dalgarno & Lee, 2010). Thanks to the highly sensory stimuli in-world (e.g., graphics, avatar movements, sounds, object building, visuals), language learning is not one-dimensional (1D), but it can take place more organically and effectively through 3D multimodal input enhancement and output reinforcement (Jauregi-Ondarra et al., 2022). With its cost-effective, social, immersive, multimodal, and collaborative perks, SL could be one of the viable alternatives for conventional language instruction.

Despite the positive claims and immense potential in using SL for education, researchers caution us not to overlook certain aspects of SL that may backfire on good teaching intentions. Technical issues, one of the most notorious downsides, have been reported in the literature. For example, high hardware demands of broad bandwidth and graphic cards, platform instability, interrupted Internet connection, poor audio quality, and background echoing are not uncommon when teaching in SL (Chen, 2016; Chen & Kent, 2020; Dawley & Dede, 2014). Along with these technical glitches, Petrakou (2010) alerted us to consider the levels of learner technical skills because the lack of needed SL skills may jeopardise their full participation and engagement in-world. Kluge and Riley (2008) also raised concerns that learners may get so "immersed" in the exciting virtual world that they "get distracted from course goals" (p. 131). Also, whilst some digital natives feel comfortable in MUVEs, others may find the 3D virtual world overwhelming. As SL mirrors RL, virtual violence, assault, and harassment still exist in-world, unfortunately. Some "griefers" (i.e., avatars who harass other residents) would also mischievously interrupt classes, impacting both teaching and learning experiences in SL. Nevertheless, setting limited access to a private class group and providing newcomers with guidelines and netiquette in SL can help mitigate in-world nuisances.

Even though SL brings a fun element to education, those caveats identified earlier need to be taken into great consideration to avoid the *double-edged sword* side effect. Mayrath et al. (2007) suggested that when designing SL activities, teachers need to (1) align those activities with both course and learning objectives, (2) consider students' level of skills and needs, (3) make sure that the time and effort required to complete a task is plausible, and (4) provide pre-course training and clear directions to facilitate transition. Trinder and Moffat (2009) also confirmed that the issues of integrating SL into instruction can be detected through piloting and serve as a baseline for further pedagogical and technological development (also see Chen, 2016; Chen & Kent, 2020). Teacher scaffolding and technical team support are the keys to tackling the aforementioned issues without eliminating the fun of teaching and learning in SL.

Virtual Identity

"Avatar", the hit movie directed by James Cameron in 2009 (the sequel coming in late 2022), imprinted this word on all moviegoers around the world. Avatar, in SL terms, is defined as "the digital persona you create and customise. It's you in the virtual world – whoever you want to be. Make a 3D version of yourself or create an entirely new identity" (Linden Lab, 2015). As previously indicated, SL residents can create their avatars in forms of humans, animals, vampires, and robots, to name a few, and change their genders and appearances as far as their imagination would take them. Therefore, the fluidity of multiple identities with which SL residents can play enables them to interact with other avatars behind the disguise and ensure anonymity. Their virtual personae also convey their sentimental connections with self-image(s) they prefer to put forth or be perceived vis-à-vis other avatars. Shielded by their masked identities and speaking through "the first and the third person" voices (Coffman & Klinger, 2007, p. 30), residents who tend to be shy or lack confidence in RL are more willing to take risks in SL (Wigham & Chanier, 2015). Being able to personalise one's self-image, customise one's desired environment, and attain communal recognition from other avatars also makes SL appealing to our digital natives.

Through an educational lens, we can see that having the autonomy to create one's avatar identities and to take risks in an anonymous MUVE supercharges learning. For example, Clarke and Dede (2005) investigated how MUVEs can empower middle school students learning science. Through immersive simulations and collaborative interactions with peers using their virtual personas, students morphed into the scientist role to identify problems, observe sites, infer and test hypotheses, and reach conclusions based on their tested results. The virtual identities students take on (e.g., as a scientist to investigate why people got sick in a city) endow them with a new self-image as a savvy professional. In one of my SL studies (Chen, 2021), I explored how avatar identities could empower English language learners' development of self-efficacy in SL, which consequently led to the improvement of their language practice and oral communication. The results were exhilarating as learners' masked identities not only boosted their sense of self-efficacy and autonomy, but fended off the embarrassment of being "watched" that was usually felt in their traditional class. My findings also echo the metaphor used by Cooke-Plagwitz (2009) of an avatar form as a virtual shield for learners, or a virtual dummy (Deutschmann & Panichi, 2013) that emboldens language learners to take risks and to make mistakes without feeling inhibited. Using a virtual "self" to "mimic face-to-face interaction" with other avatars in-world also makes learning more situated and "decrease[s] the sense of isolation students in online text-based classes often feel" (Cooke-Plagwitz, 2008, p. 549). Some introverted language learners in RL will feel more comfortable participating in SL, given the "disguises" provided by their avatars (Swier & Peterson, 2018).

Similarly, Ganem-Gutierrez's (2014) study also evidenced that the sense of learner identity and agency can be augmented through immersive avatar presence and social interaction when learners are doing tasks in SL. These positive results all point to the fact that our learners, safeguarded by their masked avatars, are more willing to take on challenging RL tasks in a trial-and-error process (Peterson, 2016b; Sadler & Dooly, 2013). Seeing and feeling that we are all *being there* in SL creates a sense of "telepresence" and *being there together* further renders the sense of "copresence" (Schroeder, 2010, p. 4). The nature of immersive involvement and the feel of proximity through avatar presence heighten the sense of telepresence/copresence (Coughlan, 2014). In other words, avatar-amplified

CHECKPOINT

- The sense of telepresence and copresence is one of the salient features afforded by SL. How does this feature come into play with teaching and learning? Wouldn't other synchronous communication tools, such as Zoom Videoconferencing or WhatsApp chat, also share this SL feature?
- Avatar identity seems to endow students with a new virtual self to take more risks in learning. Why do you think this is the case? If you have the chance to teach an SL class, will you also be conscious about how your avatar appearances are perceived by your students and other residents?
- Teaching in SL is not without its challenges, such as griefers or unexpected platform crashing. Will these issues dampen your motivation for using SL for language teaching? Some researchers offer suggestions for tackling these caveats (p. 16). How do you find these suggestions? Would you be able to set up a workable plan to pre-empt turning good teaching intentions into negative outcomes?

telepresence/copresence enables identity play and exploration that are not feasible, or difficult to take on in RL, thus allowing for experiential learning and virtual community building (Dawley & Dede, 2014; Peterson, 2016b). Hence, SL sets itself apart from other 2D platforms by creating a more inclusive virtual community to bring everyone closer together.

> ## YOUR TASK
>
> - Work in a pair or group. Reflect on the digital tools or platforms that you have used in language teaching. How will you compare them to SL? Consider using a table to lay out the comparisons across functions, practicality, costs, technical demands, target language areas, learner reactions, online community building, and (dis)advantages for remote teaching. You may also add your own aspects if need be. After completing your comparison table, discuss each aspect across the tools and rank the preferences as a team.
> - After reading the section "Second Life in Language Education", try to select 5–10 articles from the reference list that pique your interest or relate to your current teaching. Annotate each article by first summarising what the article is about and then provide your commentary. After completing the annotation of all the articles, see if you can find some common themes and implications across your annotated articles. Bring your annotated bibliography to exchange with your colleagues. Discuss what you already know, what is new, and how to apply your new understanding to your current/future teaching or research setting.

NOTES

1. Digital divide is often used to refer to matter of access, depending on socioeconomic factors. The term has been used more broadly to also signify differences in learning preferences, styles, and activities, etc., as Prensky (2001a, 2001b) indicated.
2. The term learning styles is used here to equate to learning preferences. "Styles" is the preferred term of researchers in the field of digital learning.
3. See http://teen.secondlife.com/
4. To access LindeX, visit https://www.secondlife.com/currency/buy.php
5. SL used to offer a one-semester free trial for teacher educators to experiment with SL, as well as a discount and in-world support for institutions or nonprofit organisations to purchase lands

for educational purposes. However, Linden Lab decided to end the educational discount starting January 1, 2011, but it brought back the discount offer for nonprofit and educational purposes, especially during the COVID-19 pandemic.

6 For more information about the education and nonprofit discounts, see https://community.secondlife.com/blogs/entry/3818-second-life-to-expand-support-reduce-prices-for-education-nonprofits/

7 The *Horizon Report series,* released annually by the New Media Consortium and the EDUCAUSE Learning Initiative, is a longitudinal research publication that aims to identify emerging technologies that have the potential to transform learning, teaching, and research in education worldwide.

8 For those who are keen to delve more into what defines XR, VR, AR, and MR and their configurations, please refer to both the 2019 and 2020 Horizon Reports. Given the nature of SL as a VR, I will focus mainly on VR research and its implications for language education.

9 See https://www.connect.secondlife.com/about

REFERENCES

Alexander, B., Ashford-Rowe, K., Barajas-Murph, N., Dobbin, G., Knott, J., McCormack, M., & Weber, N. (2019). EDUCAUSE horizon report 2019 higher education edition (pp. 3–41). https://www.learntechlib.org/p/208644/report_208644.pdf

Brown, M., McCormack, M., Reeves, J., Brook, D. C., Grajek, S., Alexander, B., & Weber, N. (2020). 2020 EDUCAUSE horizon report teaching and learning edition (pp. 2–58). https://www.learntechlib.org/p/215670/report_215670.pdf

Canto, S., & Jauregi-Ondarra, K. (2017). Language learning effects through the integration of synchronous socializing network opportunities in language curricula: The case of video communication and Second Life. *Language Learning in Higher Education Journal*, *7*(1), 21–53. https://doi.org/10.1515/cercles-2017-0004

Chen, J. C. (2016). The crossroads of English language learners, task-based instruction, and 3D multi-user virtual learning in Second Life. *Computers & Education*, *102*, 152–171. https://doi.org/10.1016/j.compedu.2016.08.004

Chen, J. C. (2020). Restorying a "newbie" teacher's 3D virtual teaching trajectory, resilience and professional development through action research: A narrative case study. *TESOL Quarterly*, *54*(2), 375–403. https://doi.org/10.1002/tesq.550

Chen, J. C. (2021). The interplay of avatar identities, self-efficacy and language practices. *Australian Review of Applied Linguistics*, *44*(1), 65–81. https://doi.org/10.1075/aral.19032.che

Chen, J. C., & Kent, S. (2020). Task engagement, learner motivation and avatar identity of struggling English language learners in the 3D virtual world. *System*, *88*, 102168. https://doi.org/10.1016/j.system.2019.102168

Clark, P. A. (2021). The metaverse has already arrived. Here's what that actually means. *TIME MAGAZINE*. https://time.com/6116826/what-is-the-metaverse/

Clarke, J., & Dede, C. (2005). *Making learning meaningful: An exploratory study of using multi-user environments (MUVEs) in middle school science*. Paper presentation at the annual meeting of the American Educational Research Association, Montreal, Quebec, Canada.

CNDG (2022). *Case study: Chemistry for liberal studies*. https://cndg.info/fsu-chemistry/

Coffman, T., & Klinger, M. B. (2007). Utilizing virtual worlds in education: The implications for practice. *International Journal of Social Sciences*, *2*(1), 29–33.

Cooke-Plagwitz, J. (2008). New directions in CALL: An objective introduction to Second Life. *CALICO Journal*, *25*(3), 547–557.

Cooke-Plagwitz, J. (2009). A new language for the net generation: Why second life works for the net generation. In R. Oxford & J. Oxford (Eds.), *Second language teaching and learning in the Net Generation* (pp. 173–180). National Foreign Language Resource Center.

Coughlan, T. (2014). Enhancing innovation through virtual proximity. *Technology Innovation Management Review*, *4*(2), 17–22. https://doi.org/10.22215/timreview/765

Dalgarno, B., & Lee, M. J. W. (2010). What are the learning affordances of 3-D virtual environments? *British Journal of Educational Technology*, *40*(6), 10–32. https://doi.org/10.1111/j.1467-8535.2009.01038.x

Dawley, L., & Dede, C. (2014). Situated learning in virtual worlds and immersive simulations. In J. M. Spector, M. D. Merrill, J. Elen, & M. J. Bishop (Eds.), *Handbook of research on educational communications and technology* (5th ed.) (pp. 723–734). Springer. https://doi.org/10.1007/978-1-4614-3185-5_58

Dede, C. (2005). Planning for Neomillennial learning styles. *EDUCAUSE Quarterly*, *1*, 7–12.

DeMers, M. (2010, March 17). Sloan-C Online Workshop Series: Intermediate to Second Life for Educators. *The Sloan Consortium Online Workshop*. Retrieved March 17, 2010, from http://community.sloanconsortium.org/course/category.php?id=40

Deutschmann, M., & Panichi, L. (2013). Towards models for designing language learning in virtual worlds. *International Journal of Virtual and Personal Learning Environments (IJVPLE)*, 4(2), 65–84. https://doi.org/10.4018/jvple.2013040104

Dimock, M. (2019). Defining generations: Where Millennials end and Generation Z begins. *Pew Research Center*, *17*(1), 1–7.

Frand, J. L. (2000). The information-age mindset: Changes in students and implications for higher education. *EDUCAUSE Review*, *35*(5), 15–24.

Ganem-Gutierrez, G. A. (2014). A sociocultural theory approach to the design and evaluation of 3D virtual world tasks. In M. Gonzalez-Lloret & L. Ortega (Eds.), *Technology and tasks: exploring technology-mediated TBLT* (pp. 213–238). Georgetown University Press.

Gee, J. P. (2003). What video games have to teach us about learning and literacy. *ACM Computers in Entertainment*, *1*(1), 20–24.

Gee, J. P. (2007). *What video games have to teach us about learning and literacy* (2nd ed.). Palgrave Macmillan.

Gee, J. P. (2008). Game-like learning: An example of situated learning and implications for opportunity to learn. In P. A. Moss, D. C. Pullin, J. P. Gee, E. H. Haertel & L. J. Young (Eds.), *Assessment, equity, and opportunity to learn* (pp. 200–221). Cambridge University Press.

Glover, I. (2013, June). Play as you learn: gamification as a technique for motivating learners. In *EdMedia: World ConfeRence on Educational Media and Technology* (pp. 1999–2008). Association for the Advancement of Computing in Education (AACE).

Godwin-Jones, R. (2014). Games in language learning: Opportunities and challenges. *Language Learning & Technology*, *18*(2), 9–19.

Goertler, S. (2009). Hybridizing the curriculum: Needs, benefits, challenges, and attitudes. In R. Oxford & J. Oxford (Eds.), *Second language teaching and learning in the Net Generation* (pp. 53–64). University of Hawaii, National Foreign Language Resource Center.

Humphries, S. C., Burns, A., & Tanaka, T. (2015). "My head became blank and I couldn't speak": Classroom factors that influence English speaking. *The Asian Journal of Applied Linguistics*, *2*(3), 164–175.

Jauregi-Ondarra, K., Canto, S., & Melchor-Couto, S. (2022). Virtual worlds and second language acquisition. In N. Ziegler & M. González-Lloret (Eds.), *The Routledge handbook of second language acquisition and technology* (pp. 311–325). Routledge. https://doi.org/10.4324/9781351117586-27

Johnson, L., Levine, A., Smith, R., & Smythe, T. (2009). *The 2009 Horizon Report: K-12 Edition*. The New Media Consortium. https://files.eric.ed.gov/fulltext/ED593594.pdf

Kapp, K. M. (2012). What is gamification? In K. M. Kapp (Ed.), *The gamification of learning and instruction: Game-based methods and strategies for training and education* (pp. 1–24). Pfeiffer.

Kawulich, B. B., & D'Alba, A. (2019). Teaching qualitative research methods with Second Life, a 3-dimensional online virtual environment. *Virtual Reality*, *23*(4), 375–384.

Kim, D., Vorobel, O., & King, B. (2018). Students' use of Second Life in learning Spanish as a foreign language. *Journal of Second Language Teaching & Research*, *6*(1), 109–142.

Kiryakova, G., Angelova, N., & Yordanova, N. (2014, October). *Gamification in education*. [Paper Presentation]. *9th International Balkan Education and Science Conference*, Trakya University, Edirne.

Kluge, S., & Riley, L. (2008). Teaching in virtual worlds: Opportunities and challenges. *The Journal of Issues in Informing Science and Information Technology*, *5*(1), 127–135.

Linden Lab (2011). *Second Life Education: The virtual learning advantage*. https://lecs-static-secondlife-com.s3.amazonaws.com/work/SL-Edu-Brochure-010411.pdf

Linden Lab. (2015, November 20). *Avatar* [Second Life Website]. http://go.secondlife.com/landing/avatar/

Linden Lab (2022). *Universities in Second Life*. https://secondlife.com/destinations/learning/universities/1

Lorenzo-Alvarez, R., Rudolphi-Solero, T., Ruiz-Gomez, M. J., & Sendra-Portero, F. (2020). Game-Based learning in virtual worlds: a multiuser online game for medical undergraduate radiology education within second life. *Anatomical Sciences Education*, *13*(5), 602–617.

Mayrath, M., Sanchez, J., Traphagan, T., Heikes, J., & Trivedi, A. (2007, June). Using Second Life in an English course: Designing class activities to address learning objectives. In *EdMedia+ Innovate Learning* (pp. 4219–4224). Association for the Advancement of Computing in Education (AACE).

McCrindle, M. (2021). *Generation Alpha*. Hachette UK. https://mccrindle.com.au/insights/blog/gen-alpha-defined/

McGlynn, A. P. (2005). Teaching millennials: Our newest cultural cohort. *The Education Digest*, *71*(4), 12–16.
Melchor-Couto, S. (2018). Virtual world anonymity and foreign language oral interaction. *ReCALL*, *30*(2), 232–249. https://doi.org/10.1017/S0958344017000398
Nicholson, S. (2012). A user-centered theoretical framework for meaningful gamification. In C. Martin, A. Ochsner & K. Squire (Eds.), *Proceedings GLS 8.0 Games + Learning + Society Conference* (pp. 223–230). ETC Press.
Ohashi, L. (2018, August). *Digital games in language education: Worth a closer look [Paper Presentation]*. The EuroCALL 2018 Conference, University of Jyväskylä, Finland.
Pellas, N. (2014). The influence of computer self-efficacy, metacognitive self-regulation and self-esteem on student engagement in online learning programs: Evidence from the virtual world of Second Life. *Computers in Human Behavior*, *35*, 157–170. https://doi.org/10.1016/j.chb.2014.02.048
Peterson, M. (2016a). The use of massively multiplayer online role-playing games in CALL: An analysis of research. *Computer Assisted Language Learning*, *29*(7), 1181–1194. http://dx.doi.org/10.1080/09588221.2016.1197949
Peterson, M. (2016b). Virtual worlds and language learning: An analysis of research. In F. Farr & L. Murray (Eds.), *The Routledge handbook of language learning and technology* (pp. 308–319). Routledge.
Peterson, M., Wang, Q., & Mirzaei, M. S. (2019). The use of network-based virtual worlds in second language education: A research review. In M. Kruk (Ed.), *Assessing the effectiveness of virtual technologies in foreign and second language instruction* (pp. 1–25). IGI Global. https://doi.org/10.4018/978-1-5225-7286-2.ch001
Petrakou, A. (2010). Interacting through avatars: Virtual worlds as a context for online education. *Computers & Education*, *54*(4), 1020–1027. https://doi.org/10.1016/j.compedu.2009.10.007
Pirker, J., Riffnaller-Schiefer, M., & Gütl, C. (2014, June). Motivational active learning: engaging university students in computer science education. In A. Cajander et al. (Ed.), *ITiCSE '14* (pp. 297–302). ACM, Uppsala, Sweden.
Prensky, M. (2001a). Digital natives, digital immigrants. *On the Horizon*, *9*(5), 1–6.
Prensky, M. (2001b). Digital natives, digital immigrants, part 2: Do they really think differently? *On the Horizon*, *9*(6), 7–15.
Prensky, M. (2004). *Use their tools! Speak their language*! https://www.marcprensky.com/writing/Prensky-Use_Their_Tools_Speak_Their_Language.pdf.
Prensky, M. (2008). Turning on the lights. *Educational Leadership*, *65*(6), 40–45.
Reimers, F. M., & Chung, C. K. (Eds.). (2019). *Teaching and learning for the twenty-first century: Educational goals, policies, and curricula from six nations*. Harvard Education Press.
Reinders, H., & Wattana, S. (2014). Can I say something? The effects of digital game play on willingness to communicate. *Language Learning & Technology*, *18*(2), 101–123.
Reinsmith-Jones, K., Kibbe, S., Crayton, T., & Campbell, E. (2015). Use of second life in social work education: Virtual world experiences and their effect on students. *Journal of Social Work Education*, *51*(1), 90–108.
Sadler, R., & Dooly, M. (2013). Language learning in virtual worlds: Research and practice. In H. R. M. Thomas (Ed.), *Contemporary computer-assisted language learning* (pp. 159–182). Bloomsbury.

Sadler, R. W. (2017). The continuing evolution of virtual worlds for language learning. In C. A. Chapelle & S. Sauro (Eds.), *The handbook of technology and second language teaching and learning* (pp. 184–201). John Wiley & Sons.

Schroeder, R. (2010). Virtual environments and the changing landscape of information and communication technologies. In *Being there together: Social interaction in shared virtual environments* (pp. 3–20). Oxford University Press.

Schrum, L., & Levin, B. B. (2009). Leading 21st-century schools: What school leaders need to know. In *Leading 21st century schools: Harnessing technology for engagement and achievement* (pp. 3–25). SAGE.

Schukei, A. (2021). *What you need to understand about Generation Z students*. The Art of Education University. https://theartofeducation.edu/2020/12/14/what-you-need-to-understand-about-generation-z-students/

Second Life Community (2011). *Teens, Welcome to Second Life!*. https://community.secondlife.com/blogs/entry/85-teens-welcome-to-second-life

Second Life Community (2021). *Number of Second Life users?*. https://community.secondlife.com/forums/topic/472381-number-of-second-life-users

Second Life Wiki (2022). *Second Life Education Directory*. https://wiki.secondlife.com/wiki/Second_Life_Education_Directory

Swier, R., & Peterson, M. (2018). 3D digital games, virtual worlds, and language learning in higher education: Continuing challenges in Japan. *JALT CALL Journal*, *14*(3), 225–238.

Sykes, J. M. (2018). Digital games and language teaching and learning. *Foreign Language Annals*, *51*(1), 219–224. https://doi.org/10.1111/flan.12325

The New Media Consortium (2012). *NMC Horizon Report 2012 Higher Education Edition*. https://library.educause.edu/resources/2012/2/2012-horizon-report

Trinder, K. R., & Moffat, D. C. (2009). *Trial of Second Life as a teaching aid for the curriculum in computing*. In ViWo 2009 Workshop (ICWL 2009) (pp. 1–6). 19-21 August, 2009, Aachen, Germany. https://citeseerx.ist.psu.edu/viewdoc/download?doi=10.1.1.527.5981&rep=rep1&type=pdf

UWA in Second Life (2022). *About UWA in SL: UWA in the 3D virtual world* [Blog post]. https://uwainsl.blogspot.com/p/about-uwa-in-sl.html

Vaibhav, A., & Gupta, P. (2014, December). *Gamification of MOOCs for increasing user Engagement* [Paper Presentation]. 2014 IEEE International Conference on MOOC, Innovation and Technology in Education (MITE), Piscataway, NJ, USA.

Wang, Y., Grant, S., & Grist, M. (2021). Enhancing the learning of multi-level undergraduate Chinese language with a 3D immersive experience-An exploratory study. *Computer Assisted Language Learning*, *34*(1–2), 114–132. https://doi.org/10.1080/09588221.2020.1774614

Wehner, A. K., Gump, A. W., & Downey, S. (2011). The effects of Second Life on the motivation of undergraduate students learning a foreign language. *Computer Assisted Language Learning*, *24*(3), 277–289. https://doi.org/10.1080/09588221.2010.551757

Wigham, C. R., & Chanier, T. (2015). Interactions between text chat and audio modalities for L2 communication and feedback in the synthetic world Second Life. *Computer Assisted Language Learning*, *28*(3), 260–283. https://doi.org/10.1080/09588221.2013.851702

Wood, L. C., & Reiners, T. (2012). Gamification in logistics and supply chain education: Extending active learning. In P. Kommers, T. Issa, & P. Isaías (Eds.), *IADIS International Conference on Internet Technologies & Society 2012* (pp. 101–108). IADIS.

Yeh, Y. T., Hung, H. T., & Hsu, Y. J. (2017, July). Digital game-based learning for improving students' academic achievement, learning motivation, and willingness to communicate in an English Course. In *2017 6th IIAI International Congress on Advanced Applied Informatics (IIAI-AAI)* (pp. 560–563). IEEE. https://doi.org/10.1109/IIAI-AAI.2017.40

CHAPTER 2

TASK-BASED LANGUAGE TEACHING IN SECOND LIFE

OVERVIEW

Being a language pracademic myself, I believe that teaching should be informed and guided by research-driven principles. This chapter introduces the definitions of a task, the principles of task-based language teaching (TBLT), what technology-mediated TBLT entails, how it translates into online teaching, and above all, implementing TBLT in SL. Together with Chapter 1, these two chapters lay a foundation for the book and provide readers with a sound understanding of the field before they dive into task-based teaching in the 3D virtual world.

As a practitioner, teacher trainer and researcher, I have been involved in 3D virtual teaching and research for over a decade. The unique affordances of 3D MUVEs that can turn a conventional classroom into a 3D playground never cease to amaze and excite me. Nothing would make a teacher happier than seeing students embody their avatar to perform real-world tasks and interact with peers or other SL residents in a target language through multimodal communication. It is also exhilarating to teleport students or fly from one destination to another on multiple field trips in-world, and witness SL-enabled, problem-solving tasks stimulate language output and trigger unrehearsed negotiation.

This chapter taps into my years of experience in helping and empowering (hopefully) classroom teachers to transition into the MUVE space as novice online teachers. Evidently, there is more to 3D virtual teaching than simply copying what we do in a physical class. Synergising TBLT as the pedagogical framework and the immersive and simulated nature of 3D MUVEs, such as SL, has been proven to optimise language learning and teaching as in my own research (e.g., Chen, 2016a, 2016b, 2018, 2020a, 2020b) and other studies (e.g., Canto & Jauregi-Ondarra, 2017; Lan et al., 2016; Peterson, 2016; Peterson et al., 2019; Swier & Peterson, 2018). Because theory-laden TBLT research has predominated the literature (e.g., Ahmadian & Long, 2021; Bygate, 2015; Ellis, 2003; Ellis et al., 2019; Long, 2015; Robinson, 2011), it is not my intention to exhaust my fellow teachers further here. Instead, I aim to annotate the literature on TBLT through a practical lens and focus more on its pedagogical principles and applications supported by technology. I also present an SL-enabled, task-based syllabus that I co-designed with a novice SL teacher in a teacher training project to illustrate how to operationalise these principles in SL (see Chen & Kent, 2020). Hopefully, this succinct and concrete review can ease my fellow pracademics into the realm of enacting TBLT in SL.

TASK-BASED LANGUAGE TEACHING (TBLT)

What Is a Task?

With its burgeoning popularity among task-based researchers and language practitioners, TBLT has been widely piloted and implemented in language education and second language acquisition (SLA) research over three decades. What sets TBLT apart from other traditional teaching methods (e.g., grammar translation, audiolingual method, or total physical response) is that it promotes language use for authentic purposes through communicative, meaning-focused tasks that prepare learners to potentially carry out the same tasks in the real world (Ellis, 2019; Skehan, 2003). Whilst there are different versions of TBLT, it is fundamental to understand what constitutes a task, how scholars define a task, what common traits are shared by those definitions, and how a task can be enacted following research-informed, pedagogy-sound principles.

Apparently, discussing TBLT without mentioning the late Michael Long is doing it a disservice. Long's task definition in his seminal work (Long, 1985) has been widely cited in the field of SLA: "By 'task' is meant the hundred and one things people do in everyday life, at work, at play, and in between" (p. 89). This definition, though simple and broad, rightly captures the essence of a task that is what we actually do in the real world. When a task is conceptualised in the classroom setting, Jane Willis (1996) defined it as

> a goal-oriented activity in which learners use language to achieve a real outcome. In other words, learners use whatever target language resources they have in order to solve a problem, do a puzzle, play a game, or share and compare experiences.
>
> (p. 53)

This definition gives us a workable guide as language teachers. It highlights the importance of having "a real outcome" in a task, and leaners can harness any aspect of a language in their capacity to attain the goal (outcome), rather than only resort to grammar. Following suit, David Nunan (2006) first categorised tasks into target tasks (real-world tasks beyond the classroom) and pedagogic(al) tasks (translate real-world tasks into the classroom practice). He then gave a clear definition of what a task entails and how it takes place in a language class:

> a piece of classroom work that involves learners in comprehending, manipulating, producing or interacting in the target language while their attention is focused on

> mobilizing their grammatical knowledge in order to express meaning, and in which the intention is to convey meaning rather than to manipulate form. The task should also have a sense of completeness, being able to stand alone as a communicative act in its own right with a beginning, a middle and an end.
>
> (p. 17)

A clear message is conveyed here: learner attention should be paid primarily to meaning rather than to grammar ("form"), the latter of which is typically targeted in traditional language teaching, however. That is not to say grammar is unimportant in language production but that grammatical forms should not supersede the ultimate goal to convey meaning spontaneously during task completion. It is also clear that language use through meaningful communication is the key to each phase of task completion (beginning, middle, end).

Similarly, Peter Skehan (1996), another influential TBLT scholar, stressed that a task should be:

> an activity in which meaning is primary, there is some sort of relationship to the real world, task completion has some priority, the assessment of task performance is in terms of task outcome…[and] requires personal information to be exchanged, or a problem to be solved, or a collective judgement to be made.
>
> (p. 38)

Following this lucid definition, some common ground (criteria) can be extrapolated. First, *meaning* is primary in a task activity rather than language itself. Second, the task should bear a *real-world* relevance that also enables learners to do the same outside of the class. Third, the task needs to have a *goal* for learners to work towards. Hence, the task *outcome* dictates how learner task performance should be assessed – as long as they reach the outcome by completing the task using whatever (non-)language resources are available to them. Finally, the task requires *authentic communication* that encourages learners to exchange meaningful and personal information to solve a problem or reach a consensus (Skehan, 1998).

As task-based research is evolving, task definitions are also becoming more crystalised. Rod Ellis (2003), a well-renowned TBLT guru, enriched the task definition:

> a workplan that requires learners to process language pragmatically in order to achieve an outcome that can be evaluated in terms of whether the correct or appropriate

propositional content has been conveyed. To this end, it requires them to give primary attention to meaning and to make use of their own linguistic resources, although the design of the task may predispose them to choose particular forms. A task is intended to result in language use that bears a resemblance, direct or indirect to the way language is used in the real world. Like other language activities, a task can engage productive or receptive, and oral or written skills and also various cognitive processes.

(p. 16)

This operational definition lays out a strong foundation of a task, building on various task definitions discussed previously. It highlights the key criteria that Peter Skehan (1996, 1998) put forth in a task. For example, a task serves as a goal-oriented workplan for learners, be it successfully checking in a hotel or making a restaurant reservation, as much as they would normally do in the real world. As such, it connects to a RL task scenario. Given the authenticity and learner-driven approach, students can draw upon their current language repertoires and content knowledge at their disposal to complete the task. Whilst meaning is primary in task design, Ellis argued that a teacher can still seed a target form in communicative task activities (i.e., focused tasks). The task outcome is assessed on the basis of whether the key information has been meaningfully and comprehensively conveyed to bridge the gap of the task. The task can be carried out either productively (speaking, writing; "output prompting") or receptively (listening, reading; "input providing") (Ellis, 2017a).

To help language teachers better grasp the concept, Ellis (2019) encapsulated these key characteristics to foreground the four criteria that a task should satisfy:

- The students' primary focus must be on meaning
- There must be some kind of gap.
- The students must mainly rely on their own linguistic and non-linguistic resources to perform the task.
- There is a communicative outcome.

These task criteria are helpful as they provide concrete principles that guide the task design and implementation. For example, language use over forms (grammar) is pivotal to meaningful communication. At the end of the day, it is all about how meaning can be clearly conveyed and understood during task-based communication. "Gap" built in the task is also an important concept as it stimulates information exchange and negotiation of meaning, which promotes language processing and acquisition. What makes a task different from an activity or exercise is that not only does it have a goal that guides students to attain the workable outcome(s) throughout their task completion, it also respects their *internal syllabus,* which allows them to tap into whatever resources they have, such as language, world knowledge, or even non-verbal cues like gestures. Depending on the task type (e.g., input- or output-based), a task can even be accomplished without the language use (e.g., only listening to instructions to make a cake without speaking). It is also perfectly fine that learners did not use the correct sentence structures or vocabulary in language productions as long as they get meaning across and complete the task successfully.

Interactive Tasks with SLA Underpinnings

Even though we will not exhaust the literature with theory-laden studies, it is still pivotal to form a general understanding of how and why TBLT can optimise language learning and lead to evidence-based outcomes. Understanding the SLA-TBLT synergy will help teachers and researchers make educated decisions on task design and selecting viable task types as in my own case (see for example, Chen, 2016a, 2018, 2020b).

From the SLA standpoint, TBLT is couched nicely by the interactionist theory due to its communicative, authentic, and problem-solving characteristics. It has been evidenced that learner cognitive and linguistic processes will be heightened if they engage in interactive tasks that allow for negotiation of meaning during communication breakdowns (Pica, 1988; Pica & Doughty, 1985). The corrective feedback learners receive from peers (or native speakers) will serve as a mechanism to help them *refine* input and *modify* output (Doughty & Pica, 1986), bearing on the attention paid to those "hot spots" in their current interlanguage system (Swain, 1985; Swain & Lapkin, 1995). To illustrate, learners work in pairs to guide their partner to arrive at a location on a city map in an information gap task. Without showing each other the information they are holding, both try their best to exchange information so that their partners can get to their destination. During their task interaction, a communication breakdown may occur due to mis- or non-understanding triggered by mispronunciation, accent, incorrect use of grammatical form, tense, and vocabulary, for example. The mis-/non-understanding (i.e., hot spot) is where negotiation of meaning takes place. The learners reformulate the input and modify the output using whatever (non-)language resources and communication strategies (e.g., confirmation checks) they have so that their partners can better understand the intended meaning. Hence, interactive tasks serve as a vehicle to stimulate authentic, real-time language processing (input) and production (output) from language learners. From the pedagogical perspective, communication tasks also provide learners with opportunities to use a target language spontaneously for meaningful and communicative purposes in unscripted interactional settings (Ellis, 2000). This yields practical implications for task design in both classroom and online settings.

So how do we ensure that the interactional element is effectively built into tasks to elicit negotiation of meaning that also involves communicative strategy use? Long (1980, 1990) argued that two-way information exchange tasks that are *close oriented* will trigger more negotiation and strategy use than one-way or *open-oriented* tasks. Put another way, closed, interactional tasks require that each dyad member works cooperatively and contributes equal pieces of information held by them to reach one single solution needed for task completion (e.g., jigsaw or two-way information gap task). In contrast, open, one-way tasks (e.g., opinion exchange) allow learners to "freely" exchange information based on their own opinions without having to reach the same, "predetermined" solution.

Duff (1986) also found that *convergent (closed)* or *shared-goal tasks* prompt not only more instances of negotiation in each dyad task interaction, but also prompt the use of communication strategies to resolve the non-understanding triggered in each negotiation episode. In other words, tasks that are convergent on "reach[ing] a mutually acceptable solution" (Duff, 1986, p. 150) will provide more opportunities for negotiation of meaning – an integral factor that optimises the development of language skills. In contrast, *divergent (open)* or *independent-goal tasks* promote fewer occurrences in negotiation, which leads to less use of modification strategies since the catalyst for negotiation (i.e., mis- or non-understandings) is not activated due to the "implicitly opposite or independent goals" of a task (p. 150).

Pica et al. (1993) further reiterated that optimal task conditions hinge upon:

- Each dyad member holding a portion of information that must be exchanged to reach the same task outcome,
- Each dyad taking turns to request and give information,
- Both members sharing the same goals,
- Only one single outcome being acceptable to reach the goal. (p. 17)

Once again, Pica and her colleagues validated that two-way information-exchange tasks, such as jigsaw or information gap, are more restrictive as they require each dyad interactant equally contributes their own pieces of information to reach the shared goal (convergent).

The obligatory nature triggers more cognitive and linguistic processes by pushing learners to negotiate meaning, reformulate input, and refine output to make meaning more comprehensible for the sake of task completion. In contrast, one-way or divergent tasks, such as opinion exchange, are less restrictive and allow for open-ended discussion (anything-goes), thus generating fewer occurrences of negotiation and strategy use (Pica et al., 1989).

Even after three decades, these task-based research findings still hold true and shed light on how we can design tasks that are more aligned with SLA underpinnings to yield positive learning outcomes in relation to language learners' cognitive and linguistic processes (Ellis, 2003). To put theory into practice, we will take a further look at how TBLT scholars suggest designing a task-based syllabus following research-sound, pedagogy-oriented principles.

CHECKPOINT

- Can you define a task by highlighting the key characteristics to a colleague who is new to TBLT?
- Following Ellis's (2019) criteria that a "real" task should satisfy, can you think of any activity that you usually do in class that has met all the task criteria? If not, which aspect of the activity would you like to modify to turn it into a real task?
- The two types of interactive tasks, open-ended (divergent) and closed-ended (convergent), seem to differ in quality and quantity of task-based negotiation and associated strategy use. Do you also agree that closed-ended tasks can stimulate more language acquisition than the open-ended ones? Can you share with a colleague a task example for each task type and how will you gather and analyse the discourse samples to verify this claim (i.e., convergent > divergent)?

Task-Based Syllabus Design

It is pivotal to design a task-based syllabus following the task criteria (e.g., meaning-focused, goal-oriented, outcome-evaluated, real-world-related, problem-solving; Skehan, 1996, 1998, 2003) and principles (e.g., spontaneous interaction, negotiation of meaning, trying out communication strategies; Willis, 1996). Tasks that are meaningful, authentic, communicative, challenging, and engaging will stimulate learner cognitive and linguistic processing (Ellis, 2017a, 2019). Ellis (2018) rightly argued that there is no single way of enacting TBLT as there are various methodological approaches to task-based syllabus design and modules. Some task-based syllabi may include pre-, during-, and post-task stages (see Dave and Jane Willis' (Willis & Willis, 2007) framework for doing task-based teaching), whereas others suggest following a rigorous task cycle from conducting learner needs analysis to gathering authentic target task samples to developing pedagogic tasks ready for and assessing the outcomes (for example, see Michael Long's (1985, 2015) full-blown TBLT model). Regardless of the versions, it is crucial to also point out that task-based syllabus design should also gear towards promoting language acquisition through meaningful, authentic task interaction. The myths that TBLT focuses only on the effectiveness of communication and language use, and not on language form such as grammatical accuracy and complexity, have been debunked by TBLT scholars such as Rod Ellis (2009, 2017a) and Michael Long (2016).

Take Jane Willis (1996) and later with Dave Willis' (Willis & Willis, 2007) framework for doing task-based teaching, for example. They propose a TBLT model (*pre-task, task cycle, language focus*) that guides syllabus design. The pre-task phase allows the teacher to introduce the topic and present the task to the learners such as activating student background knowledge associated with the topic, explaining how to carry out the task, and drawing student attention to some key words and expressions needed to complete the task. The teacher may also demonstrate how to do the task if time permits. Next comes the main task cycle that consists of doing the *task* itself, a *planning* phase, and a *report* phase. The task phase is the time and place in which learners can really take the reins and do the task spontaneously and collaboratively and explore different aspects of a language that can enable them to accomplish the task. The teacher only works as a facilitator to ensure students are on task or to prompt participation, for example.

In the planning phase, students prepare to report their task outcomes back to the class, similar to doing an oral presentation in public. Due to the nature of "public presentation", students will pay more attention to their language production in terms of using accurate grammar or choosing the key vocabulary. In the last phase, students do their reporting either verbally or in written form. Each pair/group can also exchange their task outcomes, followed by the teacher summary. It is in the last phase that the focus of doing a task is shifted to "language" where the teacher can draw student attention to common errors or target vocabulary, phrases, and grammatical points in the task. The teacher can also encourage students to analyse their language production using the transcript of their oral presentation, for example.

David Nunan (2006) suggested that task-based syllabus design should take into account the following principles and practices (p. 14):

- A needs-based approach to content selection
- An emphasis on learning to communicate through interaction in the target language
- The introduction of authentic texts into the learning situation
- The provision of opportunities for learners to focus, not only on language, but also on the learning process itself
- An enhancement of the learner's own personal experiences as important contributing elements to classroom learning.
- The linking of classroom language learning with language use outside the classroom

As such, the syllabus design that embodies the TBLT principles in the classroom practices aims to (1) promote authentic language processing and negotiation of meaning whilst doing RL-related tasks from the cognitive interactionist perspective, and (2) allow learners to co-construct knowledge using whatever resources they have and mutually scaffold peers through engaging in task-based interaction from the sociocognitive perspective (Skehan, 2003).

Another classic task-based design framework is proposed by Michael Long (1985, 2015). The ultimate task goal is to emulate target tasks that learners do in the real world (e.g., make a reservation) through a series of logically sequenced pedagogic tasks (e.g., compare the hotel room rates and types before booking) that will guide them to reach the goal. In this model, the task-based design should comprise key elements in

- Conducing a needs analysis to identify target tasks related to the real world
- Classifying the target tasks into overarching task types
- Developing pedagogic tasks under the selected task types
- Organising and sequencing the pedagogic tasks into a task-based syllabus

According to Michael Long, needs analysis must be addressed first and foremost when designing any type of task syllabus. It helps identify the target tasks that students are keen to do or important to them in RL, such as buying an airplane ticket, booking a table at a restaurant, applying for a job, etc. There are many ways to conduct a needs analysis by triangulating sources from involved stakeholders (e.g., students, teachers, programme administrators, domain experts) and methods (e.g., interview, survey, observation, analysis of authentic samples). After the needs analysis is completed, the syllabus developer can generate the task type from the target tasks. For example, making a reservation can serve as a task type for target tasks as in booking a table at a restaurant or renting an Airbnb accommodation.

Next, the developer can start developing and then sequencing pedagogic tasks that work as subtasks to enable students to perform the target task(s) step by step to successfully accomplish the same tasks in the real world. Note that pedagogic tasks can be carried out individually or collaboratively in pairs or groups. The main focus is to promote meaningful and spontaneous communication, though target language form can still be incorporated in task design. It is hoped that learner language acquisition can be enhanced during meaningful task-based negotiation that involves corrective feedback exchange and communication strategy use to resolve communication breakdowns. The teacher is advised not to interrupt the process of task completion but only to facilitate the task flow, monitor student task engagement and communication, and provide guidance or feedback if need be. For a large-scale programme development, the developer should also assess the effectiveness of task outcomes and student learning, paving the way for the evaluation and improvement of programme development (Long, 2015).

Rod Ellis (2017b) further suggested that task-based syllabus design should take into account the following elements:

- *Natural language use* that is unrehearsed and spontaneous
- *Course design* that consists of identifying both target and pedagogic tasks or the latter only
- *Task type* that can be either unfocused (not targeting any particular language aspect or form) or focused (with a specific target language feature in mind)
- *Task modality* that can be either output prompting (e.g., speaking) or input providing (e.g., listening)
- *Focus on form* (language focus) that can occur in any of the task phase
- *Learner-centeredness or teacher-led* approach

We can also see how TBLT scholars address the task features differently in considering task-based syllabus design as summarised in Table 2.1:

Table 2.1 Syllabus considerations across TBLT approaches

Features	Long (1985, 2015)	Willis (1996); Willis and Willis (2007)	Skehan (1998)	Ellis (2003)
Natural language use	+	+	+	+
Course design	Target + pedagogic tasks	Pedagogic tasks	Pedagogic tasks	Pedagogic tasks
Task type	Mainly unfocused tasks	Unfocused	Unfocused	Unfocused + focused tasks
Task modality	Output-based	Output-based	Output-based	Output-based + input-based
Focus on form	+ (main task phase)	+ (post-task phase)	+ (pre- and post-task phases)	+ (all phases)
Learner-centeredness	+	+	+	+/-
Rejection of traditional approaches	+	+	+	-

Source: Adapted from Ellis (2017b, p. 112).

It is also crucial to consider aspects of complexity in sequencing and manipulating the tasks in syllabus design because task complexity will affect whether learners can successfully engage in task completion. With that in mind, we will take a final look at some considerations in task design features outlined by Ellis (2019) to ensure that tasks are appropriately developed in relation to complexity and learners' current level (Table 2.2).

These guidelines posit that the TBLT design of instructional materials and tasks is based on theoretically sound frameworks that tap into goal-oriented, meaning-driven, and real-world tasks to promote spontaneous language use, and realise language acquisition in authentic discourses. This is particularly pivotal if viewed in certain instructional contexts where opportunities for unscripted task interaction and using a target language for communicative and meaningful purposes are still constrained by traditional language methods that focus primarily on language itself. A well-planned TBLT design that is driven by key elements of cognitive interactionist theory (e.g., negotiated instruction, comprehensible input and output) and grounded in methodological principles (e.g., task-oriented, communicative and real-world materials) can enhance the cognitive and interactional processes of EFL learners. Hence, implementing TBLT in class has promising implications for language acquisition to take place due to its pedagogically driven principles, such as problem-solving, negotiation of meaning, and communicative needs. We will now explore how TBLT principles and task design supported by technology can be translated into the online instructional setting, such as SL.

Table 2.2 Considerations of complexity in task design

Design features	Descriptions
± Simple input	Input-based tasks (in oral or written form) can include either simple language, vocabulary, and structure or complex ones (e.g., low-frequency words and longer sentences).
± Familiar topic	A task is simpler if it relates to a familiar topic on student personal experience, whereas a task is more difficult if it taxes understanding outside student background knowledge or experience.
± Here and now	A here-and-now task condition is more concrete than its there-and-then counterpart as the former allows students to see the object/material (e.g., picture) whilst doing the task rather than doing it without visual or additional support.
± Few elements	A task is easier if it involves fewer elements such as two characters living in the same town in a story, than multiple ones such as five different characters living in different locations.
± Structured information	If the information is structured sequentially in a task such as drawing the transit route from A to B, then it is easier than the unstructured one that involves different location points on different timetables.
± Reasoning demands	A reasoning task that requires students to explain how and why the actions took place and characters' motifs is more difficult than one that only requires retelling an event in a story narration task, for example.
± Simple outcome	If a task only requires students to only state what items they would choose to bring to an island (e.g., opinion exchange), then it is simpler than one (e.g., reasoning gap) that requires them to justify why they chose particular items over others.

Source: Adapted from Ellis (2019, Ch. 3).

TECHNOLOGY-MEDIATED TBLT IN SL

Aligning with cognitive and interactionist SLA theory (Long, 1981, 1983, 1985; Pica, 1988; Pica & Doughty, 1985; Swain, 1995), Catherine Doughty and Michael Long offered 10 methodological principles to guide the design of TBLT, particularly in a distance learning environment (for more detail about each principle, see Doughty & Long, 2003):

1. Use tasks, not texts, as the unit of analysis.
2. Promote learning by doing.
3. Elaborate input (do not simplify; do not rely solely on "authentic" texts).
4. Provide rich (not impoverished) input.
5. Encourage inductive ("chunk") learning.
6. Focus on form.
7. Provide negative feedback.

8. Respect "learner syllabuses"/developmental processes.
9. Promote cooperative/collaborative learning.
10. Individualise instruction (according to communicative needs and psycholinguistically). (p. 52)

These methodological principles of TBLT, as argued by Doughty and Long (2003), are theoretically-sound (e.g., focus on form [not forms], use of tasks, elaborate and rich input, corrective feedback) and pedagogically feasible (e.g., learning by doing, learner interlanguage processing, collaborative learning, and individualised instruction), with great potential for online language education. One of the fundamental TBLT principles, *learning by doing*, coincides rightly with the unique affordances (e.g., immersion, augmented reality, simulation) in a 3D MUVE, such as SL. For example, language teachers can hold virtual classes to simulate RL tasks (e.g., checking in an airport or visiting a museum) for student avatars to interact with other avatars around the world. The abundant 3D resources and multimodal stimuli also provide *rich input* for language learners. Another case in point is that SL allows residents to create and manipulate 3D objects. This unique feature makes *collaborative*, *problem-solving* tasks that are too costly or even risky to accomplish in RL (e.g., negotiate with team members on how to perform a surgery or fly a plane) possible in SL. It breaks down the complex procedure and makes learning more concrete and manageable through trial and error, which is particularly crucial for language beginners. Hence, RL tasks that are cumbersome or challenging to perform in a traditional language class can be seamlessly enacted in SL, thus mitigating issues related to travel arrangements or budget concerns that we have discussed in Chapter 1.

Marta González-Lloret and Lourdes Ortega also offered a practical framework for technology-mediated TBLT, aiming to integrate *tasks* with *technology* that can deepen experiential learning beyond a physical class (González-Lloret & Ortega, 2014). They argued that three conditions be met for full integration:

1. Tasks need to be real-word oriented and authentic in nature rather than copying exercise-based activities over onto a digital platform. They should also consider learner needs; interests; and their cultural, technological, and global understandings outside of the classroom.
2. Educators should be aware of the direct impact technology has on knowledge co-construction/reconstruction in language education and SLA, whilst considering wider technological applications to TBLT situated in the real world (e.g., smartphones, apps, digital maps).

3. Developing a rigorous technology-mediated TBLT curriculum needs to follow a full task cycle, such as conducting needs analysis, selecting/sequencing tasks, and assessing learner task performance. The evaluation of program effectiveness should also address technology, language, and task outcomes holistically.

This framework helps us reconceptualise the interplay of tasks and technology, considering the dynamic roles both equally play in designing task-based syllabi in online environments. To help curriculum designers and educators better develop a technology-mediated TBLT program, Marta González-Lloret (2016) provided useful guidelines in considering different aspects of needs analysis, such as student digital literacy and access to technology, as well as how to gather information from triangulated sources (Table 2.3). Getting this crucial step (needs analysis) into gear will ensure a rigorous task design supported by technology.

Evidently, the prospect of implementing technology-mediated TBLT in the 3D virtual world has encouraged language teacher researchers to experiment with innovative ways of promoting authentic language use outside of the class walls. The salient SL features— such as hands-on simulation of RL tasks, collaborative problem-solving, multimodal communication enhanced by 3D resources, and tele-/copresence that augments immersion— provide a fertile ground for task-based syllabus design supported by SLA (González-Lloret & Ortega, 2014; González-Lloret & Rock, 2022). For example, Mark Peterson in one of his studies (Peterson, 2010, also see Peterson, 2006) examined the interrelationships between task type, text-based negotiation, and communication strategy use in SL. He found that his Japanese college students were stimulated to use different multimodal communication strategies, such as emoticons and time-saving devices, to negotiate meaning with peers in interactional tasks conducted in SL. Students also perceived English learning in SL more cognitively engaging and socially collaborative, thus building a virtual community of practice (Peterson, 2012).

In several of my SL studies (Chen 2016a, 2018, 2020a), I was able to verify Peterson's findings and the positive implications drawn from interactive tasks situated in cognitive interactionist theory. Not only did I validate that convergent tasks such as two-way information gap and jigsaw can trigger more negotiation, strategy use, and quality of language production, I also proved that SLA-driven tasks can be developed and enhanced using SL features, and carried out as seamlessly in SL as in RL (if not better). Because SL also mirrors the real world that draws residents from different linguistic/cultural backgrounds

Table 2.3 Summary of considerations of sources, methods, and questions in needs analysis

Potential sources	Potential methods	Questions to consider
Students	Questionnaire Interview	What they think know and can do? Their attitudes towards it? Access to technology and training? Willingness to learn?
Students	Information technology (IT) assessment On-site observation Task interaction and performance Screen capture recording	What they actually know and can do?
Teachers	Questionnaire Interview Focus group meeting	Technology available to teachers? Teacher digital skills? What training they need?
Administrators	Questionnaire Interview	What students will need to be able to succeed? What technology is accessible? IT support for teaching staff?
Alumni employers	On-site observation Task interaction and performance	What students will need to be able to succeed? Technology available?
Job descriptions/ads	Text analysis	What students will need to be able to succeed?
IT experts	Questionnaire Interview On-site observation Task interaction and performance Screen capture recording	What is needed for task completion? IT support for teaching staff? IT training available?
Manuals/research	Text analysis	What are the technology capacities?
Scholars	Interview	The potential of digital tools for language learning? What support/infrastructure is needed? What training is needed?
Netiquette	On-site observation of task interaction Text analysis	How and what need to be done? The new digital trends?

Source: Adapted from González-Lloret (2016, Ch. 2).

in-world, researchers also found that task-based interaction in avatar form can raise the intercultural awareness of language learners, enhance oral communication skills (Canto & Jauregi-Ondarra, 2017; Canto et al., 2014; Chen, 2016b; Deutschmann & Panichi, 2013), and "stimulate learners' curiosity, empathy and openness towards the *Other*" (Jauregi-Ondarra et al., 2022, p. 318). These pedagogical benefits of "doing" tasks in SL make task-based, SLA-driven research worthwhile.

> **CHECKPOINT**
>
> - One of the "myths" in adopting TBLT is that language form should be played down (or even unattended to) during task completion. Do you also share this view? If not, when and how will you address the language aspects and draw student attention to those target areas in their language productions?
> - In Table 2.1, Ellis (2017a) provided a clear summary table comparing and contrasting different approaches to a TBLT syllabus design. Discuss with a colleague each task feature across approaches: Which approach proposed by one of the TBLT scholars do you find resonates more with your current practice?
> - Doughty and Long (2003) suggested 10 methodological principles of TBLT for distance learning. Can you connect some of the principles, if not all, to task-based instruction in an online environment? How will you operationalise them in a 3D MUVE, such as SL? Discuss the potential challenges and possibilities with a colleague using some concrete examples.
> - González-Lloret and Ortega (2014) argued that three conditions need to be met for tasks to be fully integrated with technology. How will you choose appropriate digital tool(s) that are integral to not only task completion but also construction of knowledge and language skills? Do you also think it is necessary to foster learner digital literacy skills whilst they are doing a task? How will you provide such support or training?

A CONCRETE EXAMPLE OF OPERATIONALISING TASK DESIGN IN SL

In the following, I illustrate how I conducted a teacher training project for an English bridging program to instil fun and innovation in their conventional English Support class. The English as a second language (ESL) teacher who participated in the project had observed that her students often "shut down" in class, evidenced by their lack of motivation and engagement in lesson activities. They also complained that the prescriptive syllabus that focused heavily on academic writing and structure was "boring", and not geared towards the development of oral communication. Therefore, she would like to change the status quo by bringing fun and authentic communication to student learning. Although she had never taught online before the training, much less taught in SL, she expressed interest in upskilling her online teaching through the technology-enhanced, task-based approach. As a teacher trainer, I demonstrated how to utilise different SL features in preparation for online teaching, co-designed real-world-oriented, SL-driven tasks to suit her student needs and interests, and mentored her teaching the task-based syllabus in SL throughout her journey.[1]

Considerations of Task Principles

The first thing we discussed and agreed upon was to design a syllabus that was informed by viable teaching principles. I considered not only the key TBLT principles and how to marry them with the unique SL features, but also the "fun" and "gamified" factor that would make the lessons more uplifting, interactive, and organic. Specifically, I focused on the following technology-enhanced TBLT principles (González-Lloret, 2016; González-Lloret & Ortega, 2014) in my teacher training for this project:

- **Real-world relevance:** One of the methodological principles that underlies TBLT is *learning by doing*, which "is often the case with simulations and is done in the name of 'authenticity' of materials" (Doughty & Long, 2003, p. 59). The fact that 3D MUVEs, such as SL, afford language learners to carry out RL tasks in an immersive, simulated manner epitomises this principle. Another case in point is that many authentic tasks that learners are expected to do in the real world are cumbersome to conduct in a classroom setting, or lacking the optimal resemblance. In SL, language teachers can easily teleport the class to different field trip islands (e.g., Times Square, Eiffel Tower, and an Egyptian pyramid) without worrying about physical travel arrangements. Imagine the time and expense involved if these tasks were done in a class.
- **Negotiation of meaning:** Tasks that are collaborative and problem-solving in nature can generally trigger authentic communication. Because there is a problem (gap) (Ellis, 2019), learners working in a dyad or a group would try to convey information to their partner(s) as comprehensible and clear as possible to collectively solve the problem. They would use different strategies to "push" their peers to fine-tune the language output due to mis-/non-understandings in task-based interaction (Chen, 2016a, 2018), such as comprehension check (e.g., "Do you understand what I just said?"), clarification request (e.g., "Can you repeat that, please?"), or confirmation

check (e.g., "There are two hats on the table, correct?"). Therefore, the process of negotiation of meaning is where SLA takes place, and tasks conducted in SL can promote spontaneous, unscripted negotiation using multimodal features such as text, voice, and 3D representation of objects.
- **Task engagement:** When the nature of a task is cognitively, emotionally, and socially stimulating, learners would invest more effort in task completion because they perceive the task as genuinely worth doing (Philp & Duchesne, 2016). Different from other teaching approaches, TBLT taps into the learner's internal syllabus using both linguistic and non-linguistic repertoires to complete the task, such as background knowledge about the world and home culture, and interlanguage skills (Ellis, 2019). Because learners find the task meaningful and engaging (e.g., helping each other build a 3D object in SL), their motivation would also be heightened and consequently develop into learner autonomy (Peterson, 2016; Peterson et al., 2019). Additionally, SL as an MUVE infuses gameful and fun elements in task execution, which further bolsters task engagement (Chen, 2016b).

Task Selection

Task selection was based on the alignment of SL technicality (e.g., immersive simulation, avatar tele-/copresence, multimodality, spontaneity) and TBLT principles (e.g., authenticity, respecting learner non-/linguistic resources, collaborative problem-solving, cognitively and emotionally arousing). It was important to encourage the ESL teacher to think beyond the physical class when brainstorming the potential SL tasks. Given the boundless opportunities and dynamic features afforded by SL, it made perfect sense to bring creativity and the real world to lesson planning. The tasks she considered worth doing, but decided to leave out – due to the concerns of budget, planning time, and space limitation – could be revived now, such as:

> *Wouldn't it be more fun to take students on virtual field trips to visit art galleries in SL where each team can discuss and showcase their chosen 3D art piece?*
>
> *Wouldn't it be more meaningful to celebrate their home cultures by having their avatar change into a heritage outfit given their culturally and linguistically diverse (CaLD) backgrounds?*
>
> *Wouldn't it be more rewarding to foster learner autonomy through students taking turns to guide their partners to exit a 3D Maze and collect bonus gifts?*

The sky is the limit, indeed. The golden rule is to organically immerse students in task scenarios enabled by SL features. This allows them to perform meaningful RL tasks, negotiate meaning spontaneously, collaborate towards an ultimate goal, utilise both non-linguistic and linguistic resources, and genuinely enjoy the process of task completion.

An SL-Enabled, Task-Based Syllabus

In consideration of required SL skills, task complexity and logical lesson progression, Table 2.4 outlines the co-designed task topics, task description in each SL session, and task principles related to SL affordances:

Table 2.4 An SL-enabled, task-based syllabus co-designed by the teacher and mentor

Session	Topic	Task description	SL-enabled task principles
1	SL orientation	• Introduce students to SL and basic skills • Explore SL Welcome Island • Place Curtin Island as the home landmark for the virtual class to gather in the beginning of each session • Discuss cyber safety and netiquette • Remind students to post reflection on the class blog site	• Learning by doing • Simulation • Exposure to rich input
2	Art gallery field trip	• Take the class on a virtual field trip to an in-world gallery • Instruct student pairs to take snapshots of an artwork that interests them • Use voice chat to describe the chosen piece and explain why they like it as if they were a gallery curator	• Real-world relevance • Goal-oriented simulation • Multimodal input enhancement and output production • Emotionally stimulating • Intellectually challenging • Autonomous learning
3	Dine at a restaurant	• Teleport to a 3D restaurant that resembles an Italian restaurant • Divide students into groups and assign half of the group as servers taking orders, and assign the other half as customers ordering from the menu • Students follow Notecard instructions to roleplay different scenarios, such as customer complaining about the food and asking to send it back	• Real-world relevance • Goal-oriented simulation • Negotiation of meaning • Authentic communication • Multimodal input enhancement and output production • Intellectually challenging • Emotionally stimulating • Socially collaborating • Autonomous learning

(Continued)

Table 2.4 An SL-enabled, task-based syllabus co-designed by the teacher and mentor *(Continued)*

Session	Topic	Task description	SL-enabled task principles
4	Maze exit and object building	• Students working in pairs help each other build a 3D object following the Notecard instructions • Teleport to a 3D Maze where each pair takes turns guiding their partner to exit the Maze whilst collecting bonus freebies placed inside the Maze	• Goal-oriented simulation • Negotiation of meaning • Problem-solving (information gap) • Authentic communication • Multimodal input enhancement and output production • Intellectually challenging • Emotionally stimulating • Socially collaborating • Autonomous learning
5	Avatar interview	• Teleport the class to London Hyde Park and ask them to approach an SL resident for an interview • Record their interviewee's responses to the questions as listed on the Notecard • Take a snapshot of their new avatar friend before presenting their interview findings to the class	• Real-world relevance • Goal-oriented simulation • Negotiation of meaning • Authentic communication • Multimodal input enhancement and output production • Emotionally stimulating • Socially collaborating • Autonomous learning
6	Showcasing cultural outfit	• Ask students to find a cultural outfit in SL that represents their heritage clothing • If time permits, allow students to show and tell the outfit and address questions from their audience	• Real-world relevance • Goal-oriented simulation • Exposure to rich input • Authentic communication • Emotionally stimulating • Autonomous learning • Linguistic and non-linguistic repertoires
7	Fashion runway and wrap-up	• Each student avatar wears an outfit that either represents their home culture or takes their fancy • Showcase and describe the outfit whilst walking on a runway carpet for a class photo • Guide students to write a short reflection piece on their overall task experience in SL	• Real-world relevance • Goal-oriented simulation • Authentic communication • Multimodal input enhancement and output production • Emotionally stimulating • Autonomous learning • Linguistic and non-linguistic repertoires

The first session started with the SL orientation because students needed to know the key SL functions before they could carry out those tasks. A task was sequenced earlier in the syllabus if it only required individual work (e.g., a field trip to the gallery), or was more familiar to their RL experience (e.g., eating out at a restaurant). We gradually increased task complexity that demanded more negotiation of meaning (e.g., Maze exit), taxed a higher level of SL skills (e.g., object building), or challenged them to strike up a conversation with SL residents unknown to them (e.g., avatar interview). Whilst the task in session 6 (showcasing cultural outfit) was mainly an individual oral presentation, it tapped into students' own cultural knowledge and allowed them to address questions from the audience without rehearsal. The final wrap-up session celebrated their cultural heritage and worldviews (linguistically and conceptually), culminating in the fashion runway show and group photos.

YOUR TASK

- Brainstorm with a colleague on an interactive task that you have used or would like to implement in your class (e.g., spot the difference, decide which necessities to bring to an island). Use the design features in Table 2.2 (Ellis, 2019) to help you gauge the complexity of the task. Consider modifying the task to suit the proficiency level, learning needs, and cultural/linguistic backgrounds of your students as well.
- Work in a pair or group to design a task-based syllabus for international students keen to find a job on their working holiday in an English-speaking country, such as Australia, Canada, or New Zealand. You may also think of another topic that concerns your current students and teaching practice as an alternative. Consider the following:
  1. Make a list of the potential RL tasks that students need to undertake when living and working in the target country.
  2. From the list of target tasks, identify the task type (category) to organise similar tasks in the syllabus. For example, *completing a form* can be the task type for tasks in "filling out a job application" or "responding to background check questions on an online form", etc.
  3. Under each task type, develop pedagogic tasks (subtasks) that can prepare students to perform the associated target task(s) step by step. Make sure that your tasks satisfy Ellis' (2019) task criteria.
  4. Map out the whole syllabus by sequencing the subtasks under each task type in accordance with their complexity and logical task flow.

5. Develop assessment rubrics or schemes to evaluate student task performance as well as their language learning outcomes. You may also conduct a focus group or invite students to reflect on their overall experience to help you refine the syllabus design.

- Needs analysis plays a pivotal part in any type of task design. Work with the same colleague/group to design a technology-mediated TBLT syllabus that can be carried out online this time. Use Table 2.3 (González-Lloret, 2016) as a guide to help you conduct the needs analysis. Select potential sources to gather your information based on the (re)sources available to you. Once you identify the target tasks that can be potentially delivered online, such as SL, map out both language and technology tasks students need to do in accordance with the features of the preferred digital platform.

NOTE

1 For readers keen to know more about the project, see Chen and Kent (2020) for the full study on how this new 3D approach enhanced student task engagement, and Chen (2020a) on how I mentored her throughout her maiden SL teaching journey. Chapter 20 in Part III also provides my commentaries about the two studies.

REFERENCES

Ahmadian, M. J., & Long, M. H. (Eds.). (2021). *The Cambridge handbook of task-based language teaching*. Cambridge University Press. https://doi.org/10.1017/9781108868327

Bygate, M. (Ed.). (2015). *Domains and directions in the development of TBLT: A decade of plenaries from the international conference* (Vol. 8). John Benjamins Publishing. https://doi.org/10.1075/tblt.8

Canto, S., de Graaff, R., & Jauregi, K. (2014). Collaborative tasks for negotiation of intercultural meaning in virtual worlds and video-web communication. In M. Gonzalez-Lloret & L. Ortega (Eds.), *Technology and tasks: Exploring technology-mediated TBLT* (pp. 183–212). Georgetown University Press. https://doi.org/10.1075/tblt.6.07can

Canto, S., & Jauregi-Ondarra, K. (2017). Language learning effects through the integration of synchronous socializing network opportunities in language curricula: The case of video communication and Second Life. *Language Learning in Higher Education Journal*, *7*(1), 21–53. https://doi.org/10.1515/cercles-2017-0004

Chen, J. C. (2016a). EFL learners' strategy use during task-based interaction in second Life. *Australian Journal of Educational Technology*, *32*(3), 1–17. https://doi.org/10.14742/ajet.2306

Chen, J. C. (2016b). The crossroads of English language learners, task-based instruction, and 3D multi-user virtual learning in Second Life. *Computers & Education*, *102*, 152–171. https://doi.org/10.1016/j.compedu.2016.08.004

Chen, J. C. (2018). The interplay of tasks, strategies and negotiations in Second Life. *Computer Assisted Language Learning*, *31*(8), 960–986. https://doi.org/10.1080/09588221.2018.1466810

Chen, J. C. (2020a). Restorying a "newbie" teacher's 3D virtual teaching trajectory, resilience and professional development through action research: A narrative case study. *TESOL Quarterly*, *54*(2), 375–403. https://doi.org/10.1002/tesq.550

Chen, J. C. (2020b). The effects of pre-task planning on EFL learners' oral performance in a 3D multi-user virtual environment. *ReCALL*, *32*(3), 232–249. https://doi.org/10.1017/S0958344020000026

Chen, J. C., & Kent, S. (2020). Task engagement, learner motivation and avatar identity of struggling English language learners in the 3D virtual world. *System*, *88*, 102168. https://doi.org/10.1016/j.system.2019.102168

Deutschmann, M., & Panichi, L. (2013). Towards models for designing language learning in virtual worlds. *International Journal of Virtual and Personal Learning Environments*, *4*(2), 65–84. https://doi.org/10.4018/jvple.2013040104

Doughty, C. J., & Long, M. (2003). Optimal psycholinguistic environments for distance foreign language learning. *Language Learning & Technology*, *7*(3), 50–80.

Doughty, C. J., & Pica, T. (1986). "Information gap" tasks: Do they facilitate second language acquisition? *TESOL Quarterly*, *20*(2), 305–325. https://doi.org/10.2307/3586546

Duff, P. (1986). Another look at interlanguage talk: Taking task to task. In R. R. Day (Ed.), *Talking to learn: Conversation in second language acquisition* (pp. 147–181). Newbury House.

Ellis, R. (2000). Task-based research and language pedagogy. *Language Teaching Research*, *4*(3), 193–220. https://doi.org/10.1177/136216880000400302

Ellis, R. (2003). *Task-based language learning and teaching*. Oxford University Press.

Ellis, R. (2009). Task-based language teaching: Sorting out the misunderstandings. *International Journal of Applied Linguistics*, *19*(3), 221–246. https://doi.org/10.1111/j.1473-4192.2009.00231.x

Ellis, R. (2017a). Position paper: Moving task-based language teaching forward. *Language Teaching*, *50*(4), 507–526. https://doi.org/10.1017/S0261444817000179

Ellis, R. (2017b). Task-based language teaching. In S. Loewen & M. Sato (Eds.), *The Routledge handbook of instructed second language acquisition* (pp. 108–125). Taylor & Francis Group. https://doi.org/10.4324/9781315676968.ch7

Ellis, R. (2018). *Reflections on task-based language teaching*. Multilingual Matters. https://doi.org/10.21832/9781788920148

Ellis, R. (2019). *Introducing task-based language teaching* (1st ed.). Shanghai Foreign Language Education Press.

Ellis, R., Skehan, P., Li, S., Shintani, N., & Lambert, C. (2019). *Task-based language teaching: Theory and practice*. Cambridge University Press. https://doi.org/10.1017/9781108643689

González-Lloret, M. (2016). *A practical guide to integrating technology into task-based language teaching*. Georgetown University Press.

González-Lloret, M., & Ortega, L. (2014). Towards technology- mediated TBLT: An introduction. In M. González- Lloret & L. Ortega (Eds.), *Technology- mediated TBLT: Researching technology and tasks* (pp. 1–22). John Benjamins. https://doi.org/10.1075/tblt.6.01gon

González-Lloret, M., & Rock, K. (2022). Tasks in technology-mediated contexts. In N. Ziegler & M. González-Lloret (Eds.), *The Routledge handbook of second language acquisition and technology* (pp. 36–49). Routledge. https://doi.org/10.4324/9781351117586-5

Jauregi-Ondarra, K., Canto, S., & Melchor-Couto, S. (2022). Virtual worlds and second language acquisition. In N. Ziegler & M. González-Lloret (Eds.), *The Routledge handbook of second language acquisition and technology* (pp. 311–325). Routledge. https://doi.org/10.4324/9781351117586-27

Lan, Y. J., Kan, Y. H., Sung, Y. T., & Chang, K. E. (2016). Oral-performance language tasks for CSL beginners in Second Life. *Language Learning & Technology*, *20*(3), 60–79.

Long, M. H. (1980). *Input, interaction, and second language acquisition*. Ph.D. dissertation, UCLA.

Long, M. H. (1981). Input, interaction, and second-language acquisition. *Annals of the New York Academy of Sciences*, *379*, 259–278.

Long, M. H. (1983). Native speaker/non-native speaker conversation and the negotiation of comprehensible input. *Applied Linguistics*, *4*(2), 126–141. https://doi.org/10.1093/applin/4.2.126

Long, M. H. (1985). A role for instruction in second language acquisition: Task-based language training. In K. Hyltenstam & M. Pienemann (Eds.), *Modelling and assessing second language acquisition* (pp. 77–99). Multilingual Matters.

Long, M. H. (1990). Task, groups, and task-group interactions. In S. Anivan (Ed.), *Language teaching methodology for the nineties (Anthology Series* 24, pp. 1–50). RELC.

Long, M. H. (2015). *Second language acquisition and task-based language teaching*. Wiley Blackwell.

Long, M. H. (2016). In defense of tasks and TBLT: Nonissues and real issues. *Annual Review of Applied Linguistics*, 36, 5–33. https://doi.org/10.1017/S0267190515000057

Nunan, D. (2006). Task-based language teaching in the Asia context: Defining 'task.' *Asian EFL Journal*, *8*(3), 12–18.

Peterson, M. (2006). Learner interaction management in an avatar and chat-based virtual world. *Computer Assisted Language Learning*, *19(1)*, 79–103. https://doi.org/10.1080/09588220600804087

Peterson, M. (2010). Learner participation patterns and strategy use in Second Life: an exploratory case study. *ReCALL*, *22*(3), 273–292. https://doi.org/10.1017/S0958344010000169

Peterson, M. (2012). EFL learner collaborative interaction in Second Life. *ReCALL*, *24*(01), 20–39. https://doi.org/10.1017/S0958344011000279

Peterson, M. (2016). Virtual worlds and language learning: An analysis of research. In F. Farr & L. Murray (Eds.), *The Routledge handbook of language learning and technology* (pp. 308–319). Routledge.

Peterson, M., Wang, Q., & Mirzaei, M. S. (2019). The use of network-based virtual worlds in second language education: A research review. In M. Kruk (Ed.), *Assessing the effectiveness of virtual technologies in foreign and second language instruction* (pp. 1–25). IGI Global. https://doi.org/10.4018/978-1-5225-7286-2.ch001

Philp, J., & Duchesne, S. (2016). Exploring engagement in tasks in the language classroom. *Annual Review of Applied Linguistics*, 36, 50–72. https://doi.org/10.1017/s0267190515000094

Pica, T. (1988). Interlanguage adjustments as an outcome of NS-NNS negotiated interaction. *Language Learning*, *38*, 45–73. https://doi.org/10.1111/j.1467-1770.1988.tb00401.x

Pica, T., & Doughty, C. J. (1985). Input and interaction in the communicative language classroom: A comparison of teacher-fronted and group activities. In S. M. Gass & C. Madden (Eds.), *Input in second language acquisition* (pp. 115–132). Newbury House Publishers.

Pica, T., Holliday, L., Lewis, N., & Morgenthaler, L. (1989). Comprehensible output as an outcome of linguistic demands on the learner. *Studies in Second Language Acquisition*, *11*(01), 63–90. https://doi.org/10.1017/S027226310000783X

Pica, T., Kanagy, R., & Falodun, J. (1993). Choosing and using communication tasks for second language instruction. In G. Crookes & S. Gass (Eds.), *Tasks and language learning: Integrating theory & practice* (pp. 9–34). Multilingual Matters Ltd.

Robinson, P. (Ed.). (2011). *Second language task complexity: Researching the cognition hypothesis of language learning and performance* (Vol. 2). John Benjamins Publishing. https://doi.org/10.1075/tblt.2

Skehan, P. (1996). A framework for the implementation of task-based instruction. *Applied Linguistics*, *17*(1), 38–62. https://doi.org/10.1093/applin/17.1.38

Skehan, P. (1998). Task-based instruction. *Annual Review of Applied Linguistics*, 18, 268–286. https://doi.org/10.1017/S0267190500003585

Skehan, P. (2003). Task-based instruction. *Language Teaching*, *36*(1), 1–14. https://doi.org/10.1017/S026144480200188X

Swain, M. (1985). Communicative competence: some roles of comprehensible input and comprehensible output in its development. In S. Gass & C. Madden (Eds.), *Input in second language acquisition* (pp. 235–253). Newbury House.

Swain, M. (1995). Three functions of output in second language learning. In G. Cook, B. Seidlhofer & H. G. Widdowson (Eds.), *Principle and practice in applied linguistics: Studies in honor of H.G. Widdowson* (pp. 125–44). Oxford University Press.

Swain, M., & Lapkin, S. (1995). Problems in output and the cognitive processes they generate: A step towards second language learning. *Applied Linguistics*, *16*, 370–391. https://doi.org/10.1093/applin/16.3.371

Swier, R., & Peterson, M. (2018). 3D digital games, virtual worlds, and language learning in higher education: Continuing challenges in Japan. *JALT CALL Journal*, *14*(*3*), 225–238.

Willis, J. (1996). *A framework for task-based learning*. Longman.

Willis, D., & Willis, J. (2007). *Doing task-based teaching*. Oxford University Press.

CHAPTER 3

SECOND LIFE FEATURES AND LOGISTICS

OVERVIEW

To teach and research in SL, it is imperative that teacher researchers be attuned to SL features that are integral to task design in a 3D virtual environment. This chapter serves as a step-by-step guide to show readers how and where to start as an SL newbie. Illustrated by concrete examples and vivid snapshots, it demonstrates what skills are needed for teaching in SL, ranging from the basics (e.g., creating an SL account, teleporting, changing avatar outfits) to more advanced skills (e.g., building 3D objects for class activities, customising role-play scenarios). By the end of this chapter, you should feel more comfortable to conduct your very first virtual class in SL (hopefully) if you follow the steps closely. These skills will be put in good practice in a full task-based syllabus to be presented in Part II.

I have to come clean with my fellow teachers and researchers before taking you all in-world. When I was a SL newbie back in 2009, I felt like a fish out of water as the steep learning curve did throw me off in the beginning. Along with the platform instability and technical glitches that could occur unexpectedly, it took me hours of frequent self-practice (e.g., object building) and workshop attendance to brush up on my SL teaching techniques. So my initial relationship with SL was bittersweet, though the teaching/research part was rewarding enough to offset its downsides.

It is fair to say that no digital platform can be 100% stable and bug-free, much less in its early stage of development. This is particularly the case of MUVEsth at demand high graphics quality and bandwidth, coupled with the large number of players coming in-world at the same time. Hence, getting frozen or booted out of the platform is not uncommon in SL. These drawbacks are acknowledged by the users, and Linden Lab has been working on improving the platform stability.

The good news is that SL users will find peace of mind in the Featured News[1] announced by the Linden Lab in their projected 2022 Roadmap. They are adding new features to enhance the new user experience and improve all aspects of SL functionality, including but not limited to:

- "Avatar 'expressiveness' that brings camera-based gestures and movement to your avatar for a whole new level of interaction and connectedness
- Premium Plus – a new upgrade option with added features and extras

- A new mobile viewer to enhance and improve your Second Life experience
- Improved group chat reliability
- Viewer and script performance improvements
- New user avatar customization and improvements
- Updated mesh optimiser
- Search engine improvements
- Improved materials and terrain
- Adding web marketplace variants
- …and much more!"

For the sake of demonstration, I created a new SL account so that I can be directed to Welcome Island and go through all the tutorials as a "newbie". I was also curious to see how the new features would improve my newbie experience as claimed by Linden Lab. Being an old-timer in SL, I am better positioned to provide insights on comparing the two different onboarding experiences, which are over a decade apart. The following is my guided virtual tour along with the in-world screenshots on the spot.

STEP 1. ACCOUNT REGISTRATION AND SL INSTALLATION

First things first, you need to create a new account on the SL join page (https://join.secondlife.com) by choosing a new username for your avatar and even gender (Figure 3.1). In my case, I came up with a quirky avatar name (*vivarainbow*) that only belongs to me as the system will let you know if the same avatar name has already been taken. Make sure you pick your avatar name thoughtfully because you can't change it once your username is approved by the system. I also played with the avatar gender and decided to go with the *non-binary* option this time because I was curious to see what a non-binary avatar would look like once I logged into SL. Note that you can select either "Go Basic" or "Premium" as your preferred membership. I selected the Basic account as it is free and you can always switch to the Premium account if you decide to own your private home or purchase lands in-world using the Linden Dollars (L$). Remember you can always buy or sell L$ on the LindeX Exchange (https://secondlife.com/my/lindex/index.php?) using the real-world money for currency exchange.

After successfully creating your SL account, you need to install the latest *Second Life Viewer* to enjoy the full immersive 3D experience that SL offers (Figure 3.2). Make sure your

Figure 3.1 SL join page for registering for a new account.

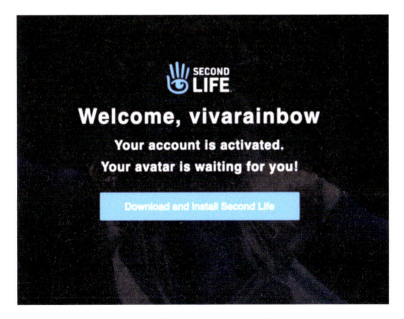

Figure 3.2 SL Account activation followed by Second Life Viewer installation.

computer is capable of running on the Viewer by meeting the system requirements (https://secondlife.com/system-requirements). Whilst users can also download mobile apps to access SL (e.g., SpeedLight on iOS and SpeedLight Viewer on Android), I personally prefer using a PC/laptop as it is easier to navigate SL and use the features to their full capacity.

STEP 2. LOG INTO SL AND EXPLORE THE LEARNING ISLAND

When you log in SL for the first time, you will be taken to the *Welcome Island* for all new SL residents. This is the learning space where you can start to explore and practise all the basic skills as an SL newbie. I was pleasantly surprised to find the new *Guidebook* popping up on the left-hand side menu of my Viewer to help new users to familiarise themselves with the SL features (Figure 3.3). Simply follow the signs and tutorials in the Guidebook to practise those skills that will enable you to function better in SL. You can stay and explore the island as long as you like until you feel more comfortable to venture into the real in-world. Once you get out of Welcome Island, you won't be able to return because you're not a newbie anymore. So please take your time and start to socialise with other SL newbies nearby using your text or voice chat function. Let's go over those basic skills following the guidebook instructions.

Figure 3.3 The SL Viewer with toolbars and guidebook displayed on the Welcome Island.

STEP 3. PRACTISE THE BASIC SKILLS

- **Walk/Run/Fly**

    Walking, running, and flying are the first three functions every newly born avatar starts. The easiest way to walk around is using the arrow keys on your keyboard: ↑ (move forward), ↓ (move backward), ← (move left), and → (move right). You can also click on a point of contact on the ground to direct your avatar to walk towards it. Alternatively, you can also use the four letter keys: W (move forward), S (move backward), A (move left), and D (move right). Similarly, if you wanted to run forward, simply double click on the W key or ↑ key, and backward by double clicking on the S key or ↓ key. If you click on the walk/run/fly button, you can control your movement and which direction your avatar likes to move towards (Figure 3.4).

    Note that flying is inactive on Welcome Island, but you can try flying in-world once you get out of the island. It is much quicker to explore in-world than walking from one spot to the other, not to mention that flying makes you feel like a

Figure 3.4 Control the movement and direction functions using the walk/run/fly button.

Figure 3.5 Avatar flying in the air by clicking on the walk/run/fly button.

superhero. Simply hold the E key or Page Up key on your PC keyboard. However, if you are a Mac user like me, simply hold down the Fn key whilst pressing the ↑ key at the same time. Both PC and Mac users can also use the walk/run/fly button key to toggle between these three movement functions as shown in my avatar flying in Figure 3.5. Finally, you can also jump upward/downward by pressing 🔼 🔽 on the movement toggle panel.

- **Camera Controls**

  There are three views that you can change in your Camera Controls button: front, side, and rear. The rear view, however, is how every avatar navigates and moves around by default. In Figure 3.6, you can see that I changed my view to the front so I can see my avatar from a different angle. The front view is particularly useful when you want to change your avatar appearances and outfits. Using your Camera Controls button, you can see a 360 degree view by rotating the cross wheel as shown in Figure 3.6. You may also zoom in or out by pressing and holding the Alt key (or Option key for Mac users) whilst using your mouse wheel.

- **Text Chat, IM, and Voice Chat**

  Chatting is one of the most pivotal features in SL that allows you to make friends and interact with other avatars nearby, privately, or as a group. Simply click on the Chat button and text chat with anyone nearby. Those who are within the range of 20 meters can see your typed message (Figure 3.7).

CHAPTER 3
SECOND LIFE FEATURES AND LOGISTICS

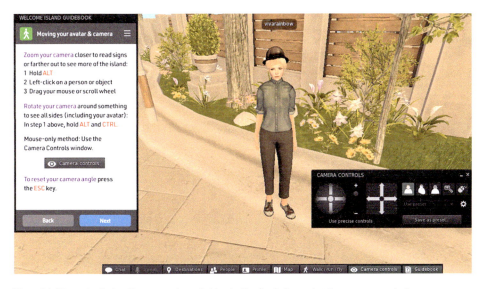

Figure 3.6 My avatar facing the screen by switching to the front view using the camera controls.

Figure 3.7 Public text chat that can be seen by everyone nearby using the chat function.

59

Figure 3.8 Send a private text chat to a nearby avatar using the IM function.

If you like to send a private instant message (IM) to an avatar friend nearby, simply right click on their avatar name from the nearby chat list and select IM (Figure 3.8). You can also right click on the name tag floating above their avatar to IM them or "View Profile" before you "Add friend" to broaden your social circle in SL.

For those who like to use voice chat to interact with an avatar friend in IM or speak in public, simply press the "Speak" button on the toolbar (Figure 3.9). You will see a small white dot enclosed by green volume waves "((( )))" above your avatar, indicating that you are speaking. Make sure that you test your microphone and speaker beforehand by selecting "Me" on the top toolbar, and scroll down to Preferences and choose Sound & Media to configure your settings. If you have a headset, it can help cancel out echoing or background noise when a number of avatars are gathering and speaking in a close vicinity.

- **Interacting with Objects**
  Because SL is a 3D MUVE, all the objects are embodied in 3D form as close to what you see and touch in the real world. To interact with an in-world object (including an avatar), simply right click on the object and you will see different options to interact with it such as edit, build, sit here, or stand up (Figure 3.10). Sometimes the object will allow your avatar to select different actions before you decide on which one to perform (e.g., leg cross, arm cross, leg up). If you want to

Figure 3.9 Use Voice chat by clicking on the speak button.

Figure 3.10 Avatar sitting on a wooden bench by right clicking on it and selecting "Sit here".

Figure 3.11 Control media (videos, music) by pausing it or adjusting the volume on the upper right of the toolbar.

know more about the object, you can move the mouse over the object and click on the information icon [i] next to the name tag.

- **Controlling In-world Media**
  When you teleport to some islands, you will hear music or videos playing in the background to set the stage for the island. You can control to start/pause the media (e.g., video) by clicking on the Pause button next to the volume button that controls turning it off or adjusting the volume on the right corner of the top toolbar (Figure 3.11).

- **Landmarking**
  It is crucial that you set the landmarks for those places that you would like to frequent or find potentially useful for your teaching or research. Landmarking is quite easy. Simply click on the World feature located on the top toolbar of your SL Viewer and select "Landmark This Place" from the drop-down menu (Figure 3.12). You can also "Set home" to the most frequently visited place as your SL landing homebase. Note that you need to become the member of the group or ask permission from the land owner to "Set home to here" because you are not the owner of the purchased land or home.

- **Taking a Snapshot**
  Whenever I teach an SL class, I usually take multiple snapshots that can capture the essence of each "teachable moment" or "learning episode". These vivid

CHAPTER 3
SECOND LIFE FEATURES AND LOGISTICS

Figure 3.12 Place an in-world landmark by selecting the "Landmark This Place" option from the world drop-down menu.

snapshots help me reflect on my teaching performance of the day and how students react to my task design in SL. To take a snapshot in-world, simply click on the camera icon on the left-hand menu of your Viewer and you should be able to see where you would like to save the snapshot (Figure 3.13). As I am still with my "Basic" membership, the options available to me are "Save to Disk" (your computer), share it to your Profile Feed, or send it to an email. If budget allows, you may purchase some L$ so that you can save those snapshots directly into your Inventory with only L$10 per snapshot.

- **Changing Profile**
Editing your avatar profile is the first step for SL residents to get the first impression of who you are, what you like, and which in-world groups you belong to before they

Figure 3.13 Take a snapshot and save it to a disk (hard drive) by clicking on the camera icon.

decide to befriend you (or not). Simply click on the Profile icon on the bottom toolbar or Me on the top and select Profile to update your biography (Figure 3.14). You can also choose a display name that you prefer others to call you (e.g., Viva for my full avatar name Vivarainbow) and can always reset it. It is quite similar to what we do in RL (e.g., Jules for Julian). As everything can happen in SL, you can also develop an in-world relationship with a special avatar as your partner (married or not), though it costs each partner L$10 and L$25 if you both decide to part ways (divorce). If you are comfortable, you can add your "Real World Bio" or even an RL picture of your true self.

In every avatar's profile, you will also see their SL birthdate. For example, my new avatar was born on 14 April 2022, and is only 5 days old as of my writing now. Whenever you are updating something in your profile, it will show your most recent activity in the Feed. After you feel comfortable with the basic skills, I would suggest starting to join some SL groups to expand your social circle. Some groups are open to anyone to join for free (e.g., EUROCALL in Second Life), but some are more restrictive and need the founders' approval (e.g., EduNation Residents). Once you successfully joined a group, it will appear in the Groups tab in your profile as well.

CHAPTER 3
SECOND LIFE FEATURES AND LOGISTICS

Figure 3.14 Updating the avatar profile by clicking on the profile icon on the bottom toolbar.

- **Changing the Environment Setting**

    Like the real world, SL also embodies the time change of a day in-world. Depending on the time difference, sometimes you will see a bright midday full of sunlight when teleporting to a new place and sometimes you can enjoy the sunset or a quiet night when all the sky turns dark in-world. What makes SL so intriguing and flexible is that you can create your own second life by manipulating the 3D environment. So if you don't like it too dark, feel free to switch it back to the daytime by clicking on the World feature on the top and select Environment from the drop-down menu. There you will see different time options that take your fancy such as sunrise or midnight (Figure 3.15).

65

Figure 3.15 Changing the in-world time by selecting the environment from the world drop-down menu.

CHECKPOINT

- To what extent would you like your created avatar to represent your true self in RL (e.g., the same first name and gender), or instead, to put on a new persona including a coined avatar name and gender that is totally opposite to who you really are? Similarly, would you allow your students to let their imagination run wild in creating their own avatar persona? How would that affect your virtual class management and teaching?
- The chat function, be it text, IM, or voice, is integral to language teaching and research as it enables students to practise the target language

> spontaneously in real time. If you are a teacher, what type of in-world tasks or projects would you develop for your students using different chat modes? If you are conducting a research study, how would you turn each mode into your data source that you can record for analysis later?
> - So far, we have covered the SL basics that every newbie should know. If it is your first time joining SL for teaching or research purposes, how do you compare this with other online teaching formats, such as videoconferencing or posting on a Discussion Board? Is it worth spending time mastering these SL skills when you can fall back on standard Blackboard, Moodle, or Zoom, for example?

STEP 4. PRACTISE ADVANCED SKILLS

Now that you have grasped the basic skills needed to function in SL, we are moving on to more advanced skills that are integral to teaching and research in SL. These skills are much needed for virtual class management or task interaction. You will note that I place "Changing your avatar" from the Guidebook here just because there is more to changing avatar appearances than what the Guidebook covers in the basics.

- **Teleporting**

    Teleporting is one of the most frequently used SL features that avatars all love. It enables you to travel instantaneously from one place to another in-world, landing gracefully upon arrival. There are different ways of teleportation. For example, you can open the Places (the globe icon) on the left-hand toolbar of your Viewer) to find the landmarks you have visited or saved as favourites. You can also open the World Map (from the World drop-down menu) to locate a place in which to teleport. You can also use the Search function ( ) to look for interesting events or places with their associated teleport links, maps, and information. Similarly, you can choose a place by looking up a wide variety of categories in Destinations, such Japan Hiroba island that is newcomer friendly (Figure 3.16).

    If you want to teleport an avatar friend or students to where you are, simply click on the People icon (People) on the bottom toolbar and right click on your friend's name to "Offer Teleport" (Figure 3.17). If they are online at the same time, they can accept your offer and teleport to you.

BEFORE WE TAKE OFF

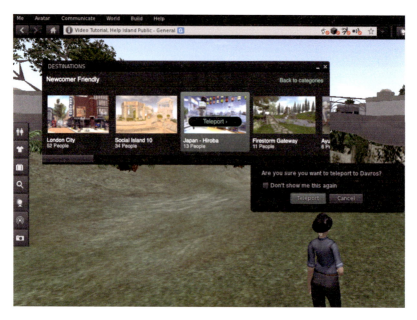

Figure 3.16 Teleporting to Japan Hiroba by choosing the newcomer friendly category from destinations.

Figure 3.17 Offer teleport to an avatar nearby by right clicking on the avatar name.

CHAPTER 3
SECOND LIFE FEATURES AND LOGISTICS

Figure 3.18 Another way to send a teleport link by clicking on copy SLurl from world map.

Another good way of sending your friend or students a teleport link to your current location is to "Copy SLurl" (a direct teleport link) from the Word Map (Figure 3.18). Teleporting is particularly useful to "heard the sheep" back to you when your students are all over the place doing their scavenger hunt in-world. Regardless of where you are, you can also "Request Teleport" from your friends or students. If they accept your request, you will be allowed to teleport to their current location.

- **Changing Avatar Appearances and Outfits**
  Maybe it is just me, but I am quite conscious of how my avatar looks and is perceived in public. After all, my created Vivarainbow is my virtual mini-me and spokesperson in SL. The last thing I would like is to have them (yes, "they" and "them" are the pronouns of my non-binary avatar) wear something inappropriate or underwhelming. When your avatar puts on some fancy outfits, your mini-me will get immediate attention or compliments from friends or other avatars nearby. You will be surprised that some of your students might spend a lot of time finding beautiful or quirky outfits for their avatars and change their clothing in every virtual class.

69

Figure 3.19 Selecting your avatar and outfits from the "Complete Avatars" list.

For an SL newbie, the quickest (also easiest) way to change your avatar appearance is to select a pre-made avatar from the "Complete Avatars" list. This feature can be activated from the "Avatar" icon located on the Viewer left-hand toolbar or simply click on "Avatar" on the top. There are several default avatar options for you to choose from without making your own avatar from scratch. These pre-made avatars come with a full package of the default body parts and clothing, ranging from new avatars and classic to fantasy and even vampires (Figure 3.19). Depending on your mood of the day, you can always switch from one avatar model to another. One anecdote is that when a newbie saw my purposefully chosen avatar on Welcome Island, he asked: "Are you a lesbian?" I found his directness "intriguing": your non-binary avatar appearances can trigger stereotypes of other SL residents about you as much as how gender-fluid folks are perceived by others in RL. In that sense, it feels as real in SL as in RL. So start to embrace the fluidity of virtual identity and enjoy being who you are and how you like to present yourself as you navigate this identity space. This may open up another interesting research avenue or teaching topic.

When you feel tired of the same old avatar, you can customise it by adjusting the body shape (e.g., taller or more muscular), changing eye colour, hairstyle, and outfits. To do this, choose "Edit shape" or "Edit outfit parts" from the top Avatar drop-down menu and start editing your avatar appearances (Figure 3.20). You will see the "Add more" button that lists available clothing items currently

CHAPTER 3
SECOND LIFE FEATURES AND LOGISTICS

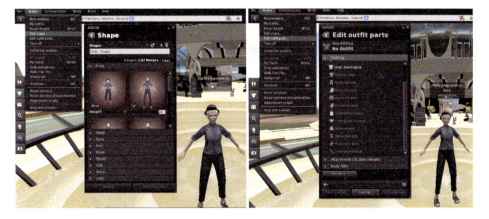

Figure 3.20 Editing avatar body shape (left) and outfits (right).

saved in your inventory. Simply select any item you want to play around and click on "Wear item". Similarly, you can edit the avatar shape by moving the scaling bar under each body part (e.g., enlarge your eye size) until you are satisfied with the change. You will see the new clothing item automatically replace your old one. Alternatively, you can also click on the little T-shirt icon to change your avatar outfits and shape[2].

In your avatar inventory, you will also see attachments that are accessories or objects attached to your avatar, such as a hat, necklace, glasses or even wings. There are many freebie places for you to shop around for some free avatar appearances (including body parts) and outfits to beautify your virtual dummy. Once you locate some goodies, there are usually floating signs above them for you to click on, followed by a pop-up window that invites you to "Keep" the free object. If you don't like what you attached to your avatar, simply right click on the object and select "Detach". As the old saying goes, "you get what you pay" – this also holds true in SL. Sometimes the free items you picked in-world might be limited or not to your fashion standards. When you start to be more discerning about your avatar appearances, you can use L$ to "Buy" custom-made attachments from the SL Marketplace (https://marketplace.secondlife.com/) that will create unique avant-garde or fashion-forward looks for your avatar and set yourself apart from other residents. Try to collect L$ by searching for "free linden" in the "Classifieds" using "Search" on the Viewer left-hand toolbar. Sometimes you will get rewards (L$) by playing newbie-friendly games or participating in-world activities.

71

BEFORE WE TAKE OFF

- **Creating Notecards**
  I use Notecards a lot as they are useful in SL teaching. For example, you can type up the task instruction on the Notecard and give it to your students in the virtual class. You can also put lesson planning notes in a Notecard to keep you on track with the lesson progression. Think of it as a worksheet for students and an index card for yourself as a teacher. For example, students will need to complete the Notecard worksheet for the task of that day and return it to you before they exit the class. To create a Notecard, click on the briefcase icon (also known as "My Inventory") on the left toolbar and you will see a + sign to allow you to add a new item. Select "New Notecard" to start editing it by adding some notes for your lesson (Figure 3.21). Depending on your lesson of the day, you can also add images or landmarks to your Notecard. If you want to upload images from your computer to the SL inventory, each image costs L$10, however. That said, the fee is relatively cost-effective and a good investment for your SL teaching.

Figure 3.21 Creating a Notecard using the new Notecard feature in the inventory.

- **Conversation Logs and Transcripts**

    By default, your SL Viewer will automatically save all the conversation logs and transcripts in a designated folder in your PC/Mac hard drive (e.g., Downloads or Documents). A conversation log documents the dates and names in your in-world conversations with other residents, including "bots" (avatars controlled by computer programs, not real humans). It helps you to keep track of who you are talking to in each SL encounter and return their messages when you are off-line. To find where your conversation logs are located, head to Chat from the menu bar of Preferences (under Me) and select a Location where you can easily find the saved logs in your hard drive. If you prefer to read the full conversation transcripts, you may select "log and transcripts" from the Save drop-down menu to keep both records (Figure 3.22). Chat logs can come in handy when you want to check the evidence of teacher-student and student-student interactions using public chat, IM, or group chat. Transcripts can serve as part of your research dataset to examine the virtual experience and interaction of the participants, or as a stimulated recall for students to raise metalinguistic awareness by evaluating their language use during authentic interaction with other avatars.

- **Group Setup**

    Class management in SL is as important as in RL. Creating a new group for your first virtual class or research project will facilitate communication with your students/participants as a group rather than chasing them up one by one in-world. To set up your first SL group, click on (People) on the bottom of your Viewer and choose the Groups tab and then the cross sign (+) to create a "New Group' (Figure 3.23). You can type up your group name, pick a group photo from the Photo

Figure 3.22 Finding the chat history automatically stored in a designated folder (right) from selecting the location in the preferences drop-down menu (left).

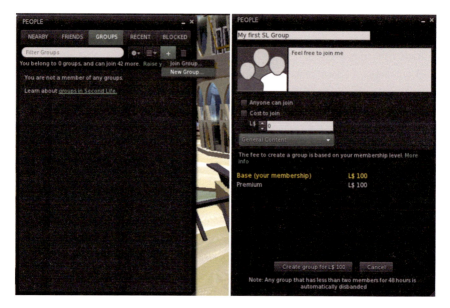

Figure 3.23 Using the groups tab from people on the bottom toolbar (left) to create a new group and modify the setting (right).

Album folder in your Inventory, and add some description for the group. You also need L$100 for the group setup fee.

To successfully retain your group status, you need to have at least two group members (including you); otherwise, your created group will be automatically disabled within 48 hours if it can't meet the minimum member requirement. You can allow anyone to join (for free) or with a fee. Because SL mirrors RL, it is better to keep your SL class private and only allow those you invite to join (Figure 3.23), or you will encounter some uninvited avatars, or even worse, SL griefers, who try to prank or disrupt your well-intentioned class. You may select "General Content" for the maturity rating for your group, similar to how movies are rated based on the level of adult content.

By the same token, you can also join up to 42 different in-world groups with your Basic account and can select one from your group list to be the most active one. Simply right click on the group name and hit "Activate" and then your avatar will be wearing the group title floating above your avatar name tag (Figure 3.24). Wearing the group title will allow others to identify your group membership and the owner to grant you access to member-only resources as well.

Figure 3.24 Wearing the group tag by activating a chosen group from the list.

To invite multiple students/participants to join your group at once, head to the "Roles & Members" tab and then click on "Invite" on the bottom of the panel before you see a "Group Invitation" window pop up. Then click on "Open Resident Chooser" and another pop-up window will appear for you to invite new members via "Search" (by typing up an avatar name), "Friends", or anyone "Near Me" (Figure 3.25). Once you finish selecting which avatars to join the group, then hit "Send Invitations". Based on my experience, the quickest way to add students/participants to your group is to invite them first to be your avatar friends so you can easily locate them under the "Friends" tab. I would also suggest doing so before creating your group.

Each group has different roles that you can assign to members of your choice. Basically, you are the "Owner" of the group and have full control of group abilities such as to add new members, assign new roles, or even kick someone out of the group. The next in line is the "Officer" role (e.g., your collaborator) who can also add or assign new members. The final role "Everyone" belongs to all members

Figure 3.25 Selecting new members to the group through open resident chooser.

(e.g., students) who only have basic abilities such as using voice or text chat to communicate with other members. Once you set up your group, you can choose the "Group Call" function (voice) or a quick IM to send task instructions, assignment reminders or simply practice the target language with them (Figure 3.26). You can also select a particular student from the Members list who seems to get lost in-world and send an IM to bring them back to the class.[3]

- **Holodecks**

  If you are a sci-fi movie fan, you probably know what Holodecks entail. A Holodeck is a fascinating SL feature that enables users to "rez" (to create or make something appear) a 3D object or even a whole environment that simulates a variety of scenarios. The rezzed scenario appears immediately and occupies the given space, allowing you to walk into another world that was just morphed in front of your avatar. I use the Holodeck feature frequently in my SL teaching to create different RL scenarios for my students to do role-plays and augment the authenticity. You don't need to create your own Holodecks as owners in some educational islands already have them available in-world (see Language Teaching Islands & Demonstrations in Chapter 21). Simply click on the Holodeck object

CHAPTER 3
SECOND LIFE FEATURES AND LOGISTICS

Figure 3.26 Inviting new members (left) and assigning different roles (right) to the group.

(e.g., the blue button in Figure 3.27), select a scenario you like to rez, and voilà, a whole new setting will presents itself to you.

- **Object Building**
  The final advanced skill, but definitely not the least, is to learn how to build 3D objects in-world. This ability is required if you like to create a poster for students to upload the screenshots taken in the gallery museum for a show-and-tell assignment, for example. One of my pilot study tasks (see Chapter 5) was to ask each student pair

Figure 3.27 Rezzing a pantheon scenario (right) by activating the Holodeck (Left).

77

to take turns telling their partners how to build a 3D object following the Notecard instructions. This helps you see how useful the building ability would be for your teaching and research. Before you get too excited about building your first object, make sure that object building is allowed in the land you visit. If you see the sign on the address bar (located on the top of your Viewer), it means that you are not permitted to build or drop an object. Fret not, as there are still some islands that allow you to practice building, such as the Ivory Tower Library of Primitives (also see Language Teaching Islands & Demonstrations in Chapter 21).

Note that what I am covering here is only object building 101. There are more complex building techniques and abilities[4] that you can acquire later if desired. However, the 101 skills covered here should set you off to a good start. For the sake of demonstration, I teleported to the Ivory Tower Library of Primitives,[5] which is a friendly Sandbox place for avatars to practise the building tools. Simply right click on the ground and select "Build" to open the pop-up window (Figure 3.28). There you can navigate the different types of object shapes listed. Choose one shape (e.g., a cube) and point it to any location on the ground you desire. The object will be rezzed immediately before you start editing it. If you want to create another object, simply click on the "Create" icon on the top of the Build window.

In the Build window, you will see different tools to manipulate the object. You can "Move" the object in any direction notated arrows in red, green, and blue to represent the X-, Y-, and Z-axes, respectively. You can also rotate the object by selecting the "Rotate" bubble and a sphere surrounded by the three coloured rings (red, green, blue) will allow you to rotate the shape in different directions. Similarly, you can also "Stretch" the prims (or "primitives", single parts of an object) to any size you like by dragging the three coloured boxes so you that you control the prim's length (red box), width (green box), and height (blue box). If you are good at maths (not me), you can adjust the "Size (meters)" by entering specific values in the X-, Y-, and Z-coordinate boxes (Figure 3.29). Also, if your "Stretch Textures" box is checked, it means that any texture (including image) in the object will be resized proportionally when you stretch it (or the texture will remain its original size).

Another useful tool to try out is editing textures on different faces of your object. Not only will changing the object texture make your creation more appealing, it will also facilitate your teaching (e.g., create a beautiful board to display an artwork) and student learning (e.g., students upload screenshot images to their created posters for oral presentation). To edit textures, first click on "Select Face" in the Build window as this will allow you to change

Figure 3.28 Selecting an object shape and starting to build it via the build window.

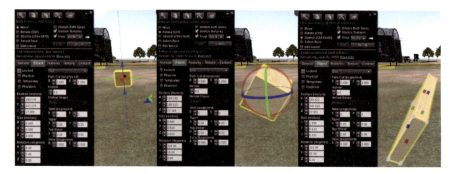

Figure 3.29 Moving, rotating, and resizing the object in different directions by the colour axes (left), rings (middle), and boxes (right).

textures per side at a time as opposed to the whole object (unless you prefer to do so). Then hit the "Texture" tab and click on the Texture box below the tab. A "Pick: Texture" window will pop up for you to change the texture style. By default, you will have some pre-made textures (also photos in the Photo Album) in the "Library" folder of your Inventory ready for you to choose from. Play around the texture options to each side of your object, which will automatically change to the style you designate. After you complete one side, remember to rotate your object to another side for editing. If there are some screenshots that you saved in the Photo Album, you can also select any of them to be the texture (Figure 3.30).

Figure 3.30 Editing textures of the object by picking different texture styles or photos in the library.

Once you are happy with your built masterpiece, you can right click on the object to "Take" it or duplicate it by clicking on "Take Copy". It will be added to your Inventory under the "Objects" folder. Please make sure that you take or remove the object in the Sandbox before you exit SL so that the landowner won't have to clean up your leftovers; this is so-called SL etiquette. Finally, if you like to rez your saved object again later on, simply drag it from your Inventory to the ground and it will appear at once. If you don't like it anymore, you can remove it by right clicking on "Delete". It is that simple.

CHECKPOINT

- Look at your own avatar (if you already created one). Do you think you would spend more time beautifying the outfits or changing your avatar appearances, or only consider it as a medium for teaching and research? In other words, do you think virtual identity matters to you or your students (participants)?
- I mentioned several ways of utilising the Notecard function for teaching (e.g., task instructions). Try to come up with other ways of using Notecards to facilitate teaching or/and enhance language learning in pairs or groups.
- If you are doing a research project on intercultural communication, how will you use chat logs and transcripts to raise the intercultural awareness of your participants before and after an SL session? Also, what type of data analysis will you conduct using the recorded chat logs and transcripts?

YOUR TASK

- First, use Destination or the Search function to look for a place that offers freebies for avatar clothing or shapes (or check out Freebie Spots in Chapter 21). Teleport to the destination and start shopping around the clothing and appearance items for your avatar. Save them in your Inventory and head to a quiet place in-world to start playing around the freebie items by giving your avatar a new look. Remember to take a snapshot of the new "you" as a proof.

- Following the instructions in Group Setup, start creating your first SL group by first updating the group profile and settings. Invite at least two of your colleagues, friends, or even better, students to join your group (within 48 hours) to keep it active. Then try out both the Group Call and Chat functions to interact with your group members, followed by sending them a teleport link to an in-world place that you have landmarked. Meet them there and take a snapshot of your gathering.
- Try to practise building your first 3D object in SL following the instructions (Object Building) or the external SL resource provided in footnote 4. See if you can upload a photo to one Face and change the texture or colour in the other Faces of the object. Take a snapshot of your masterpiece and keep it in your Inventory before you rez it in-world next time. Also discuss with colleagues in a pair/group how you will develop a task assignment for language learners using the building feature.

In this technical chapter, I have endeavoured to spell out the basics and advanced skills integral to SL teaching/research. There are definitely more upper-level skills and techniques than those covered in this chapter, and you are encouraged to take it to the next level if desired. Now that you have established your knowledge base in SL features and skills, you will time travel to my SL teaching journey through my most candid blogging in Part II.

NOTES

1. See 2021-Second Life Year in Review: https://community.secondlife.com/blogs/entry/9683-2021-second-life-year-in-review
2. For those who like to learn more about how to edit your avatar appearances, see https://community.secondlife.com/knowledgebase/english/controlling-your-avatars-appearance-r216/
3. For those who like to learn more about the Group setup, visit https://community.secondlife.com/knowledgebase/english/joining-and-participating-in-groups-r51/#Section__1_3
4. For more building practices, visit https://wiki.secondlife.com/wiki/Good_Building_Practices
5. Teleport link: http://maps.secondlife.com/secondlife/Natoma/211/163/28

PART II

LET'S GET OUR HANDS DIRTY

Chapter 4: Course preparation – A bumpy road	84
Chapter 5: Pretest: A rollercoaster ride	90
Chapter 6: Lesson 1 (Greetings)	98
Chapter 7: Lesson 2 (Food part 1)	106
Chapter 8: Lesson 2 (Food part 2)	112
Chapter 9: Lesson 2 (Food part 3)	120
Chapter 10: Lesson 2 (Food final)	134
Chapter 11: Lesson 3 (Holiday/Festival/Clothing part 1)	146
Chapter 12: Lesson 3 (Holiday/Festival/Clothing part 2)	154
Chapter 13: Lesson 4 (Music)	168
Chapter 14: Lesson 5 (Sports)	176
Chapter 15: Lesson 6 (Arts part 1)	188
Chapter 16: Lesson 6 (Arts part 2)	196
Chapter 17: Lesson 7 (Jobs)	206
Chapter 18: Posttest	216
Chapter 19: Lesson 8 (Travel & Farewell party)	228

CHAPTER 4

COURSE PREPARATION – A BUMPY ROAD

> **OVERVIEW**
>
> This chapter kicks off with what it takes to teach a 3D virtual class in SL. It breaks down the steps in preparing a task-based class and the logistics in recruiting participants, class scheduling following Second Life Time (SLT), and strategies employed to mitigate participant attrition. To keep the natural flow of blogging, I will place both the "Checkpoint" and "Your Task" at the end of each blog entry.

BLOG POST. TUESDAY, 4 MAY 2011

Well, how shall I begin here? The last time I blogged was when I was doing my pilot study (Figure 4.1), shadowing an experienced SL teacher. The difference is that I will be teaching the virtual course all by myself this time to collect data for my dissertation as opposed to coteaching with an old-timer in SL. Yup, pressure is on and I need to take more responsibility to ensure that each planned task is well executed and, above all, students will keep attending my class without dropping out in the midway, which will severely jeopardise my consistent data collection.

Even though I managed to recruit a decent number of students (around 16–17) via my SL contacts, I still have my qualms about whether they will stay with me until the end. Based on the pilot experience, students come and go and have their RL obligations to fulfil. It's hard to "force" them (I hate this word) to attend each class regularly despite the incentive that the class is FREE! I just don't want to lose them all as recruiting these students from all over the world (remotely) isn't easy at all! I can still vividly recall the bittersweet process of my recruitment of SL participants in my pilot. I was initially planning to reach out to the potential students through an instructor that I knew in-world who had taught the SL course, "Business Talking", for exchange students in Sweden. I thought the response rate would be more stable through contacting his previous and current students, hoping that his word-of-mouth recommendation would have made a difference. As much as I appreciated his kind favour, it didn't end up with the rosy picture that I had hoped to paint. First, I shot myself in the foot. When I contacted his previous students last December, most of them responded, which really pumped me up. But due to the delay of my dissertation proposal defense, I couldn't start the course until I successfully passed it. So I'd been putting it

Teaching in SL: Revisited

About Me

vivajulian

I am currently a doctoral candidate in the field of TESOL. My research study is focusing on how Second Life can enhance English language learners' language development and their perceptions about learning English in SL. I am starting to conduct my pilot study on teaching in SL. I am excited about the challenge, but also interested in the experience of teaching my first class in SL. This blog is my reflective documentation of how my teaching in SL plays out each time.

Figure 4.1 My SL teaching blog title and personal profile.

off until late March after the completion of my defense. I didn't strike when the iron was still hot so maybe most of them had lost interest. I truly feel sorry for those students who seemed quite enthusiastic about the course and contacted me quite early but couldn't join the class anymore due to the delay of the course offering.

To tackle the low response rate, I decided to send an invitation Notecard to all the members on the VIRTLANTIS Island in which I did my pilot teaching. To my surprise, more students responded to me via this platform than in RL email contact. I even got two former students who had participated in my pilot ask if they could join again this time. As much as I'd like to keep them, this course is pretty much operated in the similar task design so I didn't want them to waste their time doing the same activities. To "capture" more participants, I stay in SL these days more often to keep a close contact with those potential students who showed interest in signing up for the course. I also took the "snowballing" approach to ask those who already signed up to spread the word to anyone they know who might be interested in joining us as well. The result turned out to be positive. Thanks to the snowball sampling approach, I am able to get more students than I thought I would have gotten (almost 20 now!). Deep down I know I may still lose some of them based on my prior experience; however, 15–20 students so far sounds about right. The worst-case scenario is that at least 10 of them would still attend the class regularly (fingers crossed).

During the process of contacting students, I also asked them to sign up for the oral interview (pretest) timetable scheduled for this week before our class officially starts next week. Allowing them to fill in the time slot their preferred time/day via **Google Docs** is quite helpful. By so doing, they can see how many students already signed up for the class and how many time slots are already full (only a dyad for each slot). It also increases the visibility of the virtual community and gives them a sense of who their classmates may be. Additionally, I told them that the class will run twice a week (**Mon. & Wed.**), from **10–11:30 am Second Life Time (SLT).**[1] I reminded them of the time difference between SL and RL time and check if the timetable also fits their RL schedule (Figure 4.2).

Weird though, as I am busy with setting up the schedule for the oral interview and with the launch of the class next week, I suddenly received a lot of responses from students residing in China, and other students from elsewhere (Sweden)! I am not sure who passed the info to them, though it's going to be very late for them if they still want to attend the class (10:00 am SLT = 1:00 am in China). I may approach one of the students to ask where the info came from.

	Wednesday (4.27)	Thursday (4.28)	Friday (4.29)	Saturday (4.30)
10:00am–11:30am	Ulyo Genesis Kinda Elton	Toma Remex Profesor Korobase	Nikhil Moonsider Idea Lexenstar	Amandalarai afrdiqau (Hazrat)
11:30am–1:00pm	Annaelvit Ninoune	Hemasha Seda Noobz	TatianaRoslyakova javed hussain	
1:00pm–2:30pm	merogigo bally Rashad Ibor	Anja Lapalina Emelie Åberg	Younes Abghoui Azalia Mostof	

Figure 4.2 Students filling in time/day preferences for class timetabling via Google Docs.

To track the sources from which students got the class info, here is the list:

- Business Talking in Sweden: Annelvit, Hemasha, Anja, and Emelie
- VIRTLANTIS: Ulyo, Kinda (dropped out), Mero, Profesor, and Nikhil, Idea
- Snowballing: Ninoune, Toma, Noobz (not stable), Feng (not sure), Afridiqau, Azi, and Unessl (the last three from a student in Sweden).

Lessons learned:

1. *Strike when the iron's still hot*: Timing is important. I should've started the course right after I sent out the invitation through the email list kindly shared by the Swedish instructor. The turnout rate would've been better than when their motivation had dwindled and RL obligations had taken over their time to commit to the class.
2. *Snowballing*: I wouldn't end up with more than 15 students this time, if it weren't for the snowballing effect. Students' word-of-mouth recommendation really makes a difference. It's also crucial to seize the timing by inviting students to spread the word to the friends/classmates they know in SL who also might be keen to join the class. Furthermore, I spent a considerable amount of time hanging around in SL just because I wanted to promote the course to any potential students I bumped into in-world.
3. *Keep a close contact with participants*: To avoid losing any potential student, I've responded to students' inquiries frequently whilst immersing myself in SL. On the other hand, I've used instant messages (IMs) to follow up with those who contacted me to make sure that they've signed up for the oral interview and that the course schedule works for them. This creates the impression that the course is not too casual and has structure; hopefully they'll take the course as seriously as I do.
4. *Google Docs*: Asking students to sign up for the oral interview schedule using Google Docs has come in handy. By so doing, the whole timetable and participants available for each time slot are crystal clear, not to mention that students can freely decide their preferred time by editing the document at the same time.

UnicornG[2] is BACK!

> ## CHECKPOINT
>
> - What are the pros and cons of bringing your face-to-face (F2F) class to SL rather than recruiting new students in-world?
> - What would you have done differently to schedule the class timetable with your students? Would you also use Google Docs, for example?

> ## YOUR TASK
>
> - Teleport to VIRTLANTIS (or any of the teaching islands listed in Chapter 21) and pick the brains of those instructors who are offering language classes in-world. You may kindly invite them for a quick interview or informally chat with them about how they plan for the class and any challenges encountered.
> - Socialise with any members on those islands and conduct a brief interview with them on their language learning experience, why they come to SL, and whether they would like to learn a target language with you in the future. Feel free to add more questions and save your chat transcripts for your needs analysis.

NOTES

1 SL time (known as SLT) runs on the Pacific Time Zone (PST), which is currently 16 hours behind Western Australia where I am located. You may convert SLT (i.e., PST) to your time zone using any time zone converter.
2 UnicornG Luminos is my avatar name in addition to the new account (Vivarainbow) that I created in Chapter 3.

CHAPTER 5

PRETEST
A ROLLER-COASTER RIDE

OVERVIEW

As part of my dissertation research, this chapter outlines all things considered in preparing and administering tasks (information gap, jigsaw, decision making, and opinion exchange) in a pretest for my SL participants from all over the world. It candidly pinpoints the caveats faced by a teacher researcher and the strategies employed to tackle those hurdles in SL.

BLOG POST. FRIDAY, 6 MAY 2011

I'd have blogged the same week right after my pretest, but RL obligations (or a bit procrastination?) have put it off until now…oh well…let me turn back to the day when it started:

This week was quite intensive because I needed to implement the pretest with the students scheduled to complete four tasks in dyads before the official class starts next week. Sometimes there were three pairs of students in a row for each 90-minute session. The reason I was scheduling them to finish all the tasks a week before the class starts, rather than having them do the pretest in the first class altogether, was because of the big lesson I learned from my pilot last year. I'll never be able to finish with all the students in one sitting, compounded by the fact that other student pairs will be waiting for their turn and might lose their patience by the end. Allowing 1 week to complete the pretest before class sounds more feasible in this sense.

Before we started the pretest, I first explained the purpose of the study and the nature of the task-based class. I also gave them time to read the consent form, answered questions, and informed them to type up their avatar name and date to indicate their agreement to participate. I collected each of their consent forms before moving on to the tasks. Compared with my pilot last time, the pretest ran more effectively, despite some unexpected issues (mostly technical) as listed below:

1. My original wishful thinking was that most of my students were not SL newbies because some had already created their SL accounts and joined the VIRTLANTIS group, whereas others had also attended their first SL class with the Swedish

instructor. So, I thought they would have already got a hang of those basic SL skills. However, some students are SL newbies. They just signed up for an SL account to join my class so they were still unfamiliar with some of the SL features, which, nevertheless, would delay the flow of the task completion.

2. Because I put up all the tasks on a digital whiteboard connected to the Scribblar site (https://scribblar.com), students need to sign in so that they can see all the task images (Figure 5.1). However, some of them didn't use the SL Viewer 2 version, which created an issue of incompatibility. There were many times where I had to help them figure out why they couldn't see the images on the board. The way to bypass it was to ask them to open a new browser from their computer, but it was still inconvenient because students needed to switch back and forth between the new browser and Viewer 2 to read the instructions on the task Notecards I sent via SL.

3. Due to the frequent malfunctions encountered by the newbies, they came to me saying that they couldn't hear their partner or themselves speaking via voice chat. Even after my desperate attempts to try every way I hoped to resolve the issue, the problem still

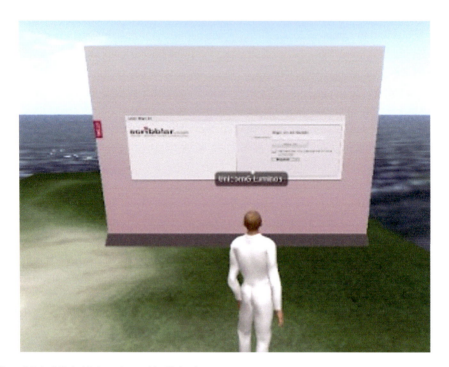

Figure 5.1 A digital whiteboard rezzed in SL for the pretest.

remained. Not until a student told me they needed to download the recent version of SL Viewer 2 to ensure compatibility did I realise the source of the problem.

4. Some students had really bad Internet connections, which unfortunately led to their **voice breaking up**. It caused a problem for his/her interlocutor to understand what was being said. However, it also increased the frequency of **"negotiation"** because each side would try hard to resolve the non-understanding due to the technical issue, though it would have been more ideal if the negotiation was triggered by something other than the connection issue.

Though it was quite mentally taxing (e.g., finishing three pairs in a row alongside fixing the technical issues), I am glad that I collected most of the pretest recordings. In my pilot, I administered six tasks, which apparently was too much to handle by myself and for students. This time, I only allocated four major tasks for them to complete in dyad, which could be done within a 1 to 1.5 hour duration, the longer of which was only due to those technical issues mentioned previously. That said, some initial observations could be made:

- Despite that I haven't got the chance to transcribe the recordings and analyse the data yet, my researcher gut feelings tell me that the **tasks of information gap (giving directions) and jigsaw (spot the differences) seemed to have triggered more negotiation.** More non-understanding seemed to occur when a student dyad needed to help each other accomplish the task by holding only part of the information given on the Notecard.
- The **opinion exchange task** didn't seem to trigger as much negotiation as the other three, mainly because students only exchanged their viewpoints without having to reach any consensus. Maybe I could have made the topic (English learning in my case) a bit more controversial so that more heated discussion could be stimulated. Also, students might feel a bit shy or too polite in their first task because they're still trying to test the water and get to know each other without sounding too overbearing. Therefore, they would simply let the non-understanding pass unless it really obstructed the flow of communication.
- As for the final task, **decision making**, I thought this one would've triggered more negotiation as the literature showed. Nevertheless, it might not have initiated more non-understanding as much as the other two tasks (i.e., information gap and jigsaw). Even though students needed to reach the same agreement based on the criteria I gave them on the Notecard (e.g., where to eat, what to order and wear, what time to meet; Figure 5.2), they compromised with each other on decision making. Non-understanding also seemed to dwindle a bit given that paired

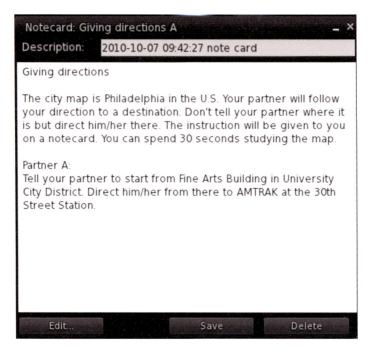

Figure 5.2 A Notecard displaying the instructions for the task of information gap.

students were somewhat used to each other's pronunciation, intonations, and expressions after having done the previous three tasks. Whether or not this task was "negotiable" enough needs to be verified later. I am also curious about how the patterns of their negotiation and communication strategy use will play out after my analysis of their recordings later.

- Using a pencil or highlighter to mark the understanding on the digital whiteboard based on the information they got from their interlocutor also facilitated the flow of communication. Multimodality definitely enhances input uptake.
- Although I gave Notecards to them in each task, I found that it's still important to brief the instructions orally because some students grasped the task requirements pretty quickly, whereas some still needed clarifications about how to proceed.
- During the process of their task completion, it's also crucial to use text chat to gently prompt them to either keep the conversation going, or address some issues occurring during the process without using voice chat that might abruptly disrupt the flow.

After the pretest, I sent them a Notecard detailing their first assignment on completing an online pre-course survey and reflecting on their experience with the task completion in SL (Figure 5.3). However, I still had to remind them one by one to complete the assignment. Without consistently documenting the data, my research study will be in jeopardy.

The truth is, even though most students answered the questions on their first task completion experience in SL as indicated in the Notecard, the depth and length of their responses varied. Some just gave a brief "yes" without explaining in detail about why they felt this way. Maybe I'll "track them down" again this weekend by probing more information. Getting a better understanding of their perspectives about their first experience with SL tasks is integral to finding out the differences between competing RL tasks in SL vs. RL. Later on,

Figure 5.3 A Notecard assignment including an online survey and student reflection on their task experience.

I'll organise their responses gathered from the Notecard and see if I could discover some common trends or patterns. BTW, I just learned from a student that there is another SL version that requires less Internet bandwidth and alleviates the pain of voice breaking up: Imprudence Viewer (https://imprudence.software.informer.com/1.4/).

So I think the daunting task I am facing now is whether I can keep these students in my class for as long as possible. Well, time will tell.

CHECKPOINT

- After reading today's blog entry, what struck you the most in conducting task-based research in SL? Further, what would you have done differently in task design and tackling technical issues?
- If you were the students, what would you respond to the Notecard assignment (Figure 5.3)? Would you benefit (or not) from doing these SL tasks with a partner through unrehearsed, spontaneous interaction?

YOUR TASK

- Notecards were used a lot in this pretest. First, come up with a task that you would like to conduct in SL whilst considering some SL features to maximise your task delivery (e.g., object building, teleporting for a virtual field trip, role-playing in a French restaurant). Create your own Notecard by adding instructions in relation to your task.
- Invite two of your colleagues, students, or your new avatar friends to undertake the task following your Notecard instructions. Record your observation in a Notecard and interview the participant dyad about their experience after their task completion. Save a transcript copy for your further evaluation of the task design in SL.

CHAPTER 6

LESSON 1 (GREETINGS)

OVERVIEW

The first SL lesson, focusing on the topic of Greetings, finally started. This chapter vividly depicts how I incorporated my careful lesson planning in my SL class (just because it's "virtual" doesn't mean no plan is needed) and built a virtual community through an ice-breaking activity facilitated by the private CALL function and Notecard instructions. I further demonstrated how to build a 3D object in preparation for a show-and-tell activity in my next class, and referred students to a class blog for posting their learning reflections right after each session.

BLOG POST. FRIDAY, 6 MAY 2011

After a long delay due to my postponed proposal defence and challenges in recruitment, our first class finally kicked off today! It's like déjà vu. Even though I followed pretty much the same course syllabus and slightly tweaked lesson plans in my pilot, starting this new SL course all by myself sans a team teacher is still nerve-racking. First, I had no idea how many students would show up today despite my constant reminders. Second, I was still haunted by the trauma of technical malfunctions arising unexpectedly in SL, which could have jeopardised a well-designed lesson plan. But again, you gotta do what you gotta do. I kept telling myself, "Just prep and pray and the rest can go with the flow".

So I've decided that I'd create an agenda for each day's lesson, following what I've got in my pilot experience. (Thank God, it really helps a lot!) Just because the course is offered in a free, virtual space doesn't mean it should have no structure. Also, my piloting experience has taught me that having a lesson plan will make the procedure flow more smoothly and make sure both sides (teacher and students) are on the right track. Below is the agenda for today's class created in an SL Notecard (Figure 6.1):

At the outset of the session, I welcomed students and thanked them for joining the class. Then I did some housekeeping business to teach them how to organise their SL inventory folders because it's important for them to find course materials (e.g., Notecards) that I send each time. I also talked about the SL etiquette in class. For example, it's better to turn off the mic when someone is speaking to minimise the background echo or noise. It is also helpful to wear a headset to cancel out the noise. I also reminded them to join our SL class group (New English Class with UnicornG) so that they won't miss any info. Above all, I told

Figure 6.1 Notecard outlining today's lesson plan.

them that as much as this course is aimed toward improving their oral communication skills, posting their learning journals after each session will also improve their writing or at least, give them more opportunities to write and reflect on what they have learned each time. Although I thought it would only take 15–20 minutes to cover the business, explaining these items in full detail and hand-holding with some newbies still took much longer than I had expected. By the time we could start the first task, 30 minutes had already passed.

I jumped right in the "ice-breaking" activity. Because this is a new course and many of them don't know each other, I thought it was important to "build our community" – a supportive, congenial, and collaborative one. The task was to find a partner they didn't know very well and then introduce their partner to the class. They did so by conducting an interview, following the Notecard prompts I gave them (e.g., find out one or two interesting facts about him/her). I asked them to use the private CALL feature to conduct the interview so that they wouldn't be disturbed by everyone talking at the same time. Some students got the hang of it pretty fast, but others were still trying to figure out how to use a private CALL.

Figure 6.2 Ice-breaking activity where students gathered to introduce their speaking partner to the class.

Also, because they didn't know each other well, I thought it might take some time for them to relieve the social awkwardness in the beginning of the interview. After a while, I invited them to report back by taking turns to introduce their partners to the class (Figure 6.2). Apparently, some students did a nice job by adding some intriguing anecdotes provided by their counterparts, whereas others only scratched the surface. That said, it's interesting to see the progress and ease of their speaking "in front of" the class as we moved along.

After the ice-breaking activity, I followed up with a bingo game, Find Someone Who, which is another community-building activity. I instructed them to use either IM or private CALL to ask their classmates or me about what's said in the Notecard (Figure 6.3). If the person said yes, they typed up his/her name under the question item and moved on to the next item. Each person could only contribute to one yes. Also, I reminded them to use a "complete sentence" to ask and answer questions by modelling it before they all started. Whoever first called out bingo on three rows (vertical, horizontal, diagonal) won. As much as I'd like to give them more time to discover something interesting about their classmates, the class time constraint forced me to cut it short. Later on in students' journals, they also voiced that they wished they could have more time completing the task because some of them started it slow and didn't get a move on until the final 2 or 3 minutes when I was about to end it.

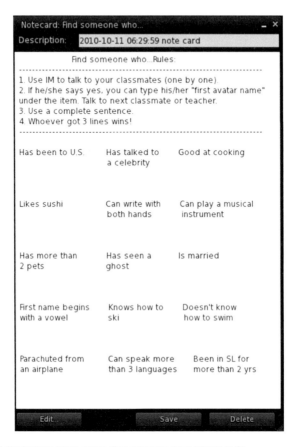

Figure 6.3 Notecard displaying a bingo game (find someone who) played in SL.

Even though I still had another task I'd like to do with them regarding comparing/contrasting the cultural differences on "greetings", I realised that I needed to move on to the last planned task for them to prepare for the show-and-tell presentation. So I made an executive decision to skip the "greetings across cultures" task and took them to the Sandbox area for their first poster-building lesson. Teaching the newbies to build their first digital poster in SL was very challenging, given that they're still trying to familiarise themselves with the basic skills, much less the more advanced skills such as rezzing an object. Much time was spent on explaining how to build from scratch, despite the fact that I gave them a Notecard with a full step-by-step detail on building. Gladly, some of them were quick learners after my explanation, whereas others were already skilled in SL functions. I asked those skilled in SL functions to help out their classmates in need.

CHAPTER 6
LESSON 1 (GREETINGS)

Figure 6.4 Class wiki for students to post their reflections on their task-based experience during each SL session.

They were told in their assignment Notecard that they would prepare a presentation to showcase a cultural artefact that represented their home culture and explained why this artefact meant a lot to them. It was going to be their first oral presentation in SL and I was also curious to see how it would play out. They were also told to post their first reflective entry on our class wiki (Figure 6.4). To protect students' privacy, I set up a class group and only my students with their assigned username and password can access the site.

Although I clearly explained in the assignment Notecard the procedure and login info for the class wiki, some students still couldn't figure it out. Even though they finally logged in, they didn't know how to EDIT the wiki page. So I had to troubleshoot the issues one by one or sometimes copy their unsubmitted posting and paste it onto the wiki on their behalf. Another issue I found, similar to the pilot study, is that students need constant reminders to post their reflection. It might be a better idea to post in the commenting space so that I can reply to their posting to keep the dialogue going and probe for more info. Looking forward to their presentation on Wed.

Lessons learned:

1. Building a supportive and collaborative community at the outset is the key to setting the congenial vibe for the class. Hopefully, the increased sense of belonging established in the virtual community will keep them staying longer with me.

103

2. Having students build objects in SL aligns with the socio-constructivism. They feel a sense of accomplishment when building objects from scratch and use the object to shape the way they think about learning and language practices in SL, thus creating something on their own in an English immersion environment. Also, they sense the power of getting peer support from their colleagues and learning from/helping each other in the joint construction process. Because they all come from different countries, English is the lingua franca for communication. Being able to use English to scaffold their classmates in object building and to understand the instructions in English further stretches their zone of proximal development (ZPD).
3. It's still hard to get everyone to post their journal entry right after each class without "shadowing" them one by one. Maybe I can try to ask them to spend 5–10 minutes after class to post their reflection instead of asking them to do so after exiting SL. Again, striking whilst the iron is still hot might be the way to go. I'll also dialogue with them by commenting on their journal entries and ask them to elaborate more on their reflections if need be.

CHECKPOINT

- There were many tasks jam-packed in this 90-minute SL session. How would you make the decision on choosing one task over the other to keep the class flow going? Give your rationale and identify the tasks in this lesson that you would like to keep or leave out.
- What is your take on spending time teaching students how to build a digital poster in SL, or would you simply ask them to practice it on their own after class to save time? If it is the latter, how would you do it differently?
- Apparently, asking students to keep their journal to reflect on their task-based experience in SL was quite challenging on my end. What strategies can you come up with to gather this type of data that spans more than one session? Additionally, how will you deal with those who never post or are always late for posting?

YOUR TASK

- Brainstorm ideas with a colleague (or in a group) to design an ice-breaking task that you like to start with in an SL class. Also consider the SL features that can help deliver the task more smoothly. Then draft a lesson plan on detailing the steps of executing this task before you pilot it in SL with your colleagues or invited students (or avatar friends).
- Teleport to the Ivory Tower Library of Primitives (http://maps.secondlife.com/secondlife/Natoma/211/164/28) and practise creating a 3D poster by using the Build feature. Try to make it more appealing by adding a picture or snapshot image to your poster. Jot down in a Notecard the steps including the position, size, and rotation (degrees) in your final product. Send this Notecard to a colleague, student, or friend to see if they could create the same poster following your steps.

CHAPTER 7

LESSON 2 (FOOD PART 1)

OVERVIEW

Due to the time constraint in each class, the second lesson (Food) was divided into four parts throughout the following weeks. (See how we LOVED different cultural cuisines!) This chapter documents the first part of the lesson where students did their first show-and-tell presentation on their cultural heritage using a 3D poster whilst communicating with each other through text/voice chat. The lesson ended with a Notecard reminder of the next assignment where they had to research and present a cultural dish and work with a partner to find and recommend a SL restaurant to the class.

BLOG POST. SATURDAY, 7 MAY 2011

The topic of today's class was scheduled to be "food", though deep down I knew I might not have time to cover all the tasks because they needed to finish their show-and-tell presentations one by one. Again, I was telling myself that I'd just play it by ear and go with the flow. To my slight disappointment, not all the students showed up this time. I knew one student (Anja) told me that she'd be late (but didn't show up by the end though), the other one (Azi) left early because she cut her hand, another one (Idea) had issues with her Internet connection that prevented her from logging back in, and still another (Toma) had to cut the class short because her computer kept crashing. Well, I thought I had seen enough in my pilot, but the karma came back biting me this time again – students still have their RL obligations to fulfil or the technical glitches just got in their way. To top it off, a student (Kinda) told me that she unfortunately had to withdraw from the class whilst the one (Rashad) I thought would attend the class didn't make it, let alone the last one (Noobz) just didn't take the class seriously. That being said, it isn't too bad as long as the rest of students (12ish) can keep attending the class regularly. Also, two more students (Feng and Barrabax) contacted me earlier and said they'd like to join the class. However, I won't collect their data until they also finish the pretest and complete the consent form.

As usual, I started the class with some housekeeping business. It's vital to remind students of what they have and haven't done to keep them on track. I complemented them on their great performance on Monday and stressed the importance of receiving notifications via our SL Group. I also walked them through our class wiki and made sure that everyone could access it without any problem. Additionally, I encouraged them to post their reflection journals as a way to practise their writing. They were also told that I'd comment on their journals and that they were welcome to read and comment on their peer postings as well. To motivate them to write more, I indicated that we might do some error correction together in class to suit the needs of some students who prefer some "focus-on-form" instruction. Whilst going through the agenda, some students IMed me about their show-and-tell presentation. Some said they still didn't know how to upload images to their posters, whereas others asked me how to buy L$ because it takes L$10 to upload an image each time. I addressed their questions one by one and told them that they would have time to prepare their posters later in Sandbox before the real presentation. I have learned since the pilot that teaching in SL requires advanced *multitasking skills* to take care of all the needs of students simultaneously. Also, we need to *improvise all the time* when the lesson sometimes doesn't go as planned due to unforeseen matters arising in-world that are beyond our control.

Because I asked them to use Teleport to go to Sandbox for the poster-building task on Monday's class, most students had no problem finding the location :-). After they all arrived in Sandbox, I told them that they could have 3–5 minutes to set up their posters even though they were supposed to prepare their own posters before coming to class. Because of some newbie students, the time given for instruction sometimes had to be doubled to ensure that everyone was on the same page. Whilst they were still working on their posters, I asked who was all set and willing to help their classmates with building and who still needed assistance. It's a strategic move to capitalise on the peer support, thus enabling those who need help to be scaffolded by their more capable counterparts in a virtual community of practice. Nevertheless, time was running so fast that I had to think on my feet and suggested that they have 3 minutes for the show-and-tell and 2 minutes for the Q&A.

I rezzed three display boards for them to put up their posters before the class (Figure 7.1). However, some newbie students couldn't figure out how to drag their posters from their SL "Inventory" directly onto the boards. Again, teaching English as a foreign language (EFL) learners in SL also requires teaching them SL skills at the same time. By the time everyone put up their poster on the boards, time was almost running out. I was also concerned about whether all the students could both finish and enjoy their first presentations in SL. Gladly, the time was well spent. I was very proud of each and every one of them who were willing to take time to prepare their presentation in RL and to share with the class their cultural artefacts. Not only did we hear colourful and interesting stories behind those showcased artifacts across cultures, but we were also impressed with the spot-on presentations everyone delivered. Students also answered the questions posed by their colleagues professionally. Whenever each presenter finished his/her presentation, the rest of the class would praise their work. Some outstanding presentations

CHAPTER 7
LESSON 2 (FOOD PART 1)

Figure 7.1 Show-and-tell presentations displayed on digital posters showcased on 3D display boards.

would also get some animated applause from the audience. I was truly proud of their excellent work; this also set the standard and model of class presentations for the subsequent lessons.

Worth noting is that I also monitored the time and flow of each presentation using public text chat without interrupting the process. It also helped set the tone and keep students on task. Later, some students chimed in with text comments to either ask questions or praise their colleagues. The supportive learning community was naturally formed. Additionally, I recorded each of their presentations for data analysis later. Due to the time constraint, I told the students who hadn't been able to present today to do their show-and-tell in the next class (Nikhil, Idea, Toma, Feng, Barrabax). I also grabbed the opportunity to commend their great work and to stress the purpose of doing each assignment like this: improving your oral presentation skills and speaking proficiency. I hope this valuable experience will serve as the drive to motivate them to accomplish each assigned task.

As expected, I couldn't finish the food topic so I gave them the assignment Notecard to remind them what they need to do for the next class: (1) research the ingredients and ways of cooking their favourite food from their country and share it with their partners; (2) work with a partner(s) to find a restaurant, bar, or bistro in SL and lead us to the place by telling us why it's worth visiting and if there are any signature dishes or ambience in the restaurant they would like to highlight; and (3) post their reflective journal on the show-and-tell experience. In particular, I would like to know how they feel about presenting in SL versus RL and what they can take away from this virtual learning experience. I decided to leave the comparing/contrasting cultural cuisines and role-play using Holodeck to the next session.

109

Lessons learned:

1. Maybe I'd extend the originally planned sessions from 10 to 15 sessions so that I can give my students more time to work on each interactive task designed for each lesson, as opposed to rushing through it.
2. Ask them as a class if they feel there is any difference in presenting in SL versus RL. If so, do they think presenting in SL is less real than in RL? Also, some students commented that they felt less nervous in SL because of the removal of eye contact with the audience. Do they think it's an advantage or disadvantage to present in SL, especially using English?
3. Because some students don't log into SL frequently to check their IMs or notifications, I showed them how to forward the IMs to their email by updating their SL account setting, under *Contact Information*.
4. I may also ask them to post their journal 5–10 minutes before (or right after) the class ends. By so doing, I don't have to "chase" each of them as if I were bugging them all the time. Also, their fresh memory will serve them right and enrich the content of their journals.
5. Having a dialogue journal with students is a good way to clarify information that still seems vague or less detailed in their original postings. Some students either overlooked my guiding prompts or wrote very brief reflections that beg further elaboration and clarification.

CHECKPOINT

- To conduct any research study, the last thing a researcher would like to see is the increasing "participant attrition" rate and inconsistent data collection. How would you tackle the issues of losing student participants in SL? What is the backup plan that you could put in place?
- Given that this class was not credit-bearing and students had no obligation to complete each assignment, why do you think they were still willing to invest their time and effort in preparing their show-and-tell presentation?
- What are the pros and cons of doing an oral presentation in SL versus RL? Do you think students would be able to transfer their skills and confidence in SL to RL later?

YOUR TASK

- Given the culturally and linguistically diverse backgrounds (CaLD) of the students, tapping into their cultural repertoires and translating them into task design had become the ethos of this class. Let's also use the same topic, "Food Culture", for your lesson planning. First, identify the age, proficiency level, and needs of your target students for this lesson. Collaborate with a colleague (or by yourself) to develop a task-based lesson on cultural cuisines and include at least two stages of task-based instruction: pre-, during, and post-task. Outline the lesson progression in each stage, time and materials needed for each step, SL features or resources needed alongside the sub-tasks in each stage, and finally, how students would be assessed for their task performance and language production.
- Pilot it with your students (if available) and survey their evaluations about this food lesson conducted in SL. Modify the lesson based on the received student feedback before testing it again.

CHAPTER 8

LESSON 2 (FOOD PART 2)

> **OVERVIEW**
>
> The second part of the Food lesson picked up where we left off in the previous session. The rest of the students took turns to complete their oral presentations, showcasing their food cultures. Following a Notecard worksheet, students in pairs started to exchange the information about different cultural cuisines. The final 5 to 10 minutes of the lesson were allocated to students posting their journal reflections before the class dismissed.

BLOG POST. TUESDAY, 10 MAY 2011

Today's lesson was a bit rough – once again, time was the killer. As usual, I started the class with some housekeeping business. I first praised them for their great work on their show-and-tell presentations last week and informed them that our course may be extended from 10 to 12–15 sessions (TBC) due to the time constraint that has rushed each lesson so far. I further stressed the benefits of sharing their journals with me – not only can I better understand what they have learned and how their feedback can help me improve the task design in SL, but they can also document their progress throughout the course as well as practice writing skills. One thing I wasn't sure that I did right was that I spent some time reminding them to set up the off-line IMs forwarded to their personal emails because I know some newbies don't frequent SL unless our class is in session. This decision may have backfired on me; when I read one of the students' journals, a student (Ninoune) felt that it was a bit time-wasting (also boring) to do the housekeeping business every time because we couldn't jump right into the lesson. Well, as much as I don't want to spend too much time on it, my concern for those newbie students who might lag behind just got the best of me. Maybe I'd spend less class time on hand-holding if students who are struggling come forward and let me know. That way it's fairer to other students who have already mastered the SL skills and just wanted to enjoy the lesson sooner.

Because some students still hadn't finished their show-and-tell presentations, we teleported back to the Sandbox to finish the unfinished business. We had two new students (Feng, Barrabax) join us, and their proficiency levels of English listening and speaking are a bit low. That said, I can see they have high motivation for and commitment to this course and try hard to complete each assigned task. Barrabax's speaking was a bit unintelligible due to her heavy accent/pronunciation and she also had trouble understanding when other classmates were speaking. But she still tried to answer questions posed by her colleagues with my help typing them up in public chat. I also reminded them to type up some culture-specific expressions/terms so that the audience would better understand their show-and-tell. As for Feng, her speaking was fine, though it seemed that she was reading her presentation script. Toma's presentation about men's clothing in the Middle East was interesting, but her strong/heavy accent kind of got in the way of our comprehension. I also had to remind her to type up some cultural usages in public chat to help her colleagues grasp what she was saying. Idea's presentation was professional and vibrant because she used a special poster frame to change her slides whilst she was talking as if doing a PowerPoint (PPT) presentation in RL. That kind of WOWed the audience, though we still needed to listen closely to her presentation due to her heavy accent. Finally, Nikhil did a nice job presenting a geographic map in Indian using different colours to represent different local cultures and languages spoken in India. That was definitely culturally informative and colourful! Actually, he was a bit shy at first and told me that he needed more time to rehearse and that's why he did his presentation today rather than last week. But his effort paid off! Like other presenters, he also spoke with a strong accent, though he seemed competent getting his meaning across.

By the end of their presentations (Figure 8.1), I commended them again for their great effort and asked the whole class to give all the presenters a big clap (using the avatar gesture feature). I also seized the moment to indicate how wonderful this class is to have so many students from different countries and cultures and speak English with a variety of accents and pronunciations. That's exactly the situation they'll encounter in RL where they'll pretty much speak English with people whose English is not their first language but as a lingua franca or World Englishes.

After we finished all the show-and-tells (thank goodness), we had roughly 30 minutes left. I asked them to quickly teleport back to the Rose Garden, which is the entry point of our class. I figured that we probably wouldn't have enough time to go over each team's restaurant field trip so I made another informed decision to focus on the task of exchanging cultural cuisines, which I asked them to prepare in advance. Originally, I intended to ask them to work in groups of three to get more opportunity to interact with their classmates as a group. Given the time constraint, I thought working in pairs would be more efficient and effective. So I gave them the Notecard detailing what they should do and asked them to use the private CALL to conduct the task with their partner. Figure 8.2 shows one of the completed Notecards submitted by a student.

CHAPTER 8
LESSON 2 (FOOD PART 2)

Figure 8.1 Students presenting their cultural heritages showcased in digital posters in front of the display board.

After reading their journals, I was pleased to know that most students expressed that they enjoyed doing this task because they could practise speaking English whilst learning a different recipe and culture at the same time. Using a private CALL seems to work for my students because they can focus on their discussion without being disturbed by other groups. Although I sent some of them IMs to ask how their pair work was going, I should probably join their private CALLs next time to check how they're doing. As much as I'd like some of the pairs to share their findings, the time didn't permit us to do so. Instead, I told them that their restaurant project will be carried out on Wednesday's class, and drew their attention again to our class wiki. I said, "I fully understand that everyone is busy with your RL obligations and sometimes it's hard to post your journal on time until I 'chase' some of you. Therefore, I decided that we'll spend 5–10 minutes right after class for everyone to post your journal before leaving the class".

So we did it the first time in class today. Although some of them did post their reflection entries, others still put it on hold. That's the double-edged sword of teaching a course in SL with a group of students from all over the world where the level of their commitment to the project is simply beyond my control. All I can do is keep reminding them of posting their journal, though there is no way I could force them to do so. Despite being cumbersome, my study would turn into a flop without the consistent data collected. Hopefully they'll make a habit of posting their learning journal right after each session.

115

LET'S GET OUR HANDS DIRTY

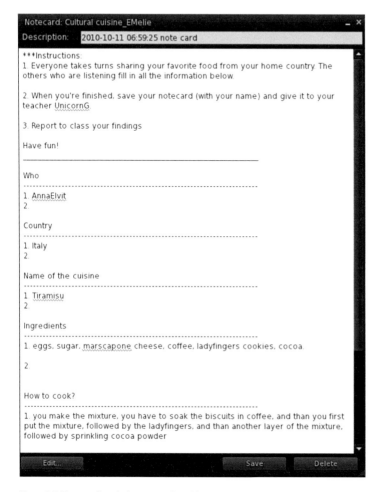

Figure 8.2 Notecard worksheet completed by a student pair on how to cook a cultural dish.

BTW, I am glad that two students worked out the issue of working as a team for their restaurant project. Earlier, Ulyo tried to contact his potential partner, Unessl, but got no reply from him. Discouraged, he decided to work on his own. I was also concerned that his frustration might get the best of him, as well as being uncertain about whether Unessl would still attend the class. That's why I did the housekeeping business in the beginning of class by asking them to keep an eye out for every IM and notice sent from SL, even when they're off-line. Gladly, both Ulyo and Unessl recouped and decided to give it a second shot.

Lessons learned:

1. I'll definitely finish the restaurant field trips on Wed. If time permits, I'll do the role-play in Holodeck because it was a successful task in my pilot.
2. I'll assign another task for them to do over the weekend (cultural clothing) for the topic on clothing (or holiday/festival?). I find that momentum helps to prepare class assignments: it's better to announce their project work on Wed instead of Monday because they get more time to work on each team project.
3. I'll spend less time on class management business but more on that day's lesson so that students get more time/chances to engage with the tasks in SL. Hopefully that will win my students back.
4. Having a dialogue journal with students is helpful. I can keep probing for more info about the intended meanings that are still vague or need more explanation in their postings. Students can also get the chance to read their colleagues' journals for inspiration.
5. I will still leave 5–10 minutes right after class for their journal writing and make it a habit for them. Hopefully they will ease into the routine and finish their posting before taking off.
6. I might do some initial data analysis of their Notecard responses during the pretest and ask some of them to elaborate more on unclear responses to the prompts.

CHECKPOINT

- How would you strike a balance between hand-holding with the newbies who still need you to cover the SL basics from time to time, and the rest of the students who just want to start the day's lesson sooner than later?
- When students were doing their pair work using the private CALL, I only checked in on them by sending IMs. What is your take on this approach? Would you rather monitor each pair work by hopping from one pair to another, or simply let them take the reins?
- As a researcher, would you also join the dialogue journaling with your students as a participant observer, or simply take on a pure observer role by letting the students post/comment on their own? If it is the latter, how will you deal with the fact that some students forget to post or do not interact with each other or only make a one-sentence reflection each time?

YOUR TASK

- I created a Notecard worksheet for student pairs to interview each other on a classic cultural dish from their home country and note down the recipes before reporting back to the class. Work with a colleague to develop your own Notecard worksheet on a similar food topic. Also brainstorm on other SL features or resources that you can utilise to deliver this task in lieu of a Notecard. Pilot it in-world and observe its effectiveness.
- Given the diverse nature of my student cohort, their spoken English came with cultural and linguistic varieties. If your class makeup is monolingual/cultural, see if you can collaborate with an avatar teacher in-world (see Table 21.5 SL researchers and specialists in Chapter 21) or a colleague to conduct a telecollaboration project on intercultural communication using SL as a platform. Meet regularly to co-design the syllabus and tasks that would suit both student cohorts. Also discuss the impact of World Englishes on student learning experience.

CHAPTER 9

LESSON 2 (FOOD PART 3)

OVERVIEW

Today's class started with my acknowledgement of students' commitments to keeping their learning reflections while addressing some of their concerns, particularly from the newbie students. A researchable moment (also a formative assessment) arose where I stimulated their discussion about a reflection prompt on which they hadn't fully elaborated in the class wiki. The highlights of the class were students taking turns to lead virtual field trips to different SL locations, whilst introducing their cultural cuisines to the class such as secret ingredients and recipes. Relevant chat logs and transcripts were also included to provide evidence for in-world lesson episodes.

BLOG POST. MONDAY, 16 MAY 2011

Today's lesson was fantastic! I am very proud of my students who took time and made the effort to prepare for their assigned task, which was taking the class on a restaurant field trip. This task also opened their eyes to what SL could offer for learning if compared with RL. At the outset of the class, I thanked them for sharing their journals with me and commented on how valuable their reflections are for me to better understand what they think about each lesson and tasks. I especially commended a student (Korobase) who tried to cook at home the recipes that his partner told him about when they exchanged recipes in the cultural cuisine task. I told them that's exactly how you can transfer SL skills and knowledge to RL. Then I addressed some "complaints" from a couple of students who mentioned in their journals that they found listening to the housekeeping business targeting newbie students a bit boring and time-wasting. I justified that the course is free and students are from a wide range of backgrounds and levels of SL skills. So I have been trying to accommodate each one of the student needs and make sure no one is left behind. I also sought their understanding and drew their attention to the class size (ironically, I got more students this time than in the pilot). Then I walked them through some tips on how to present in SL. Because our class is a replica of a global community where everyone speaks with various accents and pronunciations, it's crucial for presenters to type up some culture-specific terms/expressions in the public chat to help the audience better understand the content.

I know every second counts in each session because the planned tasks for students to undertake need to be completed within the time limit. Nevertheless, I still think it's pivotal for me to help them evaluate and reflect on what they've learned from their first oral presentation experience in SL. Similar to a focus group interview, I raised a question in the public chat:

> Some students commented in our class wiki that they felt less nervous in SL because the audience can't see them in SL (no eye contact). Do you think it's an advantage or disadvantage of presenting in SL? Does it make oral presentation less real in SL?

A lot of discussion was stimulated and I monitored by commenting and prompting the discussion further (see the text chat log and emphasis added).

[2011/05/11 10:10] Annaelvit: it's easier cause **you don't feel the pressure of the audience**
[2011/05/11 10:10] Emelie Crystal: I think is an advantage:)
[2011/05/11 10:11] Barrabax Laks: I agree.
[2011/05/11 10:11] Unessl: I guess it can be deemed as both advantage and disadvantage
[2011/05/11 10:11] ninoune: it is an advantage because I think it can be less pressure
[2011/05/11 10:11] Emelie Crystal: sure, you do not feel as stressed
[2011/05/11 10:11] ninoune: but a disadvantage because **you never know if they are intersted on what you say**
[2011/05/11 10:11] Annaelvit: cause you are sitting comfortably at home
[2011/05/11 10:11] Barrabax Laks: yes ninoune
[2011/05/11 10:11] afridiqau: a kind of disadvatage
[2011/05/11 10:12] afridiqau: cuz **u cannt apply ur SL presention skill in RL**
[2011/05/11 10:12] Annaelvit: you can pretend that no one is listening to you since you don't see other people:)
[2011/05/11 10:12] ninoune: also because **you can't see if you have to make your presentation more energetic** or not
[2011/05/11 10:12] Emelie Crystal: you can not use your verbal language
[2011/05/11 10:12] Unessl: I guess it can be deemed as both advantage and disadvantage. For the former, because it is helpful to improve speaking skills but on the other hand, it s not good due to it's drawback of **not being engaged in real life experiences**
[2011/05/11 10:13] Emelie Crystal: it is good practise to do it in SL
[2011/05/11 10:13] afridiqau: even u r laying on ur bad u can present in SL

[2011/05/11 10:13] Profesor Korobase: the only disadvange I can see presentation s in SL is the number of attendees must be limited
[2011/05/11 10:14] Barrabax Laks: **sl sometimes is not stable and has technical problem**
[2011/05/11 10:14] afridiqau: yes
[2011/05/11 10:14] fenghp99: yeah
[2011/05/11 10:14] Idea Loxingly (idea.lexenstar): yep
[2011/05/11 10:15] fenghp99: it is **different between SL and RL**

I found the discussion quite interesting, though there are mixed results. Presenting in SL is like a double-edged sword. As much as it is more at ease (presenting at home casually) and can lessen the stress of having the direct eye contact of audience, it also becomes an inhibitor because the presenter doesn't know how their audience thinks about the presentation without catching the non-verbal cues from them (e.g., gestures, facial expressions) as in RL. I tried to provide another perspective by adding that their classmates still gave them comments and raised questions in text chat during their presentation. After I pointed it out, more students started to chime in and agreed with me on that. But I do need to investigate further in this aspect, especially some newbie students' comments on "not being engaged in real life experiences" (Unessl) and "u cannt apply ur SL presentation skill in RL" (Afridi). It would be interesting to see why they think this way and if their perception will change as the course progresses. Additionally, Barrabax brought up a good point about the technical issue in SL, namely, unstable platform. I am curious about whether this issue will dampen their motivation or if other unique features in SL that make learning immersive and engaging will counteract this factor.

Here comes showtime. I can tell that students were excited about the team project of their first restaurant field trips. Each team led the field trip by teleporting us to the restaurant they're responsible for introducing. Though I told them to use the group chat to send out the teleport landmark, they still didn't figure out how to do it so I asked them to send me the link first and I would type it up in the public chat for everyone to access. I also teleported some students who still got lost to make sure that we all gathered before proceeding with each team's presentation. I am so impressed with the ways some students led the class as tour guides. Not only were they professional, they also engaged every classmate during the field trip. Ulyo and Unessl volunteered to be the first team. They took us to a mesmerising safari restaurant. Ulyo started off introducing the overall ambiance and facilities in this exotic place. We saw a lot of wildlife animals roaming around, such as tigers, elephants, and giraffes. It was as if we were in the same safari. Students were so immersed in the setting that they started to play with tigers and walking around the place. After a while, Unessl took us back to the safari restaurant and introduced us to the menu and how the food was cooked. Some students were already seated and Hemasha also volunteered to tend the bar for us. It was great fun and they were role models for the rest of the teams. Some highlights were recorded in the following chat transcript.

```
[2011/05/11 10:26]  Profesor Korobase: I'm afraid (of tigers)
[2011/05/11 10:26]  Unessl: ha
[2011/05/11 10:26]  Profesor Korobase: are these animals free?
[2011/05/11 10:26]  Unessl: dont panic
[2011/05/11 10:27]  Unessl: we already tamed them
[2011/05/11 10:27]  Barrabax Laks: lol
[2011/05/11 10:27]  Hemasha Seda: there are two birds on the table
[2011/05/11 10:28]  UnicornG Luminos: Safari in Africa
[2011/05/11 10:29]  UnicornG Luminos: so animated
[2011/05/11 10:30]  Emelie Crystal: wow
[2011/05/11 10:30]  Nikhil (nikhil.moorsider): really beautiful
[2011/05/11 10:30]  afridiqau: can I ride the elephant
[2011/05/11 10:30]  Unessl: for sure afridi
[2011/05/11 10:30]  fenghp99: so many kind of animals
[2011/05/11 10:30]  Barrabax Laks: its a beautiful place:)
[2011/05/11 10:31]  UnicornG Luminos: indeed
[2011/05/11 10:31]  Barrabax Laks: no bite?
[2011/05/11 10:31]  UnicornG Luminos: haha funny
[2011/05/11 10:33]  UnicornG Luminos: many ppl are taking snapshots
[2011/05/11 10:33]  UnicornG Luminos: ok, leaders, pls take us to the restaurant
[2011/05/11 10:33]  UnicornG Luminos: we'd like to dine
[2011/05/11 10:36]  Cornish Game Hens with Figs in Port Reduction: Enjoy a delicious
     Roast Game Hen, Idea Lexenstar!
[2011/05/11 10:36]  UnicornG Luminos: can we sit down?
[2011/05/11 10:36]  Unessl: ulyo is there anything u wanna add?
[2011/05/11 10:36]  Unessl: I think so
[2011/05/11 10:37]  UnicornG Luminos: wow, we're eating
[2011/05/11 10:37]  Unessl: Bon appetite
[2011/05/11 10:37]  Barrabax Laks: jajajaa
```

[2011/05/11 10:37] ulyo Genesis: the word safari means "long journey" in sawhili and has its origin from an arabic wor"safar"
[2011/05/11 10:37] UnicornG Luminos: Hemasha is tending the bar
[2011/05/11 10:38] Hemasha Seda: anyone want drinks? i offer any drink, haha
[2011/05/11 10:38] UnicornG Luminos: thank you…very informative
[2011/05/11 10:38] Profesor Korobase: Congratulations. Very well worked
[2011/05/11 10:38] UnicornG Luminos: any questions or comments for our wonderful leaders
[2011/05/11 10:39] Mero (merogigo.baily): great work ulyo and unessl
[2011/05/11 10:39] Emelie Crystal: you did a really good job
[2011/05/11 10:39] Profesor Korobase: Ho did you domesticate tigers?
[2011/05/11 10:39] Unessl: Thanks a million
[2011/05/11 10:40] Nikhil (nikhil.moorsider): BRAVO!!!!!!
[2011/05/11 10:40] Nikhil (nikhil.moorsider): *****APPPPPLLAAAUUUSSSEEE***

Next, Afridi and Emelie took us to a restaurant that was classy with an open space (Figure 9.1). There were many tables already set up for the diners and some dance animations were also ready for couples to activate if they wished to dance. Emelie was supposed to lead the first part of the field trip. Unfortunately, her voice chat had some glitches, making her voice break up constantly. So Afridi had to take over her role to lead the rest of the session. I was so pleased to see that Afridi was quite composed to take the lead to introduce the venue and

Figure 9.1 Snapshot of the restaurant field trip led by a student pair.

how to prepare the food. Diners were allowed to activate the menu and order the food, which was brought to them instantly. As the text chat log shows below, students were all engaged/immersed in the SIM and enjoyed the simulated ambiance, animated food, and dance. The chat transcript also revealed the excitement, fun, and immersion they felt. Afterward, each of them commended the leaders on their excellent work. A student (Barrabax) also thanked Afridi for his clear explanation during the whole dining experience.

> [2011/05/11 10:47] Dim Sum Platter: Enjoy your Dim Sum, Unessl Resident!
> [2011/05/11 10:47] Emelie Crystal: my sound is not workung
> [2011/05/11 10:48] UnicornG Luminos: Emelie, try to log off and log back in again. maybe that will help
> [2011/05/11 10:48] Emelie Crystal: ok
> [2011/05/11 10:48] UnicornG Luminos: guys, shall we take a seat while afridi is talking
> [2011/05/11 10:48] Barrabax Laks: i can hear birds:)
> [2011/05/11 10:50] Emelie Crystal: pls follow me
> [2011/05/11 10:52] Unessl: Voice is not clear
> [2011/05/11 10:53] Emelie Crystal: I am so sorry
> [2011/05/11 10:53] UnicornG Luminos: yes, Emelie's voice is a bit breaking up…but that is fine
> [2011/05/11 10:53] Emelie Crystal: I have some problem with my sound
> [2011/05/11 10:53] Emelie Crystal: I tried to sort it out, but it did not help
> [2011/05/11 10:53] Hemasha Seda: afridi
> [2011/05/11 10:53] UnicornG Luminos: maybe u can fix it next time…or use text chat to help explain
> [2011/05/11 10:54] UnicornG Luminos: Emelie, talk to me after class and see if we can fix it
> [2011/05/11 10:54] Emelie Crystal: sure:)
> [2011/05/11 10:54] Emelie Crystal: thank u
> [2011/05/11 10:54] UnicornG Luminos: now, Emelie, pls use text to help explain for Afridi
> [2011/05/11 10:57] Greek Gyros Platter: Enjoy your plate of Greek delicacies, Barrabax Laks!
> [2011/05/11 10:58] Emelie Crystal: good choice Barrabax:)
> [2011/05/11 10:58] Barrabax Laks: jajaja
> [2011/05/11 10:58] Profesor Korobase: Lobster is really nice

[2011/05/11 10:58] Tiramisu Cake: Enjoy your Tiramisu, Barrabax Laks!
[2011/05/11 10:59] UnicornG Luminos: haha
[2011/05/11 10:59] JC Designs Martini: whispers: JC Designs Martini
[2011/05/11 10:59] UnicornG Luminos: hmm, i am drinking martini
[2011/05/11 10:59] Unessl: Come on man
[2011/05/11 10:59] Unessl: we were invited by you
[2011/05/11 10:59] UnicornG Luminos: it's on the house this time, Afridi
[2011/05/11 10:59] Barrabax Laks: 2 euros
[2011/05/11 11:00] Mero (merogigo.baily): thanks afridiqau
[2011/05/11 11:00] Unessl: How we can dance here?
[2011/05/11 11:00] Emelie Crystal: you rock afridi
[2011/05/11 11:00] Emelie Crystal: you did a great job
[2011/05/11 11:01] UnicornG Luminos: can we have someone dance?
[2011/05/11 11:01] Waltz (slow): whispers: synchronising
[2011/05/11 11:02] Ballroom Dance 1: whispers: synchronising
[2011/05/11 11:02] Barrabax Laks: fun
[2011/05/11 11:02] Unessl: very very gooooooooood
[2011/05/11 11:02] Mero (merogigo.baily): nice
[2011/05/11 11:02] afridiqau: thanks
[2011/05/11 11:02] Profesor Korobase: Congratulation
[2011/05/11 11:02] ulyo Genesis: good presentation
[2011/05/11 11:02] afridiqau: thanks every one
[2011/05/11 11:02] Unessl: How can I stop dancing?
[2011/05/11 11:03] Barrabax Laks: your explanation was very clear
[2011/05/11 11:03] afridiqau: thanks
[2011/05/11 11:03] Idea Loxingly (idea.lexenstar): claping
[2011/05/11 11:03] Nikhil (nikhil.moorsider): BRAVO!!!!!!

Following up, Barrabax and Korobase took us to sample Spanish cuisine. Barrabax taught us how to make a tortilla and displayed all the ingredients in front of us with name tags above the food objects. Due to their unfamiliarity with sending the teleport landmark to the group, I was teleporting back and forth from the new place to copy the link and back to where most students were located by pasting the link in the public chat so everyone could teleport. When we all landed, another SL resident happened to be there as well. She asked us what we were doing and I had to text chat with her that we were having a class now and would appreciate it if she could kindly give us some space. That's exactly what happens when teaching in SL! You never know who will be there because some lands are open to the public. Though there are some griefers that may interrupt the class, most residents would respect what we're doing. Barrabax seemed quite comfortable with her demonstration, despite it sounding a bit scripted. Nevertheless, she helped us understand the ingredients and steps in the recipe by typing up some terms in the text chat. Throughout her presentation, students also expressed some palpable RL feelings such as "I am hungry now", "mouth-watering", or "looks yummy!" She was also kind enough to give a copy of the finished tortilla as a digital object to everyone in class.

Korobase followed up with his impressive, informative, and professional presentation. He put up a storybook menu that can be flipped through with a food picture on one page and the text next to it, side by side with his oral explanation. He broke down each step of making paella and tried to engage his audience without sounding like he was reading a script (Figure 9.2). After his presentation, gracious Korobase gave away a copy of the menu book to the class. Unessl even checked the origin of the word, saffron, by looking it up on the web and typed up the definition for us. Again, it was a very successful presentation that inspired all the students, as evidenced in the following chat transcript below.

[2011/05/11 11:16] UnicornG Luminos: yes, Korobase, pls start
[2011/05/11 11:17] UnicornG Luminos: also, what is the place?
[2011/05/11 11:17] Profesor Korobase: chiringuito

Figure 9.2 Snapshot of a student explaining how to make paella displayed in a 3D menu booklet.

CHAPTER 9
LESSON 2 (FOOD PART 3)

[2011/05/11 11:18] Annaelvit: chiringuito is a place where you can have meals or drinks on the Beach
[2011/05/11 11:18] Unessl: it must be free of charge
[2011/05/11 11:18] UnicornG Luminos: haah Unessl, don't be naughty
[2011/05/11 11:18] ulyo Genesis: that tastes good!
[2011/05/11 11:19] afridiqau: wow
[2011/05/11 11:19] Hemasha Seda: like sea food…: D
[2011/05/11 11:19] Idea Loxingly (idea.lexenstar): good
[2011/05/11 11:19] UnicornG Luminos: i love seafood, too
[2011/05/11 11:19] UnicornG Luminos: mussels
[2011/05/11 11:20] UnicornG Luminos: i want to cook it myself next time
[2011/05/11 11:20] Unessl: You are really great Korobase in explaining this
[2011/05/11 11:20] Unessl: I am writing this
[2011/05/11 11:20] UnicornG Luminos: isn't he, Unessl?: -))
[2011/05/11 11:20] UnicornG Luminos: fish broth
[2011/05/11 11:20] Annaelvit: couple of spoons maybe?
[2011/05/11 11:20] Unessl: yes, he really is
[2011/05/11 11:20] UnicornG Luminos: yes, good, Annaelvit, sounds u're a good cook
[2011/05/11 11:22] Emelie Crystal: you are good!
[2011/05/11 11:22] Unessl: The English word saffron stems from the Latin word safranum via the 13th-century Old French term safran. Safranum in turn derives from Persian (za'fer√¢n).
[2011/05/11 11:22] afridiqau: u r really great
[2011/05/11 11:22] ninoune: so cute
[2011/05/11 11:22] Barrabax Laks: great work Korobase
[2011/05/11 11:22] ulyo Genesis: congratulations
[2011/05/11 11:22] UnicornG Luminos: how do we buy it
[2011/05/11 11:22] Barrabax Laks: tengo hambre
[2011/05/11 11:23] UnicornG Luminos: right click?
[2011/05/11 11:23] Barrabax Laks: jajajaa
[2011/05/11 11:23] Unessl: it was fantastic, dude
[2011/05/11 11:23] Hemasha Seda: can you cook for me… i go to your home.:)
[2011/05/11 11:23] Unessl: what about me?
[2011/05/11 11:23] UnicornG Luminos: that would be helpful for everyone to get a copy
[2011/05/11 11:24] UnicornG Luminos: we're so lucky
[2011/05/11 11:24] UnicornG Luminos: thanks so much, Korobase…

[2011/05/11 11:24] UnicornG Luminos: i got it
[2011/05/11 11:24] Hemasha Seda: yes
[2011/05/11 11:25] Nikhil (nikhil.moorsider): another good presentation
[2011/05/11 11:27] UnicornG Luminos: so gracias, Korobase
[2011/05/11 11:27] Unessl: Thanks a lot. It is free
[2011/05/11 11:27] afridiqau: u r great Prof
[2011/05/11 11:28] Unessl: you have a heart of gold
[2011/05/11 11:28] Barrabax Laks: thank you

The last field trip was led by Mero, Ninoune, and Annaelvit's team. They took us to a very classy Italian restaurant and the decor and ambiance set the tone for the restaurant. We were able to touch the lamp to change the colour of the light (e.g., from white to purple) (Figure 9.3). Originally, another team (Idea, Nikhil, and Feng) also found the same restaurant so I suggested that they coordinate with their counterpart to make sure that the restaurants they were planning to introduce would not overlap. Perhaps Idea's team was so impressed with the other teams' great performance that she IMed me in private saying that they had reached the agreement to search for another restaurant and do the field trip on Monday. I was pleased that they'd like to make more effort to polish their teamwork, despite Nikhil needing to prepare for his school exam. Additionally, Mero told me that she needed to leave early (only 5 minutes left before the class ended)

Figure 9.3 Snapshot of a student team ushering the class to fine dining at an Italian restaurant in SL.

so she started to introduce the restaurant first. Each team member also coordinated pretty well. Annaelvit continued by talking more about the ambiance. Because Ninoune majors in Hospitality and Tourism Management, she was able to deliver her presentation as if she was working as an on-site manager in this restaurant. The following chat log transcript says it all!

[2011/05/11 11:33] UnicornG Luminos: can u type the name of the restaurant?
[2011/05/11 11:33] ninoune: al peperoncino piccante
[2011/05/11 11:34] UnicornG Luminos: Unessl, u're already seated
[2011/05/11 11:34] UnicornG Luminos: nice intro
[2011/05/11 11:35] Unessl: good job, Anna
[2011/05/11 11:35] UnicornG Luminos: tks, Annaelvit
[2011/05/11 11:35] [Ploreho] Wall lamp (take 4): Switching light intensity to medium.
[2011/05/11 11:35] [Ploreho] Wall lamp (take 4): Please say the new color in chat channel 47 (example:/47red), you have 30 seconds.
[2011/05/11 11:36] UnicornG Luminos: very elegant
[2011/05/11 11:36] Unessl: exactly
[2011/05/11 11:36] UnicornG Luminos: Ninoune, u sound like a waitress
[2011/05/11 11:37] UnicornG Luminos: or manager of the restaurant: -)
[2011/05/11 11:37] UnicornG Luminos: wow, the color changes
[2011/05/11 11:38] UnicornG Luminos: perfect!!!
[2011/05/11 11:38] Unessl: Really informative
[2011/05/11 11:38] ninoune: thanks
[2011/05/11 11:39] Emelie Crystal: a good presentation:) well done
[2011/05/11 11:39] Unessl: Very organised
[2011/05/11 11:39] Profesor Korobase: Very good presentation
[2011/05/11 11:39] ulyo Genesis: dreaming presentation! congratulation
[2011/05/11 11:39] Unessl: fantastic
[2011/05/11 11:39] Profesor Korobase: and the place is fantastic
[2011/05/11 11:40] Barrabax Laks: this place is very elegancy but its very expensive?
[2011/05/11 11:40] Unessl: for sure lol
[2011/05/11 11:40] Barrabax Laks: APLLAAAUSEESEEEE
[2011/05/11 11:40] Annaelvit: thanks!
[2011/05/11 11:40] Nikhil (nikhil.moorsider):. ;:+*¨'* APPPLLLAAAUUUSSSEEE*¨'*+
[2011/05/11 11:40] Hemasha Seda: BRAVO!!!!!!

Lessons learned:

1. It was a great class today. Students finally witnessed the potential SL can offer for learning through simulation of the RL restaurants and immersive engagement. They learned different ways of dining and picked up some new vocabulary during the virtual field trips. Each one of them took the autonomy of being a guide to introduce the restaurant they researched. I can see that they really enjoyed collaborating with their team members to accomplish the assigned task. Other students also felt as if they were dining at different RL restaurants, augmented by interacting with animated 3D replicas of RL venues. I had a quick chat with a student (Nikhil) after class to ask about his virtual field trip experience in today's task (his texts are bold for emphasis).

    [2011/05/12 07:31] UnicornG Luminos: did u enjoy the field trips?
    [2011/05/12 07:31] Nikhil (nikhil.moorsider): **yeah**
    [2011/05/12 07:32] UnicornG Luminos: me, too…i am so proud of you all
    [2011/05/12 07:33] Nikhil (nikhil.moorsider): **activities are so interesting that can't distinguish we are learning with enjoying or enjoying with learning**
    [2011/05/12 07:33] Nikhil (nikhil.moorsider): **lol**
    [2011/05/12 07:33] UnicornG Luminos: well said, Nikhil :-))

2. This is what language learning in SL is about – immersing yourself in RL tasks that are made possible in SL. It's reassuring to know that students are learning for pleasure, not pressure, and just having fun. In the next session, I may ask them as a focus group about their restaurant project experience. We'll see if Nikhil's virtual learning experience will also be shared by his peers.

CHECKPOINT

- In the beginning of the lesson, I allowed them to have a say about some students' dissatisfaction about time spent on accommodation made for the newbies (e.g., SL basics). While I justified the purpose of doing so, do you think I might have also let the "researcher bias" sneak into the study ecology, swaying participants' views into mine?
- Do you think students will be able to transfer their oral presentation skills developed in SL to RL? Consider the factor of "eye contact" that makes students feel nervous.

- How does today's lesson make you feel about conducting virtual trips in SL? What are the challenges or/and benefits of having students collaborate (outside of class) on finding a restaurant in-world and introducing it to the class?
- I peppered today's blog entry with recorded chat logs and transcripts to highlight the lesson progression and learning episodes in-world. If you are a researcher, how would this approach help you analyse your data? Similarly, how would you turn this documentation into a learning activity for your students if you are a teacher?

YOUR TASK

- Have you conducted any field trip for your RL class? If you have, think about a topic from your previous experience that you can turn into an SL field trip as well (or you can use the same topic on dining at a restaurant in-world). Plan ahead by searching for one or two locations in SL that you would like to take your students to. You may use Destination in your SL Viewer to find the venues, ask your avatar friends, or simply explore them on your own. After you decide where to go, take your students (or a colleague) on a virtual field trip there.
- The second task is to replicate this lesson by asking your students to take the reins to find their preferred SL restaurant and be the guides to teleport the class there. You may demonstrate first (i.e., your first task above) so that they know what to expect and how to carry out this task. To evaluate student performance, you may design two rubric Notecards (teacher feedback and peer feedback) so that each team can benefit from the comments and suggestions from you and their classmates.
- If you have time, follow up with your students by asking about their first virtual field trip experience and their opinions about task collaboration in SL.

CHAPTER 10

LESSON 2 (FOOD FINAL)

> ## OVERVIEW
>
> This is the final part of the Food topic – we must have LOVED food a lot! A few more students pairs, who didn't complete their presentations last time, took us on field trips to their favourite restaurants in SL and informed us to interact with animated dishes available in each 3D restaurant. To wrap up the lesson, I rezzed a 3D pizzeria using the Holodeck feature in VIRTLANTIS for a role-play activity. In this activity, students were assigned to two groups as either servers or customers. Both groups followed the role-play instructions on the Notecard to take orders from their diners or order dishes from the menu, simulating their dining experience in a RL pizzeria

BLOG POST. WEDNESDAY, 18 MAY 2011

I must love FOOD (big time), so much so that I have four sessions allocated to this single topic! Though it's a bit behind my original lesson scheduling, I think it's worth allowing students to undertake each task that was successfully implemented in my pilot. Their task learning experience will further provide me with a better understanding of the effect that task-based language teaching/learning in SL can have on students' perceptions and language production.

Some students were late in the beginning of the class. To give them the benefit of the doubt, they were probably using the last minute to prepare their field trips for us. Therefore, I filled in the time by doing another focus group interview on their experience with their first virtual field trips to those restaurants in SL. I input the question in public chat: *"What is the difference between doing the task in SL versus RL? (How different is it to go on field trips to SL restaurants versus RL restaurants?)"* Maybe I didn't phrase my question clearly or maybe the question was a bit too long. I didn't get as many discussions flowing as last time. Korobase used voice chat to express his opinion, which was recorded, whilst others used text chat to chime in. The following is the text chat log.

[2011/05/16 10:08] UnicornG Luminos: any thought?
[2011/05/16 10:08] Barrabax Laks: sl helps to make a presentation, 3D settings, voice, etc.
[2011/05/16 10:08] UnicornG Luminos: just briefly brainstorm here

[2011/05/16 10:10] fenghp99: we can use gestures in RL but less in SL
[2011/05/16 10:11] UnicornG Luminos: SL class vs. RL class
[2011/05/16 10:11] UnicornG Luminos: Afridi
[2011/05/16 10:11] UnicornG Luminos: u said you feel like a king when ppl are listening to you
[2011/05/16 10:11] UnicornG Luminos: but ppl can still listen to you in RL
[2011/05/16 10:12] UnicornG Luminos: but how about the language learning…do u think you can learn more?
[2011/05/16 10:14] Unessl: In terms of conversation, I did not see any difference in each RL and SL. But regardless of eating sth in RL, participating in such a party or gathering we had in previous session, was profoundly informative and recalling lots of useful expressions
[2011/05/16 10:14] Unessl: exactly

After the debriefing, we were waiting for the remaining two teams to take us to their discovered hidden gems. Uncannily, both teams said they found the same restaurant but decided to introduce the same place from different angles. Hemasha went to the restaurant and came back by pasting the SLurl in the public chat so that everyone could teleport to the same location at once. I was so proud of these two teams! They were well prepared and each member took a different role to usher the class to different features of this restaurant (Figure 10.1). This restaurant was too beautiful to be true. Diners could enjoy their meals whilst overlooking the breath-taking view through the windows. Toma started off by telling

Figure 10.1 Snapshot of a student team ushering the class to fine dining at a romantic restaurant in SL.

us how we could use the facilities in this restaurant. We were seated around the tables and activated the user-friendly menu with a wide range of selections. After clicking on our preferred meal, we were automatically served different animated dishes, as evidenced in the following chat transcript.

[2011/05/16 10:17] salute assistance: Welcome, UnicornG to Salute'….Please have a seat and look through our menu.
[2011/05/16 10:18] Unessl: I love this music
[2011/05/16 10:19] UnicornG Luminos: very romantic
[2011/05/16 10:19] UnicornG Luminos: i love the view
[2011/05/16 10:19] afridiqau: nice resturant
[2011/05/16 10:20] UnicornG Luminos: guys, take a seat
[2011/05/16 10:20] UnicornG Luminos: and then click on the menu
[2011/05/16 10:20] UnicornG Luminos: wow i got caviar
[2011/05/16 10:20] afridiqau: wow
[2011/05/16 10:21] UnicornG Luminos: i am eating lunch now
[2011/05/16 10:21] Idea Loxingly (idea.lexenstar): yummy
[2011/05/16 10:21] Emelie Crystal: mmmmmm blueberry cheesecake
[2011/05/16 10:21] afridiqau: I am taking sea food
[2011/05/16 10:21] afridiqau: Nikki
[2011/05/16 10:22] afridiqau: u r enjoying the lunch
[2011/05/16 10:22] UnicornG Luminos: yes, just click on the food
[2011/05/16 10:22] UnicornG Luminos: so nice and easy to order
[2011/05/16 10:22] Barrabax Laks: my plate is too full
[2011/05/16 10:22] Profesor Korobase: I like Lobsters very much
[2011/05/16 10:22] Emelie Crystal: and cheap
[2011/05/16 10:22] Profesor Korobase: thanks Toma
[2011/05/16 10:23] UnicornG Luminos: Emelie, is it cheap? lol
[2011/05/16 10:23] Barrabax Laks: I will be very fat
[2011/05/16 10:23] Emelie Crystal: haha
[2011/05/16 10:23] UnicornG Luminos: shall we go to next leader
[2011/05/16 10:23] Unessl: Is it possible to download these music?
[2011/05/16 10:23] Unessl: They are so nice

Hemasha led us to the bar after we were all content with our dinner. Since the last field trip, I noticed that she seems to like to tend the bar. So she was our bartender again and

Figure 10.2 Student acting as a bartender whilst introducing dumpling making in a 3D restaurant.

introduced different kinds of wine/liquor to us. It's also interesting to see that the whole class interacted with her by asking her to prepare some wine for them (e.g., Korobase: "Red wine, please"). Later, she sent us a 3D display of dumpling making though it took a few students some time to figure out how to receive it. Even though introducing dumplings in this western style restaurant might be a bit "out of place", Hemasha did a very nice job detailing how to make the dumpling recipe whilst the class looked at the picture in real time (Figure 10.2).

The other team (Idea, Nikhil, and Feng) started to take the leading role after Toma's team. Idea did a professional job taking us to the surroundings outside the restaurant, which was breathtakingly beautiful and romantic that all of us hoped we could live there forever (Emelie's testimony :-)) (Figure 10.3). We went to the waterfall to swim with the cute ducks,

Figure 10.3 Snapshots of a student team taking the class on field trips to beautiful venues in-world.

animated the "Will you marry me" balls for couples, hiked up to the cliff to appreciate the colourful foliage of trees, learned how to become a painter by playing with the painting animation, and took a whole group photo. Nikhil followed up by leading us to a Roman-style plaza circled by stoned-wall colosseums. He told us that we could also activate the dance balls to pair with any classmate for a dance. The whole presentation ended with big applause from other students and huge compliments. It was truly another immersive, engaging, and interesting SL field trip experience for both the students and me. The following chat transcript and snapshot capture it all.

[2011/05/16 10:41] afridiqau: wow, nice music
[2011/05/16 10:41] Nikhil (nikhil.moorsider): boat is demolished… boom boom
[2011/05/16 10:41] Barrabax Laks: is fantastic
[2011/05/16 10:41] Hemasha Seda: everyone can try the gun… that's fun: D
[2011/05/16 10:41] Idea Loxingly (idea.lexenstar): please click link http://maps.secondlife.com/secondlife/Morfina/46/53/26
[2011/05/16 10:42] Mero (merogigo.baily): do we have to teleport
[2011/05/16 10:42] UnicornG Luminos: not a gun. it's called canon ☺
[2011/05/16 10:43] UnicornG Luminos: sorry, guys, i was falling off the hill: -(
[2011/05/16 10:43] afridiqau: lol r u okay
[2011/05/16 10:45] UnicornG Luminos: Nihil is painting!!
[2011/05/16 10:46] Profesor Korobase: nice painting Nikhill
[2011/05/16 10:47] UnicornG Luminos: korobase is swimming
[2011/05/16 10:47] Nikhil (nikhil.moorsider): lol… with ducks!
[2011/05/16 10:48] Nikhil (nikhil.moorsider): Desclaimer: this is just a demo
[2011/05/16 10:48] Hemasha Seda: do you want to marry me.
[2011/05/16 10:48] Hemasha Seda: haha
[2011/05/16 10:48] UnicornG Luminos: look at those ducks and ducklings
[2011/05/16 10:48] Toma Remex: very cute
[2011/05/16 10:50] Emelie Crystal: indeed lovely
[2011/05/16 10:50] Emelie Crystal: I could stay here for the rest of my life:)
[2011/05/16 10:50] UnicornG Luminos: hehe, me, too Emelie
[2011/05/16 10:51] afridiqau: wonderful place
[2011/05/16 10:52] Idea Loxingly (idea.lexenstar): and click on rainbow ball
[2011/05/16 10:52] Intan Couple Dance Ball: Touch again to get menu.
[2011/05/16 10:52] Idea Loxingly (idea.lexenstar): dance pose will go to you

[2011/05/16 10:52] Idea Loxingly (idea.lexenstar): try it as a couple… animate dance will work
[2011/05/16 10:53] Emelie Crystal: well done:)
[2011/05/16 10:54] Idea Loxingly (idea.lexenstar): thank you ^^
[2011/05/16 10:54] UnicornG Luminos: BRAVO!!!!!!
[2011/05/16 10:54] UnicornG Luminos:. ;:+*'"'* APPPPLLLAAAUUUSSSEEEE *'"'*+:;.

The final task of the day was having the students role-play in a pizzeria rezzed through the Holodeck in VIRTLANTIS. This task was great fun and positively received by my participants in the pilot, so I was curious as to how it would play out this time. Rather than taking them to the pizzeria and giving them the role-play Notecard there, I assigned individual students to play either the server or customer role on the class wiki site in advance. I soon realised that I should've done it the other way around because I found that some of them got a bit confused. After we teleported to the Holodeck, I also forgot to tell them not to touch it because I would lose the Holodeck control if someone else activated it at the same time. So I had to ask Korobase (who was already playing with it) to select the pizzeria for us. As soon as we entered the restaurant scene, students were seated automatically and then started to role-play based on the roles originally assigned to them (Figure 10.4). However, there was some confusion because some students didn't sit with their assigned customer group so the student sever didn't know who to serve. To top it off, a few residents who were

Figure 10.4 Students role-playing in a 3D pizzeria rezzed through Holodeck.

not in our class also popped in so I had to make sure that they were not interrupting the task flow whilst being present. After we were all on the same page, I taught them how to use the private CALL to carry out their role-play at each dining table by using the CONTROL key to select their members and right clicking CALL to start the private conversation.

More confusion arose when some students didn't know where to find the menu. I quickly directed them to the menu by walking to the counter and told them that it was above my avatar. They were informed that they could use the camera Object View to zoom into the menu, and that they could read the Notecard instructions to act out their assigned role (Figure 10.5). However, Nikhil still couldn't figure out how to start as a server and he also didn't get my earlier tutorial on using the Group CALL. Thank goodness, Korobase and Mero's teams seemed to play their roles pretty well and they also interacted with their customers professionally, judging by the fact that their customers (manager of the pizzeria) told me in the text chat that they enjoyed the service provided to them.

Figure 10.5 Role-play Notecard assigned to students to play either a server or a customer.

I monitored the whole progression by reminding them to check the bill brought by the server and leave the tip based on the quality of the service. Students seemed to engage in the role they were assigned to play. Some students were even naughty and gave their server a hard time or complained about the food (e.g., "there was a fly in my pizza"; "I need to see the manager of the restaurant".) It showed that students felt at ease playing their roles and had fun with the simulation of a pizzeria scenario augmented by Holodeck. The roles they played, coupled with the embodiment of an RL pizzeria, maximised the task interaction in a spontaneous and non-rehearsed manner. See some of the following highlights in the chat transcript.

[2011/05/16 11:23] UnicornG Luminos: guys, don't give your servers a hard time: -))
[2011/05/16 11:23] UnicornG Luminos: be generous on the tips as well if you think they serve you right
[2011/05/16 11:24] afridiqau: lol I forget my purse at home
[2011/05/16 11:24] afridiqau: I forgot
[2011/05/16 11:26] Unessl: Afridi, do you think this pizza will quench our hunger?
[2011/05/16 11:27] UnicornG Luminos: good question, Unessl
[2011/05/16 11:27] RASHAD Ibor: guys are you on group chat voice?
[2011/05/16 11:28] UnicornG Luminos: pls bring the check to ur customers
[2011/05/16 11:29] UnicornG Luminos: if u are finished, let me know
[2011/05/16 11:29] Profesor Korobase: finished
[2011/05/16 11:29] Unessl: i am still Hungryyyyyyyyyyyyyyyyyyyyyyy
[2011/05/16 11:29] UnicornG Luminos: Korobase, ur customer is complaining: -p
[2011/05/16 11:30] Emelie Crystal: where is our dessert?
[2011/05/16 11:30] Emelie Crystal:: (
[2011/05/16 11:30] Profesor Korobase: perhaps he would like to take another pizza
[2011/05/16 11:30] Profesor Korobase: because it was free
[2011/05/16 11:30] UnicornG Luminos: guys, 1 last minute
[2011/05/16 11:30] Profesor Korobase: All ordered cake
[2011/05/16 11:30] Unessl: I will leave no tip, sorry
[2011/05/16 11:30] Emelie Crystal: haha, so swedish;)
[2011/05/16 11:31] Profesor Korobase: Unicorn, I think all is happy
[2011/05/16 11:31] UnicornG Luminos: good to hear
[2011/05/16 11:31] Unessl: Come on, I need to see the manager of this restaurant
[2011/05/16 11:31] UnicornG Luminos: if customers are complaining, i'll fire you
[2011/05/16 11:31] UnicornG Luminos:: -p

[2011/05/16 11:31] sypy1: there is a fly on my Pizza!!

[2011/05/16 11:31] afridiqau: eat the fly

[2011/05/16 11:32] Unessl: I just enjoying my cold pizza

[2011/05/16 11:33] Unessl: why did you get my dish?

As we were winding down, I quickly distributed the assignment Notecard on the cultural clothing project they were to undertake in the next class (Figure 10.6). I included some freebie sites for them to look for their cultural outfits, and also informed them that they could join their ethnic group in SL to ask for further info among the group members. If they still have trouble finding the outfit, they could still use a poster to present it. I didn't have much time to cover the holiday/festival task, which definitely needs to be accomplished next week along with students' show-and-tell on their cultural outfits.

Figure 10.6 Assignment Notecard on the cultural outfit project and suggested freebie sites.

Lessons learned:

1. The two communication modes in SL (voice + text chat) are conducive to input enhancement. For example, students can use text chat to provide additional explanation to the culturally bound words/expressions that are voiced out. They also foster a strong bond through community members texting/voicing encouraging compliments to their peers. The two modes can operate simultaneously, which also maximises the sense of immersion and engagement (versus RL).
2. I need to figure out how to join the private Group CALLs from one team to another. I was wondering if there is a way that I could still participate in their conversation even after the private CALL already started.
3. As much as I'd like them to write their journal right after class, I found it a bit rushed and there were also some residents not in our class who entered the pizzeria at the same time. I probably would teleport them back to our home base (Rose Garden) so that they feel more comfortable doing so as a class. It's interesting to see that different SIMs in SL would create different vibes for learning as in RL.
4. Time management needs to be more on point as I've spent nearly four sessions on the same topic. Whether or not I can cover all the well-designed tasks in SL is still a question.

CHECKPOINT

- From the perspective of a language teacher, what are the challenges and benefits of organising field trips for your students in RL and SL? How do you feel about having your students plan their own field trip(s) and lead the class in RL compared with what I did in this lesson?
- How would you deal with the fact that "anything could happen in SL" where some avatar strangers might enter your class site out of the blue?
- If you wanted to carry out the same role-play task in SL, how would you do it differently? For example, would you also use the same role-play Notecard to provide guided instructions? How would you assign the roles?
- Similarly, how would you record the data in the role-play task where student groups are seated at different tables if you are a researcher? How would you observe each group at the same time?

YOUR TASK

- Holodeck is a fantastic feature that allows teachers to select a wide variety of scenarios for role-play. With a simple mouse click, you can rez a venue that simulates an RL scenario such as a class, a library, or a pub. You can also let your imagination run wild to rez a fantasy world. Your new task is to develop a role-play activity, similar to the pizzeria scenario in this lesson. First teleport to either VIRTLANTIS or EduNation Islands (see Table 21.3 Language teaching islands & demonstrations in Chapter 21) and select from the Holodeck menu an ideal scenario that works for your role-play activity. Then create a role-play Notecard that details the instruction about how students will play the role assigned to them. You may decide on the role assignment at your disposal.
- Test it out with your class by teleporting them to the Holodeck area and explain the role-play task. Record the session and use either the public or group chat to monitor their progress. See if you can also join their Group CALL.
- Debrief their performance with them and how they feel about their first role-play experience in SL.

CHAPTER 11

LESSON 3 (HOLIDAY / FESTIVAL / CLOTHING PART 1)

OVERVIEW

We finally started a new topic today that incorporated the *Holiday, Festival*, and *Clothing* themes. This chapter presents the first part of the lesson in which students played charades by taking turns describing a food item on a digital poster without naming it so their classmates could guess the food item. They moved on to interview each other in pairs about the holidays and festivals in their home country, following a Notecard worksheet. The lesson ended with students doing an oral presentation showcasing their cultural clothing either worn directly by their avatar or displayed in a digital poster. Students also received an assignment Notecard for them to find free cultural outfits in several freebie places in-world.

BLOG POST. FRIDAY, 20 MAY 2011

We finally started a new topic today. However, some students were absent (a bit disappointed ☹) due to their RL obligations or other reasons (Emelie had to move to London, Toma needed to prepare for her final exam, Idea got her Internet disconnected for hours, Ulyo didn't inform me yet of why he didn't attend the class, and Feng told me yesterday that she couldn't make it). That's exactly what happens when teaching a free course in SL. Because it's not a credit-bearing, compulsory course, students may come and go as they wish and it's hard to FORCE them to stay throughout the course. Hopefully the rest of the students can stay with me till the last session (fingers and toes crossed).

Because we were still waiting for other students to arrive, I rezzed a Holiday/Festival poster as a warm-up game (Figure 11.1). They were told to take turns to describe any picture on the poster without naming the holiday or festival and the other students had to type up the name in the public chat. Whoever got it right first won. I thought students would easily get all the answers and we would just spend less than 10 minutes to finish this warm-up. To my surprise, students were a bit shy to take the initiative when asked to volunteer. For example, Korobase thought he had to figure out all the names of the holiday pictures before feeling more confident to describe any of them. It took a bit longer to go around, and I also needed to supply information about holidays unfamiliar to some students (e.g., Easter).

Figure 11.1 Digital poster displaying selected holiday pictures for a charade activity.

After the warm-up, I introduced the holiday/festival topic before we started the show-and-tell on the cultural outfit. Due to the time constraint, I only asked them to finish the first half of the task, which was how New Year's is celebrated in their partner's country, and assigned the second half as homework (a special holiday/festival only celebrated in their partner's country) (Figure 11.2). They were told to use the private CALL to conduct the interview and report back later. So far, I think most students are acquainted with talking to a classmate using the private chat to finish the assigned task. Not only do they get more chance to talk one-on-one, they also develop intercultural competence by learning certain cultural aspects from their partner not privy to them before. It took a bit longer than expected, but my teacher gut feelings sensed that students seemed quite engaged in this task and would like to have more time to talk to their partner. Even though I tried to join each pair's private chat this time, I couldn't figure out how to do it because the student would lose their original partner if they started a new private CALL with me. Later after the class, I tried it out with two other students and finally figured out how to do it: three of us needed to start a new private CALL by selecting all the members so that no one was left out.

I asked each pair to share what they knew about the New Year's celebration in their partner's country. Even though it took time to go around with each pair, I think the time was worth spent because students were able to learn from each other whilst practising how to summarise their points in public. I also reminded them to type up some cultural terms/expressions for the class because these usages were not familiar to those of us who are not from the same

```
Notecard: New Year                                      _ x
Description:  2010-10-19 17:06:10 note card

*****Holidays and Festivals around the World***********

1. Share with your partner how you celebrate New Year's in your country.
When you're done, take notes on how he/she celebrates his/hers.

2. We'll compare/contrast how New Year's is celebrated in each country.

Partner's name/Country
---------------------------------------------------

When
---------------------------------------------------

Traditions/Customs (how to celebrate)
---------------------------------------------------


Festive food
---------------------------------------------------

---------------------------------------------------

****Homework*******

3. Share one interesting holiday/festival in your home culture with your
partner. After that, take notes on his/hers.

Partner's holiday/festival
---------------------------------------------------

When
---------------------------------------------------

Traditions/Customs (how to celebrate)

     Edit...                    Save            Delete
```

Figure 11.2 Notecard worksheet on exchanging information about New Year's and holiday/festival celebrations across cultures.

cultural background. We talked about interesting facts across cultures, food they prepare during New Year's, and how New Year's falls in different national calendars. Interestingly, when we talked about how New Year's is celebrated in Iran, students also learned the new word "fasting" from Unessl, the Iranian student. I was amazed to see that he even wanted to explain more about the concept by volunteering to speak up first and typing up a weblink to the information about fasting (see the following chat transcript). Later, I also exercised an error correction on the pronunciation of "calendar" in response to some students' comments in their journals that they hoped their errors could be "corrected" sometimes. So I took the liberty of the teachable moment and demonstrated how to pronounce calendar.

[2011/05/18 10:55] UnicornG Luminos: good, Unessl is typing to help explain
[2011/05/18 10:55] Unessl: lunar calendar is for Arabian countries
[2011/05/18 11:01] UnicornG Luminos: Moon calendar (lunar)
[2011/05/18 11:01] UnicornG Luminos: lunar-moon
[2011/05/18 11:01] UnicornG Luminos: solar-sun
[2011/05/18 11:02] UnicornG Luminos: fasting?
[2011/05/18 11:02] afridiqau: yes
[2011/05/18 11:02] UnicornG Luminos: fasting….not fast/quick: -p
[2011/05/18 11:02] UnicornG Luminos: for religious reason
[2011/05/18 11:03] UnicornG Luminos: stop eating and drinking, in a nutshell
[2011/05/18 11:03] Unessl: to improve your ability to say no to what which is really tempting
[2011/05/18 11:03] afridiqau: Eid
[2011/05/18 11:03] Hemasha Seda: thanks afridi
[2011/05/18 11:03] Unessl: it is also proved that fasting is really good for internal organs
[2011/05/18 11:04] afridiqau: yes
[2011/05/18 11:04] UnicornG Luminos: thanks, Unessl, for the explanation
[2011/05/18 11:04] Unessl: welcome
[2011/05/18 11:10] Unessl: may I say sth more about fasting?
[2011/05/18 11:10] Unessl: I just typed for u
[2011/05/18 11:10] afridiqau: yes
[2011/05/18 11:10] Unessl: Fasting is primarily the act of willingly abstaining from some or all food, drink, or both, for a period of time. An absolute fast is normally defined as abstinence from all food and liquid for a defined period, from sunrise to sunset, for one month. The fast may also be intermittent in nature.
[2011/05/18 11:11] Hemasha Seda: thanks Unessl
[2011/05/18 11:11] Unessl: ur welcome

The session ended with students showcasing their cultural outfits. They either wore the outfit in avatar form or presented it in a poster (or both). I reminded them that they could type up the cultural terms in text chat during their presentation. Annaelvit volunteered to introduce the outfit her avatar was wearing. Because she's from Milan, she talked about this fashion city by asking us if we knew how many famous brands were made in Italy. It's a smart presentation skill by interacting with the audience before getting into the content. Students were hooked by her interesting and smooth show-and-tell. Next, Mero introduced a traditional outfit worn by Egyptian women. She rezzed a poster for her presentation (Figure 11.3). In the middle of her presentation, I had to use text chat to remind her to type up some culturally

CHAPTER 11
LESSON 3 (HOLIDAY/FESTIVAL/CLOTHING PART 1)

Figure 11.3 Snapshot of a student rezzing a digital poster to present the cultural clothing worn by Egyptian women.

bound vocabulary for her classmates as it would help them better grasp what she was talking about without losing the thread of her talk. Because Unessl is from the Middle East, he also helped out Mero with further explanations through the public chat. It's interesting to know that the colour (red) of the outfit suggests that the woman is married. We really appreciated her talk that was both educationally entertaining and culturally enlightening. Hemasha was the last presenter who introduced "qipao", the traditional clothing worn by Chinese women. She also wore a modern version of qipao popular with younger women alongside a poster to describe the cultural outfit. She even provided a link to a site for students who were interested to find out more about qipao. Unessl, a male student who usually likes to joke around in class, asked Hemasha to turn around to showcase her qipao as a model.

Again, time was a killer. We couldn't finish the rest of the student presentations and some of them also IMed me that they needed more time to prepare. So I announced that the rest of the class will do their show-and-tell next Monday, followed by a reminder to post reflection journals and finish the second part of the assignment on the Notecard.

Lessons learned:

1. A student (Ninnoune) emailed me before the class and said that she decided to quit the course because she didn't feel her English had improved due to the "big" class size and the fact that she didn't get a lot of time to practice speaking or have her grammatical errors corrected by me. I genuinely appreciated her candid

feedback, pinpointing that SL is not unanimously embraced by all students. They still want to get down to the nitty gritty of what is generally expected in an RL language class, which is grammar, error correction, etc. I get it. But this course is not operated as forms-focused instruction but as a task-based one that capitalises on the unique features of SL to provide the best practices for language teaching and learning. If we had to follow the same route as we usually see in a language-focused class, there would be no point to copy it again in the 3D virtual world. That said, a couple of students (Feng, Hemasha) also raised a similar issue in their journals that they would like to have more error correction and grammar instruction, as well as a mini-lecture on oral skills. As much as we'd like to ride on the wave of virtual learning in SL, these students' voices can't go unheard. Maybe I should start to think about how to address their forms-focused needs without sucking the fun out of task-based learning in the virtual world.

2. The two communication modes (text and voice chat) not only provide more options for interaction, but they also enhance comprehension when the meaning doesn't get across in the initial voice chat. For example, when we talked about New Year's celebrations in different countries, some culturally bound vocabulary was so dense that it's hard to understand the content without reading those terms (text chat) and listening to students' oral explanations (voice chat) at the same time. The combination of these two modes embodies multimodality that can facilitate the presentation delivery as well as make meaning more comprehensible to the audience.

3. Capitalising on students' cultural repertoires is conducive to stimulating more language output and boosting engagement. Because the topic is closely related to their cultural root and reinforces what they're knowledgeable about, they feel motivated to invest more time and effort to polish their work and to ensure that the content is accurate and appealing to their audience. Acting as culture ambassadors, some students even went great lengths to research more information about the origin of their heritage clothing to enrich their oral presentation (as previously shown in Unessl's case).

4. When students see their peers deliver well-prepared and professional presentations, they feel "pumped" to make their own as high calibre as their counterparts. Whilst I can sense the competition vibe, it feels positive as the peer competition sets the benchmark for this SL task. Even though students couldn't see facial expressions from or have eye contact with the audience, they take it seriously and don't want to "lose face" in front of their classmates. The sense of a supportive learning community also allows them to feel more comfortable practising English speaking and sharing their know-how in class.

CHECKPOINT

- If you were me, what would you have done differently with the Holiday Charade game as a warm-up?
- How would you treat "errors" in a task-based course in SL (using explicit, implicit, or recast approaches)? Would you also take time in each class to work on the grammatical errors or wrong expressions observed in student language outputs? Why or why not?
- The topic was purposefully chosen to tap into students' cultural repertoires, which triggered spontaneous discussion and language production from the students. For example, Unessl initiated the chat by explaining what "fasting" means for Islam in Iran. If you are a teacher, how would you profile these valuable reference points to foster student intercultural competence and language acquisition?
- If you are a researcher, which aspect(s) of today's lesson would you consider potentially useful for your research project? Also, what type of data analysis would you utilise to examine the naturally occurring data?

CHECKPOINT

- Replicate the Notecard worksheet (Figure 11.2) or create a new one on having students exchange information about how holidays/festivals are celebrated in their own country. Pilot it with your own class or consider inviting your avatar friends to join the class so that students can have the chance to interact with real SL residents or partners outside of the class.
- Alternatively, ask your students to explore SL and find a friendly resident who is willing to conduct this task with them. Remind them to record the responses in the Notecard and take a snapshot of their interaction. Ask them to bring all the information back to the class for discussion.
- After each student pair reports back to the class, conduct a focus group interview with them on any suggestions or feedback about the task design as well as their cultural exchange experience in SL. Record the session and take notes for your reference in modifying the task.

CHAPTER 12

LESSON 3 (HOLIDAY / FESTIVAL / CLOTHING PART 2)

OVERVIEW

This chapter reports on the technical issues encountered in the second part of the lesson topic (*Holiday, Festival*, and *Clothing*) and how they were resolved. The lesson plan was improvised due to the time spent on troubleshooting those technical issues. Students took turns finishing up showcasing their cultural clothing, highlighted by their in-depth descriptions about the origin of the clothing as well as fabulous outfits worn by student avatars. Recorded chat logs and transcripts were also included in the blog entry to support my teaching observations and reflections.

BLOG POST. TUESDAY, 24 MAY 2011

Today's lesson backfired because of the technology devil in SL! At 1:00 Second Life Time (SLT) sharp, I started to feel that the loading was getting slow after logging into VIRTLANTIS. Some students also texted that they couldn't hear each other's voices. I was wondering if the problem was from the VIRTLANTIS SIM (i.e., region simulator) or something to do with the whole SL platform. I kept logging off and back in again to see if that would resolve the issue. Apparently, this measure didn't work today. I was a bit panicky about the time we'd wasted and wondered if students would stay till I/we sorted it out. When I finally got the voice working, despite sluggish loading still, I asked them to teleport to Sandbox to prepare for their cultural outfit presentation. Two of the most tech-savvy students, Barrabax and Korobase, flew to another SIM to test out the voice issue. Whilst I was monitoring students' preparation in the Sandbox area, they IMed back that the voice function was working properly there. I asked the class to stay here whilst teleporting to meet with Barrabax and Korobase to ensure that voice chat was actually working. That said, I was anxious that students might lose patience and just leave early today. Although the voice was working fine in the new SIM, I still found it a bit slow to load the content.

By the time I finally got all the students to teleport here (between monitoring students who were already here and teleporting Ulyo who seemed to get lost), half an hour had gone. I was a bit frustrated by the technical glitches. Oh well, you just gotta do what you gotta do. I apologised to the class for the terrible delay and SL malfunction. Gladly, most students still stayed and Korobase also told me that it's not my fault (Nikhil was absent for attending a family wedding in his village and Emelie was late from her first intern job

Figure 12.1 Student rezzing a large digital poster to showcase Iranian clothing for men and women.

in London). In my original lesson plan, I was hoping to finish all the cultural outfit presentations and move on to the new topic, music. Because we lost the first third of the class time, the remaining tasks had to be postponed for the Wednesday session.

Unessl started the second half of the class by introducing the cultural clothing worn by Iranian men and women. He rezzed a big poster to showcase the outfits, whilst explaining the origin, functions, and fabrics of each of the items (Figure 12.1). He talked about each item clockwise from the poster and typed up some culturally related vocabulary to help us better understand his description. Despite a well-detailed show-and-tell, his presentation went a bit over time because he had more than one picture on his digital poster.

Ulyo followed up with his poster presentation of showcasing what beauty pageants would wear in France, which was quite entertaining. Gladly, all the student members are all adults who are mature enough to know more about those "sensual" words introduced by Ulyo, such as panties. He did a fine job detailing those outfits women wear in the beauty contest and recounted some anecdotes, such as judging a woman's status by the dress she's wearing. The following chat transcript captures some of our interaction.

[2011/05/23 10:52] UnicornG Luminos: beauty contest?
[2011/05/23 10:52] UnicornG Luminos: in France?
[2011/05/23 10:52] ulyo Genesis: panty

[2011/05/23 10:52] UnicornG Luminos: hmm, panties are sexy for women
[2011/05/23 10:52] ulyo Genesis: embroidered petticoat
[2011/05/23 10:52] UnicornG Luminos: beautiful
[2011/05/23 10:52] ulyo Genesis: laces and frills
[2011/05/23 10:53] ulyo Genesis: adorned with laces
[2011/05/23 10:53] UnicornG Luminos: wow
[2011/05/23 10:54] UnicornG Luminos: interesting to know u can determine her status by her dress!
[2011/05/23 10:54] fenghp99: i had heard about that
[2011/05/23 10:54] UnicornG Luminos: Feng, u're also well-cultured. Miss France: -)
[2011/05/23 10:54] fenghp99: thank u
[2011/05/23 10:55] Unessl: Bravo
[2011/05/23 10:55] Mero (merogigo.baily): nice thanks u ulyo

Idea was wearing a stunning outfit usually worn by Thai women on special holidays and festivals. I like the way she used her avatar as a model to showcase the cultural clothing (Figure 12.2). She seemed quite composed about her presentation and the class was also impressed with her gorgeous outfit whenever she turned or moved around. After her presentation, I pointed out one pronunciation hot spot, which was "silk". The reason I did the error correction was to address the needs of some students who mentioned in their journal reflections that they hope we could also address the grammar and pronunciation errors (see transcript).

[2011/05/23 10:56] Idea Loxingly (idea.lexenstar): northern east of thailand
[2011/05/23 10:57] UnicornG Luminos: diamond, hmm,
[2011/05/23 10:57] Idea Loxingly (idea.lexenstar): loincloth
[2011/05/23 10:57] UnicornG Luminos: silk… very expensive texture
[2011/05/23 10:57] Idea Loxingly (idea.lexenstar): weave silk
[2011/05/23 10:59] Barrabax Laks: thank you
[2011/05/23 10:59] fenghp99: nice
[2011/05/23 10:59] Profesor Korobase: fantastic Idea
[2011/05/23 10:59] ulyo Genesis: beautiful clothes, you looks like a queen
[2011/05/23 11:00] UnicornG Luminos: silk
[2011/05/23 11:00] Idea Loxingly (idea.lexenstar):; -)

Figure 12.2 Student avatar donning a traditional outfit worn by Thai women on a special occasion.

Afridi's presentation was short and sweet. He introduced Pakistani men's casual wear (Figure 12.3). He explained every part of the outfit very clearly, in a way that his audience could follow along easily. He also typed up key vocabulary in public chat throughout his presentation. He appeared relaxed and spoke as if he were talking to his audience in RL. He's definitely a natural for public presentation as endorsed by his classmates in the chat log.

[2011/05/23 11:01] UnicornG Luminos: he's handsome: -)
[2011/05/23 11:01] Unessl: Shalvar
[2011/05/23 11:01] khan (afridiqau): Shalwar Kameez
[2011/05/23 11:03] Unessl: Shalwar is actually sth like trousers
[2011/05/23 11:03] UnicornG Luminos: tks, Unessl, for the explanation
[2011/05/23 11:03] khan (afridiqau): Dupata
[2011/05/23 11:04] Unessl: good afridi

CHAPTER 12
LESSON 3 (HOLIDAY/FESTIVAL/CLOTHING PART 2)

Figure 12.3 Student displaying a poster to showcase Pakistani men's casual wear.

[2011/05/23 11:04] UnicornG Luminos: very short and sweet
[2011/05/23 11:04] khan (afridiqau): thanks
[2011/05/23 11:04] Unessl: fantastic
[2011/05/23 11:04] UnicornG Luminos: concise
[2011/05/23 11:04] Unessl: The best presenter I've ever seen in this planet
[2011/05/23 11:04] khan (afridiqau): thanks: -)

Feng was absent last time so she did her presentation today by introducing "qipao", the same one that Hemasha presented because they're both from China. She was also wearing a qipao today, which gave another boost to her presentation. One thing she did very well is that she interacted with her audience by asking them a question before getting into her presentation, such as "Has anyone seen the movie, Lust & Caution?" This is the movie directed by the famous Taiwanese director, Ang Lee, in which the actress wore different kinds of qipaos. Some students didn't get her question so she had to repeat the question; I also typed it up in the text chat, as requested by Mero in the text chat log. Feng also provided a weblink for those who would like to delve more into qipao.

[2011/05/23 11:05] UnicornG Luminos: can u ask the question again
[2011/05/23 11:05] fenghp99: lust, caution
[2011/05/23 11:06] fenghp99: in the mood for love
[2011/05/23 11:06] Mero (merogigo.baily): write the question

[2011/05/23 11:06] UnicornG Luminos: by the famous director, Ang Lee
[2011/05/23 11:06] UnicornG Luminos: how many of you have watched the movie
[2011/05/23 11:06] khan (afridiqau): wow
[2011/05/23 11:06] UnicornG Luminos: Lust and Caution
[2011/05/23 11:06] Mero (merogigo.baily): not me
[2011/05/23 11:06] Barrabax Laks: no
[2011/05/23 11:06] fenghp99: Qipao
[2011/05/23 11:06] Barrabax Laks: sorry
[2011/05/23 11:06] UnicornG Luminos: but the actress wore different kinds of qipao
[2011/05/23 11:07] fenghp99: http://upload.ouliu.net/k/3ef948c8a7dac39191a4118825065905.jpeg
[2011/05/23 11:09] khan (afridiqau): fantastic
[2011/05/23 11:09] ulyo Genesis: nice colors

Barrabax's fabulous presentation was the showstopper of the day. I was so impressed with the effort and time she devoted to the presentation, which totally blew us away. Apparently, she was the one who came to the class with the lowest oral proficiency, due to her formal English schooling that was exclusively grammar-translation oriented. But in SL, she's found her voice. She seemed more comfortable and confident when she presented, strengthened by her exceptional SL skills. I think her advanced SL competence complements her low English proficiency, and the solidarity and praise she got from her classmates also fosters her motivation and self-efficacy. I also think each RL task assigned in SL is so meaningful and interesting to her that she'd go to great lengths to accomplish those tasks (also verified in my personal communication with her via IM). Barrabax took her presentation of the iconic Spanish dance, Flamenco, to the next level. Not only did she display a slideshow on a big poster, she also explained it by typing up the vocabulary for each part of the Flamenco dress and the venue for dancing (Figure 12.4). Being a Spaniard, Korobase also helped out by typing up those words and expressions related to Flamenco. Above all, she taught us how to dance Flamenco by rezzing the dance box, from which we can click and animate our avatars to dance to Flamenco. Everyone enjoyed the dance and was WOWed by her exceptional presentation, whilst being totally immersed in the dance and music (see the following chat transcript). I couldn't be more proud of her! Worth noting is that Korobase and Annaelvit corrected my typo on "flaminco" in the text chat. Another evidence of getting more input through different modes of communication. After her presentation, Barrabax addressed the question that I raised in text chat about the Spanish word (Caseta) I didn't hear clearly, indicating that she's attentive to her audience.

CHAPTER 12
LESSON 3 (HOLIDAY/FESTIVAL/CLOTHING PART 2)

Figure 12.4 Student avatar wearing a traditional Flamenco dress accompanied by animated Flamenco dancing.

[2011/05/23 11:10] UnicornG Luminos: so beautiful… Flaminco
[2011/05/23 11:10] Profesor Korobase: Flamenco
[2011/05/23 11:10] Annaelvit: flamenco
[2011/05/23 11:10] Profesor Korobase: Andalucia, the South of Spain
[2011/05/23 11:11] UnicornG Luminos: thanks, Korobase, for the explanation
[2011/05/23 11:11] UnicornG Luminos: thanks for the tyo correction, Annaelvit and Korobase: -)
[2011/05/23 11:12] UnicornG Luminos: wow, i feel like dancing to Flamenco now
[2011/05/23 11:12] UnicornG Luminos: the elements of flamenco. accessories
[2011/05/23 11:13] Barrabax Laks: flowers, necklaces, big earrings, fan, hair combs
[2011/05/23 11:13] Barrabax Laks: shawls
[2011/05/23 11:14] UnicornG Luminos: the poster slide show reminds me of Idea and Korobase's presentation last time
[2011/05/23 11:14] Unessl: exactly
[2011/05/23 11:14] UnicornG Luminos: it's also called carriage… horse and cart
[2011/05/23 11:15] Profesor Korobase: FERIA

161

```
[2011/05/23 11:15]  UnicornG Luminos: thanks, Korobase
[2011/05/23 11:16]  MACETA DISCO FLAMENCO3: whispers: Playing…
[2011/05/23 11:16]  UnicornG Luminos: what's it? can u explain? Caseta?
[2011/05/23 11:16]  UnicornG Luminos: we can hear the music now
[2011/05/23 11:17]  UnicornG Luminos: wow, u are dancing flamenco now, Barrabax!!
[2011/05/23 11:17]  Toma Remex: very nice:)
[2011/05/23 11:17]  Profesor Korobase: wowww
[2011/05/23 11:17]  Barrabax Laks: touch the box please
[2011/05/23 11:17]  Profesor Korobase: everybody know how to dance FALMENCO
[2011/05/23 11:18]  UnicornG Luminos: just touch the pink box and we can dance
[2011/05/23 11:18]  Toma Remex: wooww i like it:)
[2011/05/23 11:18]  khan (afridiqau): I'm not gonna stop now
[2011/05/23 11:18]  Idea Loxingly (idea.lexenstar): good it's fun
[2011/05/23 11:18]  Mero  (merogigo.baily): bravo
[2011/05/23 11:18]  Profesor Korobase: Fantastic Presentation Barrabax. Congratulations
[2011/05/23 11:19]  Toma Remex: gooood barrbax:) i love it
[2011/05/23 11:19]  ulyo Genesis: maravilosa
[2011/05/23 11:19]  Unessl: fabulous
```

Toma talked about the traditional Saudi Arabian clothing and she uploaded a picture of a cute baby wearing the outfit. Apparently, she spoke with a heavy accent that made it hard for us to understand what she said, especially introducing such a culturally dense topic. But I think she still tried her best to explain the outfit in a short-and-sweet fashion.

Korobase's presentation nicely wrapped up today's lesson. As we have witnessed, he's more like an SL wizard in our class (Unessl likes to tease him as an "SL geek"). He always gives away handy SL presentation tools to the class. Today, he introduced a new SL presentation approach via "video projector". It projected each slide show on a poster controlled by the presenter avatar by animating the remote controller (Figure 12.5). He introduced the Medieval clothing in Spain and traced back to the history of that era. He told us about how he researched this topic by looking up those vocabulary words on wiki and other sources because he didn't know how to translate the Spanish meaning into English in the beginning of his preparation. Then he got hooked by the research and researched more, which also gave him the joy of being more knowledgeable about this topic. When he flipped through the slides and explained each term, I also added more explanations in text chat. I also found Korobase a very professional and attentive presenter. He responded to my explanations in

CHAPTER 12
LESSON 3 (HOLIDAY/FESTIVAL/CLOTHING PART 2)

Figure 12.5 Student rezzing a video projector to display traditional clothing in Medieval Spain for his show-and-tell.

text with oral comments. To top it off, he also used the Scribblar, the interactive whiteboard that I introduced to the class, to complement his presentation. He uploaded additional pictures to the digital whiteboard for our further reference. Finally, he gave away this hands-on tool to the whole class for FREE! The following chat log transcript speaks it all.

[2011/05/23 11:27] Unessl: video projector?
[2011/05/23 11:27] Unessl: You are SL geek, aren't you?
[2011/05/23 11:27] Unessl: I am green with envy
[2011/05/23 11:28] UnicornG Luminos: he is, Unessl: -)
[2011/05/23 11:29] UnicornG Luminos: he tried to find vocabulary to explain Spanish clothing in English
[2011/05/23 11:29] Unessl: nice presenter. so cool
[2011/05/23 11:31] UnicornG Luminos: yes, the tower usually connects to the gate
[2011/05/23 11:31] UnicornG Luminos: a bit like Great Wall in China
[2011/05/23 11:31] UnicornG Luminos: battlements
[2011/05/23 11:32] fenghp99: yep
[2011/05/23 11:32] UnicornG Luminos: to protect from the invasion of the barbarians
[2011/05/23 11:32] UnicornG Luminos: i hate dungeon

[2011/05/23 11:33]   Profesor Korobase: http://www.scribblar.com/rjph6ws
[2011/05/23 11:34]   UnicornG Luminos: i just saw the pix
[2011/05/23 11:34]   Unessl: we need username to enter the website you gave us. why?
[2011/05/23 11:34]   UnicornG Luminos: just type ur first name
[2011/05/23 11:34]   ulyo Genesis: yes
[2011/05/23 11:35]   Barrabax Laks: thanks korobosa
[2011/05/23 11:35]   Unessl: Thanks
[2011/05/23 11:35]   Toma Remex: thank u
[2011/05/23 11:36]   Mero (merogigo.baily): thanks
[2011/05/23 11:36]   UnicornG Luminos: we always got some goodies from Korobase: -))
[2011/05/23 11:37]   Unessl: He has a heart of gold

Lessons learned:

1. I found students didn't ask as many questions after each presenter's presentation as they used to. Being conscious of the limited class time could be one of the reasons. I'd have prompted them more if had we more time. However, I've also noticed that students are getting less nervous about their SL presentation and speaking English in front of the class. The support and encouragement they have received from each other is truly reassuring and positive. The sense of belonging to the virtual community they have built since they joined the class has become stronger and bound them closer.

2. Although the task of showcasing different outfits across cultures allows students to learn from each other, I've also found it a bit challenging due to the variety of accent, pronunciation, and culturally dense vocabulary. I assume some students might feel a bit overwhelmed, but hopefully they would take it as a positive challenge to hone their listening comprehension when communicating with global citizens speaking English as a lingua franca. It would be also interesting to see how students use communication strategies to resolve communication breakdown in SL due to mis-/un-understanding triggered by varied pronunciation and accent.

3. A couple of students seemed to occasionally read over their scripts during their presentation. I probably will remind them next time that it is more vital to speak/ present spontaneously and naturally as if they are talking to their audience rather than relying too much on their typed up script.

4. Assigning students to culturally responsive, RL-driven tasks in SL is a good way to keep them engaged, motivated, and immersed. They spend time researching the

topic by building on their cultural knowledge whilst exposing themselves to more input. Not only do they learn new vocabulary associated with their culture, they also test out their interlanguage system by processing how to integrate both new and existing linguistic knowledge to get their meaning across. It further "pushes" their language production.

5. Many students have repeatedly commented in their journals that they feel less nervous and more confident when speaking English and presenting in public. They feel the pressure level drops in SL as opposed to presenting in RL where the eye contact, gestures, and the presence of an audience, are just too intimidating. When asked if it's an advantage or disadvantage to have no eye contact and see no facial expressions from the audience in SL, their responses are mixed with a tendency toward the positive side. Even though some students feel that the lack of non-verbal cues makes SL presentation a bit less REAL, a majority of students feel otherwise; it's this very reason that makes them feel more liberated from the stress and pressure of speaking in RL. The tricky part is that they still feel they're talking to a group of RL people because they can still see each other in the same place, at the same time (tele/copresence), despite the absence of non-verbal features. This "masking" presence through their avatars also resonates the sense of security found in most SL research, which is particularly beneficial for EFL learners.

6. Given the fact that my students are EFL learners who don't use English on a regular basis in their RL, they find SL a viable environment for them to practice English with people around the world and to learn from each other. Each of them brings to the class their unique cultural repertoire, expertise in SL skills, knowledge across subject matters, and varied English proficiency. Some of them also commented that they wouldn't have gotten the chance to learn and practice English in RL through such vibrant and immersive ways as they do in SL (e.g., Mero). Ulyo also mentioned that SL is a potential platform for shy students like him to step up and talk without worrying how people will watch or judge him because he's secure in his avatar. Korobase, our SL geek, also favours SL so much that he thinks it has the potential to empower language learning and teaching.

7. A couple of students (Ninoune, Anja) dropped out of the class because they either thought the class was too task oriented, not business oriented for their career, or the class time was not fully allocated to speaking practice. Now I am wondering if students only care about speaking more in class rather than spending time exploring different interesting SIMs that embody RL scenarios. I probably can ask them further in the focus group, journal prompts, or post-course survey later.

CHECKPOINT

- Despite her lower English proficiency compared with that of her peers, Barrabax started to rise to the occasion by impressing the class with her tech savvy and capacity to turn her presentation into animated show-and-tell in SL. She also appeared more confident in delivering her oral presentation professionally. Can you think of any factors that led to her positive learning outcome? Also, how did her advanced SL skills and language production come into play?
- A lot of students commented that they felt less nervous and more confident when presenting and speaking English in front of the class in SL than in RL. Do you think the masked identity safeguarded by their avatar makes a difference in their growing self-efficacy? Also, do you think that the lack of eye contact and non-verbal cues in SL would make the transfer of students' gained confidence and improved speaking skills less effective to the RL context?

YOUR TASK

- Based on the same lesson topic (clothing), develop a fashion week project by asking students to explore SL freebie spots (see Table 21.1 SL Basics and wikis in Chapter 21) and find their favourite outfits that are either avant-garde and fashion-forward (if you have a homogenous class) or culturally relevant to their heritage (if you have a culturally/linguistically diverse student cohort). Ask students to do some research about their chosen outfit (e.g., textile, purpose, origin, etc.) so that they can describe it to the class. Prepare a Notecard to guide the student planning if deemed necessary, especially if you have a class of lower proficiency. Remind them to change their avatar outfit by donning the new one before coming to the class for a show-and-tell.
- After each student finishes introducing their outfit and taking questions from the audience, invite them to walk on a red carpet one by one for the fashion runway show (you can also find a red carpet from one of the freebie spots or create your own). Finally, take a snapshot of all the students showcasing their outfits on the red carpet and give it to them afterwards.

CHAPTER 13

LESSON 4 (MUSIC)

> **OVERVIEW**
>
> Today I took them on a field trip to *Virtual Morocco* where they were able to try out different Muslim outfits as an extension of the previous lesson (clothing) before starting the new topic on music. In the music lesson, I activated their background knowledge by asking them to describe those well-known music icons in the world (e.g., Elvis Presley, Madonna) via an interactive whiteboard rezzed in SL. Then we went on another field trip to *Magnatue* where they could "play" a wide variety of animated 3D musical instruments and work with a partner to decide which one they liked the best following a Notecard worksheet. Each pair was also required to report back to the class.

BLOG POST. FRIDAY, 27 MAY 2011

Student turnout rate was a bit low today, which was a bit disappointing. ☹ Even though a couple of students told me in advance that they couldn't make it today due to their RL commitments (Nikhil attending a wedding ceremony, Hemasha a conference), others were absent (Barrabax taking care of her family, Annaelvit her hospitalised friend, and Afridi unknown) or late (Korobase out dealing with personal business in RL) without advance notice. Oh well, the show still needed to go on regardless.

Today's topic was about music, but I still liked to wrap up the clothing topic with a field trip to *Virtual Morocco* (Figure 13.1), hoping that those who were absent might join us a bit later. The reason I took them to Morocco was because they could try out the Muslim outfits (free for male students and low cost for female students) and get to know the Muslim culture (e.g., taking off the shoes before entering the Mosque and stepping on the carpet). I also walked them around the SIM and showed them those exotic Persian rugs and Genie lamps, which gained their attention and interest at once, especially of the Middle Eastern students (e.g., Unessl and Toma). I am glad that the only two male students today, Unessl and Ulyo, were able to put on their male Muslim outfits and experience the immersion with me.

Because music is today's lesson topic, I planned a warm-up activity to activate their background knowledge about some famous celebrities in the music industry. I rezzed an interactive whiteboard that connected to Scribblar where I had already uploaded the pictures

Figure 13.1 Virtual field trip to a Moroccan shrine in SL.

of five celebrities and text boxes for them to type up what they know about each superstar (Figure 13.2). I first asked them to log in Scribblar either through the whiteboard or a new browser if they're not using the SL Viewer 2. Thanks to the pretest, they should have been comfortable with this tool by now. However, I noticed that they seemed more familiar with the chat room tool embedded in the interactive whiteboard, and some already started to brainstorm ideas in the chatroom without my cue. Interestingly, their knowledge about the celebrities varied, from knowing none of them (Feng from China) to a walking dictionary that could provide juicy anecdotes about most of the celebrities (Ulyo). I tried to prompt them by asking, for example, "How do you call them if their job is to dig into the private lives of celebrities" or "Michael Jackson was the King of the ___" to engage them more.

Figure 13.2 Warm-up activity on describing five music superstars/bands through an interactive whiteboard.

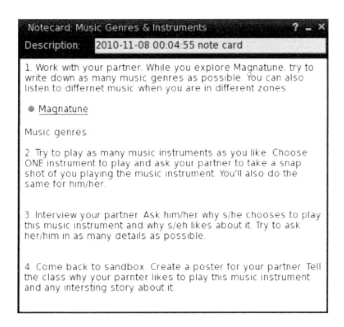

Figure 13.3 Notecard instruction for collaborating on a music instrument project on the virtual island (*Magnatue*).

After that, I sent them to *Magnatue*, a SIM where they can play different kinds of musical instruments whilst exploring different music genres (e.g., classical, pop, electronica, etc.). I gave them a Notecard detailing how to complete the task, followed by my oral explanation (Figure 13.3). This task required them to work in pairs or a group of three to go around the SIM, note down all the music genres floating above the 3D instruments, and then play each musical instrument as they wish. After that, each partner would decide which music instrument they liked the most, and then asked each other to take a snapshot of them playing the chosen instrument. They also had to tell their partner why they chose this musical instrument (e.g., they didn't have the chance to learn how to play it when they were young and would love to give it a try after growing up). Collectively, they needed to make a poster to showcase the snapshot they took for each other and report it back during the class next time.

Interestingly, when we first arrived in Magnatue, two male students couldn't wait to explore the fun place before I even asked them to. It indicated that they're already hooked by this SIM and ready to explore. Although Korobase arrived a bit late, he picked it up right away after reading the Notecard instruction and my further explanation. Each group seemed so "immersed" in exploring the SIM and playing different musical instruments that I noticed that some students (e.g., Emelie and Unessl) were only playing one musical instrument because they enjoyed it so much that they didn't want to leave. So I had to remind them to try out some other instruments and give their classmates the chance to also try the instrument that had been occupied by them. Further evidence to show that students were fully immersed and engaged was that Unessl asked whether he could get a harp here for free. I told him that all the musical instruments can only be played here, though he might be able to buy it if he had enough linden dollars. Due to the time constraint, I'll finish the music topic next Monday and move on to a new topic, sports. The following chat transcript documents today's lesson episode.

[2011/05/25 10:53] UnicornG Luminos: pls take a snapshot of u playing the instrument
[2011/05/25 10:55] Unessl: we have to upload the snapshot of the partner?
[2011/05/25 10:56] Emelie Crystal: yes
[2011/05/25 10:58] UnicornG Luminos: just right click on the musical instrument
[2011/05/25 10:59] UnicornG Luminos: and then u'll play it
[2011/05/25 11:01] UnicornG Luminos: go around, play and have fun
[2011/05/25 11:02] UnicornG Luminos: remember, u have to work with a partner
[2011/05/25 11:10] Idea Loxingly (idea.lexenstar): nice *GIGGLES*:) ~~~~
[2011/05/25 11:11] Idea Loxingly (idea.lexenstar): wow unicon you play nice music; -)
[2011/05/25 11:11] UnicornG Luminos: WOW, Emelie, u are a drummer now!
[2011/05/25 11:11] Emelie Crystal: hahaha
[2011/05/25 11:12] UnicornG Luminos: don't forget to write down the name for each instrument and music genre on your notecard
[2011/05/25 11:15] UnicornG Luminos: guys, have fun so far?
[2011/05/25 11:15] Idea Loxingly (idea.lexenstar): yep ^
[2011/05/25 11:16] Profesor Korobase: the picture is very nice Unless
[2011/05/25 11:16] Profesor Korobase: Toma, Why did you prefer piano?
[2011/05/25 11:17] Toma Remex: mmm it's b/c make lady in good look and cool when they play piano
[2011/05/25 11:17] UnicornG Luminos: make sure u got the chance to play other instruments
[2011/05/25 11:21] Unessl: come on guys, let's go to try sth else
[2011/05/25 11:21] UnicornG Luminos: Ulyo, did u get the chance to play some instruments?
[2011/05/25 11:21] ulyo Genesis: yes
[2011/05/25 11:21] UnicornG Luminos: Emelie, try to explore other instruments as well
[2011/05/25 11:21] ulyo Genesis: guitar

[2011/05/25 11:22] Emelie Crystal: http://www.youtube.com/watch?v=xEHdb1LgLZY
[2011/05/25 11:22] UnicornG Luminos: and let Ulyo know which one u'd like him to take a snapshot: -)
[2011/05/25 11:30] UnicornG Luminos: pls finish the task with each other
[2011/05/25 11:30] UnicornG Luminos: follow the instruction on the notecard
[2011/05/25 11:31] UnicornG Luminos: u guys can come here anytime this week to finish it
[2011/05/25 11:31] fenghp99: okay~~
[2011/05/25 11:31] Idea Loxingly (idea.lexenstar): ok we finish interview; -)
[2011/05/25 11:34] Profesor Korobase: Unessl asks if he can get the Harp?
[2011/05/25 11:35] UnicornG Luminos: well, i think it can only be played here
[2011/05/25 11:35] UnicornG Luminos: but u might be able to buy it if you like, Unessl
[2011/05/25 11:35] UnicornG Luminos: since u're a poor student, i think just play here: -)
[2011/05/25 11:35] Profesor Korobase: hahaha
[2011/05/25 11:36] Unessl: ha
[2011/05/25 11:36] Profesor Korobase: From my side I am ready to work in the presentation about what Uneless and Toma like
[2011/05/25 11:36] UnicornG Luminos: good, but u only choose one person to talk about
[2011/05/25 11:36] Unessl: me also ready
[2011/05/25 11:37] Profesor Korobase: Prefect UnicornG
[2011/05/25 11:38] UnicornG Luminos: also, don't forget that u have to take snapshots of ur partners, not yourself
[2011/05/25 11:40] Profesor Korobase: Thanks Unicrong
[2011/05/25 11:41] Profesor Korobase: Despite I arrive late I think I could capture the idea
[2011/05/25 11:41] Emelie Crystal: thanks for today:)
[2011/05/25 11:41] Emelie Crystal: have a lovely evening everybody

Lessons learned:

1. Although I couldn't record each pair's interaction via voice chat or their private chat log, my own public chat log helps me trace back what's going on in each session (audit trail) and provides another data source that consistently triangulates with their journal, informal focus group interview, and my researcher blogging. It also serves as another layer of data validation in consideration of rigor.

2. Whenever students went near each music zone, they would see the name of the music genre already appearing in front of them. Also, when they started to play a musical instrument (activate it), they'd also see the floating name tag of the musical instrument they're playing. These unique SL features not only deepen students' learning experiences, but they also foster their vocabulary acquisition by exposing them to more input anywhere, anytime.
3. Asking students to take a snapshot of their partner playing a favourite musical instrument and explaining why they chose it is an effective approach to peer collaboration, whilst putting a twist on the poster presentation. It has dawned on me that students by now may have been too familiar with the digital poster for show-and-tell to find it a bit repetitious if asked to do it all the time. Today's task put the old wine in a new bottle. Even though they're still asked to do a poster presentation, they're doing it not for themselves, but for their partner. Not only did they need to take the responsibility of taking a snapshot of their partner, they also had to interview him/her about the reason behind choosing a particular musical instrument and to make a poster out of it. This a great way to enact TBLT because students have the ultimate goal to achieve (a show-and-tell poster presentation about their partner's chosen instrument), each sub-task helps them reach the goal (interviewing, taking a snapshot), the task is meaningful and motivating to them (learning by doing: avatar virtually playing the musical instrument), and they need to accomplish the task collaboratively during the whole process.
4. To ensure that students complete their task assignments, checking in on them with friendly reminders is crucial. Students may procrastinate or do the last minute thing. However, a lot of assignments are group work so they need to coordinate with each other (in-world and in RL) to make the project work. As such, my teacher role is as a facilitator and as a manager, frequently reminding them to contact their partners before the next class. It's cumbersome, but without doing so, I might end up with a loose data collection.
5. Several students couldn't make it to class this week due to personal business in RL, which worries me. Because consistent data collection is paramount to the whole research study, the only way to tackle it is to ask those students to make it up in the next class so that they still get the chance to produce their language output for me to record. To do so, I have to keep a close track of their progress by sending IM reminders. I also need to log in SL all the time with hopes to "catch" them on the spot. Nevertheless, this approach is still not well rounded because their RL commitments and schedules are killing off this resolution. Maybe I could use

the percentage of T-units divided by the number of their oral productions when analysing the data as a way to average out the unequal numbers of presentation. Another issue is how to deal with students who may drop out of the class in mid-course. Shall I still keep their data and analyse it using the percentage as a copying mechanism, or just sadly leave them out?

CHECKPOINT

- Which sub-tasks of today's music lesson do you find effective? What would you have done differently if you were me?
- Which aspects of SL features do you find useful to facilitate the music project? How would you prepare for the same music lesson if it was done in RL?
- In my last reflection point (Lessons learned), I was struggling with how to encourage some students to attend the class regularly due to their RL obligations. The worst-case scenario is that they still withdraw from the course in the middle of the study. If you were me, how would you tackle the dilemma of analysing the data already collected from them, or removing them for the sake of data consistency?

YOUR TASK

- Replicate today's lesson and test it out with your class. First, explore SL and search the Destination guide to find a SIM that is music oriented and affordable so guests can play different musical instruments. If you can't locate any of the in-world places that meet these requirements, consider tweaking your lesson plan by developing a music project that allows your students to attend live performances or music events in-world. Develop the sub-tasks around this modified lesson accordingly.
- Take observation notes when the class is in session and ask students to send you their chat transcripts as an exit slip. Also, conduct a focus group on what they think about this collaborative music project in SL.

CHAPTER 14

LESSON 5 (SPORTS)

> **OVERVIEW**
>
> The class started with students who were absent in the earlier session presenting their show-and-tell presentations on cultural clothing. Students then worked in pairs to report to the class their partner's favourite musical instrument, the reason for choosing it, and a snapshot of the partner playing the chosen instrument as displayed in a digital poster. Afterwards, I introduced the new lesson topic on Sports and teleported the class to an ice skating rink for them to experience being a professional figure skater by activating different figure skating styles. We had a blast in that day's class!

BLOG POST. FRIDAY, 31 MAY 2011

The low student turnout rate today worries me. As much as I know they all have their RL business to attend to (Toma and Afridi preparing for final exams; Feng needing to fix her computer; Annaelvit and Barrabax dealing with family issues; and Hemasha, Idea, and Unessl just being absent), getting fewer students in these couple of sessions really concerns me regarding the inability to gather consistent data. Although I might tackle this by asking those who are absent to catch up on the work in the next class (e.g., Mero and Nikhil), not every student will follow suit. So I will still lose some student data, to say the least.

Because Nikhil missed both classes last week, I asked him to make up the cultural outfit presentation today. As usual, he's very well prepared. He changed his avatar outfit to the traditional Indian male clothing, called a "Dhoti-Kurta" (Figure 14.1). Even though I can tell he was trying to explain the outfit in as much detail as possible, the mediocre Internet connection he had caused some problems getting his meaning across, nevertheless. It's also why the other students didn't provide much feedback after his presentation, though I tried to chime in by offering positive feedback on everyone's behalf.

After Nikhil's presentation, I cut to the chase by asking them to take turns presenting their music project where they needed to report why their partner chose the musical instrument with a snapshot taken. Ulyo volunteered to show-and-tell his partner's, Emelie, favourite musical instrument. His presentation went smoothly as he provided sufficient information about why Emelie chose piano as her favourite instrument, who her favourite pianist was,

Figure 14.1 A Student changed his avatar outfit to the traditional Indian male clothing for a show-and-tell.

and so forth. Although Ulyo's pronunciation and French accent still got in the way of us comprehending his intended meaning, he did a better job this time and most of us seemed to follow along. Because Ulyo and Emelie worked as a pair, I took the liberty of asking her to talk about Ulyo's favourite musical instrument as well. Despite the connection issue, Emelie did a nice job trying to speak as slowly and clearly as possible so we could grasp her points. She let us realise that Ulyo is very talented at playing guitar, thanks to his former musical training and his passion for music (Figure 14.2).

After Emelie, I asked Mero to take the lead because she had been waiting for a while. As a SL teacher, I have to be very attentive to student learning needs and styles to make sure that everyone has a say and stays motivated. Mero's partner was Nikhil. I am glad that her connection was so much better today so she could deliver her presentation intelligibly and professionally. Nikhil's favourite musical instrument is tabla, a popular Indian musical instrument that is like a drum, which fortunately can also be found and played in *Magnatune*! Because Mero and Nikhil worked together, I asked Nikhil to follow up with introducing Mero's favourite musical instrument. Again, Nikhil's voice wasn't that clear due to the unstable Internet connection, but he still managed to make it informative and handled my questions well. I am also relieved that he and Mero could pull it off right after their absence. If they hadn't been fully engaged or motivated, they wouldn't have made any effort to work on this music project after the SL class.

CHAPTER 14
LESSON 5 (SPORTS)

Figure 14.2 A Student rezzed a digital poster with a snapshot of her partner playing his favourite musical instrument.

As known to the class, Korobase is the "overachiever or technology guru" so I saved his presentation for the last as the final highlight. Again, he used an SL presentational tool to showcase the snapshot of his partner, Toma's favourite musical instrument, the piano. Interestingly, we found that most female students in our class inadvertently chose piano as their favourite instrument. A couple of students (Nikhil and Ulyo) also commented that they found that the piano suited the style and elegance of the girls. Korobase first talked about why Toma picked the piano as her favourite instrument (Figure 14.3). Then, in line with our expectations, he started to delineate that he went back to *Magnatune* again to explore more of those musical instruments and that he got so hooked that he did some research online by looking up the history and new information about some instruments which he wasn't familiar with or had never heard of. His presentation inspired the whole class – not only because of his advanced SL tool for presentation, but also because of the way he delivered it. He was natural, spontaneous, animated, and unscripted. Once again, he gave away another technological tool to the class as a generous gift (see the following chat transcript).

[2011/05/30 10:38]   UnicornG Luminos: Toma is playing
[2011/05/30 10:38]   Emelie Crystal: well done
[2011/05/30 10:40]   UnicornG Luminos: Korobase, you are piquing our curiosity: -)
[2011/05/30 10:40]   UnicornG Luminos: a very good storyteller
[2011/05/30 10:40]   Mero (merogigo.baily): he is
[2011/05/30 10:41]   Emelie Crystal: amazing:)

179

Figure 14.3 A student rezzed an SL presentation tool with a picture of his partner playing piano.

[2011/05/30 10:41] UnicornG Luminos: u're not alone...many of students here do the same like u...they all went back to the place to play

[2011/05/30 10:43] UnicornG Luminos: when u clicked on the instrument, it will show u the name, Mero

[2011/05/30 10:44] UnicornG Luminos: another new tool, eh, Korobase: -)

[2011/05/30 10:45] UnicornG Luminos: another gift again?: -))

[2011/05/30 10:46] Nikhil (nikhil.moorsider): really cool

[2011/05/30 10:47] rozalia54: thnx

[2011/05/30 10:47] Nikhil (nikhil.moorsider): woooooooooooo

[2011/05/30 10:48] Binnocence: Hello, I'd like to participate:)

[2011/05/30 10:48] ulyo Genesis: Kerobas has a teaching gift

[2011/05/30 10:49] Nikhil (nikhil.moorsider): BRAVO!!!!!!

[2011/05/30 10:49] Nikhil (nikhil.moorsider): ***APPPPPPLLLAAAUUUSSSEEEE***

Finally, we moved on to today's topic on sports. Two non-registered students privately IMed me that they'd like to join the class. Since many students were absent today, I decided to welcome them to today's session. I noticed that students liked the paired activity where they had more chance and time to practice their speaking whilst interviewing and knowing more about their partner at the same time. Using a private CALL, they were paired to exchange

Figure 14.4 Notecard worksheet on student paired interview about sports.

information about sports as indicated in the Notecard given to them. They also needed to note down the information shared by their partner and report to the class later (Figure 14.4).

Whilst they were taking turns sharing interesting facts about their partner's favourite sport, I also provided additional language input, especially new vocabulary around the subject. For example, Mero didn't know the word "ankle" when I typed it up in the public chat. I took the "teachable moment" and asked the class what ankle meant. Students tried to decipher its meaning using paraphrasing or any way they could come up with, which was conducive to second language acquisition (SLA). Why? Because they're trying to process the input and push the output by stretching their current interlanguage repertoire. As a whole group, they co-constructed the meaning together and the more capable students would push more output, which also struck a chord with the less capable or shyer students in class, and in return fed more input into these students' interlanguage system. Additionally, through information exchanging, new vocabulary was introduced, enhanced, and solidified by my further explanation using both voice/text modes of communication. The following chat history encapsulates this teachable moment.

[2011/05/30 11:18] UnicornG Luminos: rugby… interesting
[2011/05/30 11:19] UnicornG Luminos: a sprained **ankle** or something
[2011/05/30 11:20] Binnocence: we're ready
[2011/05/30 11:20] UnicornG Luminos: ankle is on which body part?
[2011/05/30 11:20] Binnocence: foot
[2011/05/30 11:20] kratos512: in ur feet
[2011/05/30 11:21] kratos512: the part that allows u to move ur feet i think no?
[2011/05/30 11:21] Nikhil (nikhil.moorsider): ankle— joints
[2011/05/30 11:21] Mero (merogigo.baily): hi kratos:)
[2011/05/30 11:21] kratos512: hi mero:)
[2011/05/30 11:21] UnicornG Luminos: cute!!
[2011/05/30 11:21] UnicornG Luminos: pinpong=talbe tennis
[2011/05/30 11:23] UnicornG Luminos: Nikhil, would you like to tell us something about ur partner?
[2011/05/30 11:25] UnicornG Luminos: Nihil, are u still here?
[2011/05/30 11:25] Nikhil (nikhil.moorsider): yup
[2011/05/30 11:25] UnicornG Luminos: did u turn on ur mic
[2011/05/30 11:25] Nikhil (nikhil.moorsider): yeah can u hear me or not?
[2011/05/30 11:25] Emelie Crystal: no: (
[2011/05/30 11:26] Nikhil (nikhil.moorsider): oops!
[2011/05/30 11:26] Profesor Korobase: I can't hear you
[2011/05/30 11:26] UnicornG Luminos: we can hear u now
[2011/05/30 11:27] UnicornG Luminos: tennis…interesting….
[2011/05/30 11:27] Nikhil (nikhil.moorsider): pikball
[2011/05/30 11:28] UnicornG Luminos: wow, 20 years playing tennis!!
[2011/05/30 11:29] Binnocence::)
[2011/05/30 11:30] UnicornG Luminos: badminton
[2011/05/30 11:30] UnicornG Luminos: tennis's cousin; -)
[2011/05/30 11:30] Profesor Korobase: Casillas
[2011/05/30 11:31] UnicornG Luminos: quarter back

[2011/05/30 11:31] UnicornG Luminos: jogging…i like that
[2011/05/30 11:31] Binnocence: hehe
[2011/05/30 11:32] UnicornG Luminos: skydiving!!!
[2011/05/30 11:32] UnicornG Luminos: wow, challenging but very exciting
[2011/05/30 11:34] Profesor Korobase: rafting
[2011/05/30 11:34] UnicornG Luminos: river rafting
[2011/05/30 11:34] Emelie Crystal::)
[2011/05/30 11:32] Binnocence: thank you Professor and thanks Unicorn
[2011/05/30 11:34] Profesor Korobase: thanks Binnocence. Yo told all the true about me

Because we only had 5 minutes left before the class ended, I asked them whether they'd like to teleport to a new SIM for figure skating or if they preferred to do it next time. Gladly, most students chose to stay and seemed quite excited about doing figure skating in SL. So we teleported there together with the two new students. When we arrived, I began to introduce some key words for figure skating, such as jumps, spins, spirals, and axels, as shown in the text chat log below. The reason for doing so is that I wanted them to know that SL is not only for fun, but can be educational as long as the language teacher knows to conduct mini-lessons and scaffold students throughout the immersive learning experience. After the warm-up session, I ushered them to the ice skate freebie box where they could get two pairs of free ice skates for both men and women. I asked them to put them on. Some students (Mero, Ulyo, and Emelie) seemed to have trouble figuring out how to put on the ice skates so I had to spend some time assisting them on the spot. That said, other students had already advanced to animate the "Singles Tricks Skaters", enabling them to skate as a professional figure skater (Figure 14.5). Whilst they were enjoying their first figure skating experience in SL, the three students still couldn't figure out how to animate the ball – Singles Tricks Skaters. So I used both text and voice chat to explain to them and they finally got the hang of it, though we'd already run out of time. By the time I bade them goodbye, Korobase asked me if they had another assignment. I was very delighted to see students getting so motivated and engaged that they would take the initiative to ask for the next task. I told them to post their journal and that we would talk about a new project on Wednesday.

[2011/05/30 11:40] UnicornG Luminos: jumps
[2011/05/30 11:40] UnicornG Luminos: spins
[2011/05/30 11:40] UnicornG Luminos: footwork
[2011/05/30 11:40] UnicornG Luminos: spirals
[2011/05/30 11:41] UnicornG Luminos: short and long program

Figure 14.5 Simulating figure skating in a mesmerising ice skating SIM in SL.

[2011/05/30 11:41]   UnicornG Luminos: triple loops
[2011/05/30 11:41]   UnicornG Luminos: axels
[2011/05/30 11:44]   Singles Tricks Skaters 2.1: whispers: pause for 0.000000 seconds
[2011/05/30 11:44]   Binnocence: still loading, the skates
[2011/05/30 11:45]   UnicornG Luminos: u will see the freebie
[2011/05/30 11:45]   Singles Tricks Skaters 2.1: whispers: pause for 0.000000 seconds
[2011/05/30 11:45]   UnicornG Luminos: go to inventory
[2011/05/30 11:45]   UnicornG Luminos: u will see the folder called "Free Ice Skates"
[2011/05/30 11:45]   UnicornG Luminos: yes, Emlie, u are wearing them
[2011/05/30 11:46]   UnicornG Luminos: good, now u can skate
[2011/05/30 11:46]   UnicornG Luminos: click on singels trick skating
[2011/05/30 11:46]   UnicornG Luminos: u can play it now
[2011/05/30 11:46]   Mero (merogigo.baily): it is very lagging for me i can't wear them
[2011/05/30 11:46]   Profesor Korobase: you can hear music if you like
[2011/05/30 11:46]   rozalia54: woow
[2011/05/30 11:47]   Mero (merogigo.baily): i can 't wear them
[2011/05/30 11:49]   ulyo Genesis: how to make a figure?
[2011/05/30 11:49]   Binnocence: Thank you Unicorn for the wonderful lesson

[2011/05/30 11:49] UnicornG Luminos: single trick skating
[2011/05/30 11:49] UnicornG Luminos: right click on it
[2011/05/30 11:49] Binnocence: Mero, it was nice meeting you sister
[2011/05/30 11:49] UnicornG Luminos: and choose SKATE
[2011/05/30 11:49] Binnocence: hope to have the chance to talk to you soon: D
[2011/05/30 11:49] Binnocence: take care
[2011/05/30 11:49] Singles Tricks Skaters 2.1: whispers: pause for 0.000000 seconds
[2011/05/30 11:49] UnicornG Luminos: Mero,
[2011/05/30 11:50] Singles Tricks Skaters 2.1: whispers: pause for 0.000000 seconds
[2011/05/30 11:50] rozalia54: in the balll
[2011/05/30 11:51] Emelie Crystal: lol very funny
[2011/05/30 11:51] Nikhil (nikhil.moorsider): Mero skating with one skate…
[2011/05/30 11:51] UnicornG Luminos: i'll see u on Wed.
[2011/05/30 11:52] UnicornG Luminos: feel free to come here anytime… it's a very beautiful place
[2011/05/30 11:52] rozalia54: ok
[2011/05/30 11:52] Profesor Korobase: do you have some assignment for us?
[2011/05/30 11:52] UnicornG Luminos: we'll talk about a new topic on Wed
[2011/05/30 11:53] Emelie Crystal: I am sorry unicornG I have to go:) thank you for another wonderful lecture
[2011/05/30 11:53] Profesor Korobase: OK
[2011/05/30 11:53] Emelie Crystal: take care and speak on wednesday:)
[2011/05/30 11:53] Profesor Korobase: see you next Wednesday
[2011/05/30 11:53] Mero (merogigo.baily): thanks:) see u all
[2011/05/30 11:53] Profesor Korobase: Great class!!

Lessons learned:

1. Reading Mero's journal made me realise that sometimes the technical issues or patchy Internet connection of some students causes incomprehension and difficulty providing feedback and raising questions by other students. It is definitely an issue that we all want to resolve when teaching in SL. However, when students are located all over the world, it's really challenging to troubleshoot each individual student's Internet connection because it's totally out of the teacher's hands. All I can do is act on the student's behalf by asking questions and providing further feedback, whilst encouraging them to do the same at the same time.

2. Because many students were absent today, I will send them the teleport landmark for figure skating to remind them of what we did today, and to entice them to come to the next session. Even though I know using some monetary incentive, such as rewarding them with L$ if they can attend class regularly, as suggested by my dissertation committee, might keep students, deep down I know this incentive will still be hijacked by their RL obligations or whatever reason they come up with. I can only pray to the SL Gods that students will stay with me for the last 2–3 weeks before the whole course comes to a close.
3. The music project went quite well. From students' journals and feedback, I think it is another solid testament that students can virtually play the instrument in SL as much as they usually do or don't have the chance to do in RL. Students also commented that they got so motivated by playing those musical instruments that they'd like to actually play it in RL! Also, they learned new vocabulary and expressions, such as vocabulary and music genres, by interacting with each musical instrument in *Magnatune*. Korobase even did research to delve more into the instruments that he was really interested in playing in RL but didn't have the chance to. It is definitely a pedagogical implication that we can draw from virtual learning in SL; that is, that knowledge and motivation can be transferred to RL, or even further, create new knowledge about the subject matter students were unfamiliar with or lacking the chance to touch upon in RL.
4. A keen observation from the music project is that the language input students exchanged with each other is surprisingly effective and conducive to incidental learning. For example, in her journal Mero talked about how she learned new things and vocabulary just from watching Korobase's presentation. She thought she was playing piano without realising that she was actually playing the harpsichord, just because they look similar. Not until she saw Korobase introduce this instrument did she realise that it was the harpsichord she was playing. Students' exposure to new knowledge associated with each RL topic, especially at the lexical level, proves that the immersion and engagement afforded by SL stimulates their current interlanguage repertoire and takes their SLA to the next level.
5. Using the public chat in each SL session really helps me trace back what's going on in the task-based classroom discourse aside from the voice chat. Acknowledging the constraint of retrieving students' own private chat logs and recording their voice chat in pair/group work, the public chat logs and transcripts I have kept so far help capture another spectrum of student language practices in SL. They serve as a useful research tool that triangulates my researcher journal.

CHECKPOINT

- As a researcher, would you offer your participants L$ as an incentive to keep them more committed to your study? What are some considerations of putting this monetary incentive in place?
- Some students expressed that they "picked up" new vocabulary or content knowledge without realising that they were actually learning it whilst being fully immersed and engaged in doing SL tasks, such as playing animated musical instruments. Have you also observed incidental learning in your RL class? Why do you think this effect takes place in SL and how would you assess student retention of the newly learned language items?
- Would you also provide some keywords related to sports as a pre-task, or draw student attention to them when they occur naturally during the task, or simply wait until the task is completed? What is your rationale for choosing one over the other?

YOUR TASK

- Develop a new lesson on sports. For your pre-task activity, create a similar Notecard worksheet for students to interview each other in pairs using a private CALL. They can exchange information about their favourite sports, the one(s) they are good at or like to learn how to play, etc. Alternatively, you can turn it into a jeopardy game by grouping them in several teams competing to answer the questions around sports.
- To prepare for your main task, explore Destination Guide in SL or ask your SL contacts about a SIM where students can play sports virtually. Ideally, the SIM would allow residents to animate different kinds of sports or at least target one particular sport category, such as figure skating in this lesson. Teleport your class there and give them some guidance on how they should play/animate the sport(s) and any sub-tasks they need to complete whilst immersing themselves in playing the sport. Use your creativity to make the task fun, collaborative, and engaging for the students.
- Invite students to report on their thoughts about this task experience afterwards. You may also work with them on some target items observed during their task interaction, such as new vocabulary, pronunciation, grammar, or content-related knowledge.

CHAPTER 15

LESSON 6 (ARTS PART 1)

OVERVIEW

Despite the absence of several students, we started a new lesson on *Arts*. This chapter illustrates the first part of the lesson. To connect them to the topic, we did a cloze test using the lyrics of *Starry, Starry Night* alongside *Van Gogh*'s paintings displayed in a slide show. Then we teleported to the *Sky Sculpture Gallery* where they worked in pairs as gallery curators, following the Notecard instruction. They needed to negotiate with their partner on choosing a preferred 3D artwork and discussed its most interesting and salient aspects before introducing it to the class.

BLOG POST. THURSDAY, 2 JUNE 2011

Another student (Annaelvit) just emailed me an hour before the class that she unfortunately had to withdraw from the course due to her hectic RL schedule. Even though she expressed her appreciation for this virtual language learning experience and cross-cultural communication with her peers worldwide, her RL obligations outweighed her well-intentioned commitment to the class. Despite this being understandable, I still feel regret seeing students so eager to join the class in the very beginning but inevitably quitting midway. ☹ Also, several students who didn't show up last time were still absent today (Hemasha, Idea, Feng, Afridi, and Barrabax). Even Ulyo, the student who is always present in class, didn't show up today – hmm, I am deeply concerned about the consistency in my data collection now. Before the lesson, I told them that we only have one to two more weeks to go before we say adios to each other. As such, I was hoping that they could try to make it to every session and stay until the end because the opportunity to learn and grow with all the wonderful students around the world in the same place, at the same time, is just too valuable to pass up. I am not sure about the extent to which the "pep talk" will translate into their attendance. I guess that's the only thing I could do at this point.

Today's topic was Arts. In my pilot study, I did an activity that included listening to the song, *Starry Starry Night*, in the Music lesson whilst we were watching Vincent Van Gogh's paintings in the slide show. But this time I decided to put this activity in the Arts topic because Van Gogh's artwork perfectly couched today's topic. I went ahead to rez the whiteboard and load the song from YouTube but somehow a couple of students couldn't watch it on the spot. So I

LET'S GET OUR HANDS DIRTY

Figure 15.1 Notecard worksheet on fill-in-the-blank of the song lyrics for Vincent (*Starry Starry Night*).

typed up the link in the public chat for them to open a new browser on their end. That way, everyone could be on the same page. To enhance their listening comprehension as well as appreciation for the art, I gave them a Notecard of the song lyrics in which I took out some key words for them to fill in the blanks (Figure 15.1). I asked them to listen and appreciate the art slideshow for the first time before paying attention to the lyrics the second time I played it. Then I asked them to compare what they had noted down with a partner. I figured the task might be a bit hard for them ("Emelie Crystal: quite hard words ☹") and they didn't seem able to tell me some missing words (except for Emelie) when asked to share as a class. Fair enough – I may revamp this task in the future. I probably will still play the song and invite them to appreciate Van Gogh's paintings. Instead of asking them to fill in blanks, I may ask them to discuss what they like or dislike about his paintings, which painting strikes them the most and why, what they think about him as an artist, and how they will introduce his paintings to their friends who haven't heard of Van Gogh before.

Because Toma and Unessl missed the last session, I asked them to make it up today. As observed, Unessl is not as skilled in using SL features as his counterparts because he only accesses SL when the class is in session, much less using SL for socialising on his own. Therefore, it took him a bit longer to set up his digital poster so I asked Toma to get it started first. To my pleasant surprise, Toma was very composed today and did her presentation smoothly. I used to have a hard time trying to make out what she was trying to say because of her heavy accent. But today, I could follow along with her and complimented her on her delivery. As for Unessl, he's just a natural presenter. He seemed as at ease telling us about his partners as if he was talking to us in RL.

After that, I took them on a field trip to *Sky Sculpture Gallery*. I sent them the Notecard, explaining that they needed to work with a partner and played the role of curator (Figure 15.2). I figured the word, "curator", might be new to some students so I tried to prompt them to come up with some definitions for this word. Gladly, they were able to define the word nicely (see the following chat log) and I further summarised it by telling them that a museum/gallery curator should be able to interpret a collection of artwork, whilst informing, educating, and entertaining the audience. They were required to explore this gallery with their partner and use the private CALL to discuss how they like each object, what concept the artist was trying to convey, and how they could inform and entertain their audience who rely on their interpretations. After negotiation, they reached the consensus on two chosen objects they would like to present to us with some interesting anecdotes. They had 15 minutes or so to finish the task, though I kind of knew this time was too tight given the enormous gallery that deserved more time to explore.

[2011/06/01 10:47] UnicornG Luminos: gallery curator
[2011/06/01 10:47] Unessl: guardian
[2011/06/01 10:48] Unessl: take care of objects
[2011/06/01 10:48] Mero (merogigo.baily): he is lead people
[2011/06/01 10:48] Toma Remex: guid people
[2011/06/01 10:48] Mero (merogigo.baily): guide

After making sure that they understood the task, I walked them around the 3D gallery before setting them off for their task. I suggested that they fly around this vast gallery because some gigantic sculptures are too huge to just stand and look at from below. When I asked them to

LET'S GET OUR HANDS DIRTY

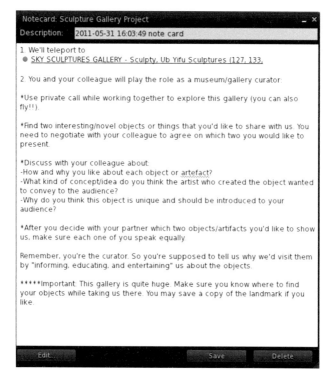

Figure 15.2 Notecard instruction on how to play the role as a curator in pairwork to complete the gallery project.

fly with me to check out a sculpture in full size (Figure 15.3), Unessl didn't know how to fly. Before I instructed him how to take off, some of his classmates already chimed in to take the lead (see the following chat log). Once again, it proves that the virtual learning community has been established among students, evidenced in the zone of proximal development (ZPD) where more capable students offer to scaffold less SL-proficient peers throughout the course.

[2011/06/01 10:56] Emelie Crystal: move
[2011/06/01 10:56] Emelie Crystal: fly
[2011/06/01 10:57] Nikhil (nikhil.moorsider): press 'page up'
[2011/06/01 10:59] Emelie Crystal: yes
[2011/06/01 10:59] Mero (merogigo.baily): yes
[2011/06/01 10:59] Unessl: yes
[2011/06/01 10:59] Unessl: sorry for delay
[2011/06/01 11:00] Emelie Crystal: great

Figure 15.3 Snapshot of my avatar flying around the funky sculpture installations in an art exhibition.

I paired them up by assigning students to work with others they don't usually work with. Whilst they were exploring the gallery, I flew around to monitor and offer help if necessary. For example, I'd ask them if they were still using private CALL to connect with their partner. Mero asked me that if they could use an outside source, such as doing a Google or wiki search, to make their content more substantial and richer. It's another example of seeing students "immersed and engaged" in the virtual role they're playing and gain the sense of autonomy of being responsible for their task. They could have just taken an easy route for this task rather than making more effort and time to capitalise on the RL sources. It's interesting to see that the boundary between SL and RL is blurry and both optimise the extension of their knowledge construction and empowering their learning experience. Korobase came in late (but still made it to class in the final 20 minutes) and I took some time to explain to him the required task and offered him the Notecard. Because Mero, Toma, and Unessl were in a group of 3, I asked if anyone of them would like to work with Korobase. Toma kindly agreed to pair up with Korobase. I took a look at the time again and there was only 3 minutes left and Mero told me that she had to leave. (Originally, she couldn't make it to class due to her doctor's appointment. I am so pleased that she didn't just take the class lightly but decided to attend the session by all means.) So I told them to coordinate with their partner curator to schedule the time to finish the task this week and then they will do the gallery walk next Monday. They seemed quite excited about the project and told me that this gallery is amazing and that they would like to have more time to explore it.

Lessons learned:

1. I can't help but reiterate that teaching a virtual course in SL with students from all over the world is particularly challenging, as opposed to bringing a compulsory, credit-bearing class to SL where students have more responsibility. Motivation or "fun" can no longer retain student attendance as RL obligations and unexpected scheduling would still hold them back and eventually kill off their "free" commitment to this course. Worse off, I am not sure if I can still analyse the data gathered from them as of now given the data inconsistency. My contingency plan is that I might use their journal data for qualitative analysis because their reflections still account for what they honestly thought about each lesson session among others. However, their oral productions recorded during show-and-tells will be problematic for quantitative data analysis. If I remove their recordings out of the data pool, it definitely will weaken the quantifications of the overall analysis, but if I use the percentage as an analysis measure, it might work for examining the quality and quantity in student oral productions as a whole. Regardless, I may still have to leave them out in the pretest and posttest data pool because they will no longer participate in the posttest.
2. The chat log transcripts really help capture a full SL classroom discourse by distinguishing the interaction between me and the students, among students, and which student(s) take more initiative. It can also help a teacher to track some students who tend to take a back seat, and reveal which lesson scenario or task stimulates more active participation from these students.
3. Another teaching strategy is to vary the tasks to sustain student motivation and engagement without boring them with the same routine. By now, they seem quite familiar with the poster presentation. In today's main task, they were required to take on the curator role in the museum. Whilst the task was RL relevant and also meaningful to them, it also could be challenging for some students who were not confident or into arts. But if they saw the value of accomplishing the task whilst enjoying the process of doing it, they would invest time and effort to achieve the ultimate goal. Collaborating with a partner also encouraged them to co-construct the knowledge and learn from each other, rather than in isolation.
4. Note to myself: Ask them next time how they felt about walking and flying to browse around so many quirky, enormous sculptures in the 3D museum. Did they feel as if they were visiting an RL gallery? How does this virtual gallery walk experience compare with an RL field trip?

CHECKPOINT

- Apparently, the warm-up exercise (fill-in-the-blank of the Song Lyrics for Vincent, *Starry Starry Night*) didn't work well. My intention was to use Van Gogh's paintings alongside the song to activate their background knowledge about arts. If you were me, how would you modify this activity or have done it differently?
- Today's curator task tapped into different levels of skills of a student pair. To accomplish it successfully, each student pair needed to draw upon their SL skills (flying, private CALL, landmarking), task interaction (description of and negotiation on two objects to present), research skill (looking for information about the chosen objects), and oral communication (introducing objects with educational and interesting anecdotes). Discuss these pedagogical aspects underpinning this task with a colleague.
- In the final lesson learned, "note to myself", I was planning to ask my students about their SL gallery walk experience and how it compared with their RL experience. By the same token, how would you compare these two field trip experiences from the standpoint of a teacher? Specifically, what are the benefits and drawbacks of teaching/learning in each setting?

YOUR TASK

- Replicate the same curator task for your class. As part of the lesson planning, it may be worth spending some time looking for a suitable gallery museum in-world. If you can't find any ideal one, feel free to teleport to *The Free Museum* (http://maps.secondlife.com/secondlife/Leodegrance/169/) where students can take as many art pieces for free as they want. After you finish exploring the museum, take your students on a field trip here and show them around the museum before introducing curator project. You may model how to work as a curator by showcasing a unique sculpture or painting found in the museum.
- To guide students, feel free to adopt the Notecard (Figure 15.2) that I created for this lesson or create your own. Ideally, you would like students to work in pairs or groups. However, it is also fine to turn it into an individual project if you have a more advanced class. Allow students to have time to prepare for this task (e.g., as a take-home project) and record their oral productions afterwards.

CHAPTER 16

LESSON 6 (ARTS PART 2)

OVERVIEW

In the beginning of today's session, I gave the class a gentle reminder that the posttest interview would be scheduled by the end of the course. Continuing the final part of the *Arts* lesson, we teleported to the *Sky Sculpture Gallery* for each student pair to take on the curator role and introduce their favourite 3D artwork to the class. Students and I were impressed with the time and effort each pair invested in this project, which paid off with their professional presentations, engaging discussions, and genuine praise from the audience. The art lesson ended on a high note, after all.

BLOG POST. WEDNESDAY, 8 JUNE 2011

Today's lesson went smoothly, I think. When I saw more students gathering around in the Rose Garden, our class site, my heart just leapt. I first told them that our class will come to a close next week with only three sessions left. Because the main factor that dictates student turnout rate is their RL scheduling and commitment, I'd like to start the posttest a week earlier whilst they're still in class. That way, I can hopefully pre-empt the risk of student no-show after the class ends and they are all gone. They were also informed that the format of the "final oral interview" will be quite similar to their pre-course interview (I don't want to use the word "posttest" with them as an "interview" sounds more friendly than a "test"). With that said, I sent them the link to the Google Docs where I already set up the schedule for them to fill in any time slot that would work for them. I think it's better to schedule it when everyone was here at the same time, rather than letting them do it after class as it is usually more cumbersome. Gladly, I was able to pair most of the students before the class dismissed, except that Emelie still needs a partner.

We teleported to the *Sky Sculpture Gallery* again for today's gallery walk. Each member of the team worked as a curator, who would guide, inform, educate, and entertain us. Mero and Unessl volunteered to be the first curator team. He told us that Mero would fly to the sculpture first and sent him a teleport link, but I thought it would have been better if all of us could tag along with her. After we all arrived near the Pharaoh Abu Simbel statue, Mero started her guided tour talk. I can tell that she did her research on the history and

Figure 16.1 Student introducing the Pharaoh sculpture to the class in her guided tour as a curator.

facts about the Pharaoh and also typed up some key words for us. She also sounded like an experienced curator (Figure 16.1). I showered her with praise as she set the bar high for the following groups.

Unessl followed up by taking us to the statue of Angel De La Independecia, the landmark in Mexico city. He's such a natural. He impersonated the curator role by telling us that he's been working as a curator for this gallery for a long time and was delighted to introduce the statue to us. He talked about why and how the Angel De La Independecia was built and its importance in the history of Mexico City (Figure 16.2). Though I sensed that both Mero and Unessl were reading from the script/notes when talking about the history, they articulated it clearly. I also wonder if they had rehearsed it in RL before today's SL gallery walk. Interestingly, the Angel statue also glittered from time to time and oozed an ethereal feel to his presentation.

Next, Korobase and his curator team took the lead. We flew with him to the destination of the statue of Plato, one of the greatest Greek philosophers. What I liked about Korobase's presentation was that it was not scripted. He was playing the curator role so well that we felt as if he was speaking in front of us in RL. He joked that never in a million years did he think a person with an engineering background would fall for the arts and now philosophy. Not until he conducted research on this project to better understand Plato's life did he become fascinated by the history and story of this famous Greek philosopher. He presented in a way

CHAPTER 16
LESSON 6 (ARTS PART 2)

Figure 16.2 Student introducing the statue of Angel de la Independecia to the class in his guided tour as a curator.

that was articulate and organised so all of us could follow along easily (Figure 16.3). After each curator's talk, I asked the class if they had any questions or comments for the curator, but most of them only gave heartfelt compliments without further questions raised, which also made me wonder if it's because they didn't catch most of what each presenter said, or they were too "nice" to ask any hard question. That said, Mero asked Korobase a question about why Plato was built on a big palm of a hand. Korobase answered that "it is built in a hand because that represents the common sense".

Figure 16.3 Student introducing the portrait bust of Plato to the class in his guided tour as a curator.

Also part of the curator team, Toma came next by asking us to fly with her to the giant statue of Gulliver's Travels with which most of us are familiar from English literature or the fable story. However, I found her pronunciation and accent still got in the way of most of her talk. I may need to replay the recording multiple times to figure out what she's talking about. After that, Ulyo also took us back to the statue of Pharaoh Abu Simbel. It's interesting to see that both Mero and Ulyo showed great minds think alike by choosing the same statue. I told the class that Ulyo would talk about the statue from his own interpretation (as Unessl put, "what a nice coincidence"). I felt that Ulyo was a bit nervous as he stuttered several times, even though his classmates all praised him for his nice presentation afterward. I also tried to reassure him that we really liked his presentation through a private IM. He told me that he really learned a lot from presenting this statue to us because he did research on Pharaoh Abu Simbel, which is a famous sculpture that was new to him before this project. This provides more evidence of how simulating and immersing oneself in RL tasks in SL can lead to the construction of new knowledge.

Idea asked us to fly with her to a gigantic statue of "In Out There", which is a man sitting with his left hand holding his head in a pensive position (Figure 16.4). As usual, Idea was very composed when she led the group. She shared with us her own interpretation of "In Out There" and the creator's intended meaning. She also showed us how to "interact with" the sculpture by clicking on "Sit", which allowed us to swim around the sculpture along with the fish. It was just amazing to see how SL can instil a more animated and fun twist to an unmoving object. This unexpected animation also propelled Korobase to ask Idea the question, "Where is this sculpture in RL…I would like to find it in RL so I would fly there". This shows that RL task simulation and engagement has piqued his interest and motivation to extend this SL experience to RL, more evidence of how immersive learning can be transferred to RL. Idea addressed Korobase's question with ease. She already did her homework before today's presentation: she went to great lengths to ask the creator/owner of this gallery and was told that this one and only statue could only be found in SL.

Here came the last curator team. We flew with Barrabax to a unique installation with an artist's 3D painting on the ground. Barrabax did a wonderful job by explaining what ground painting was and used very effective expressions, such as "Art is accessible to all" and "Each artist is unique". She also provided some outside sources to connect us to other "ground paintings". It appears that she's become more comfortable speaking English in public, at least in a virtual world like SL, and the quality of her language output has improved leaps and bounds. I'm so moved to witness how much she has

CHAPTER 16
LESSON 6 (ARTS PART 2)

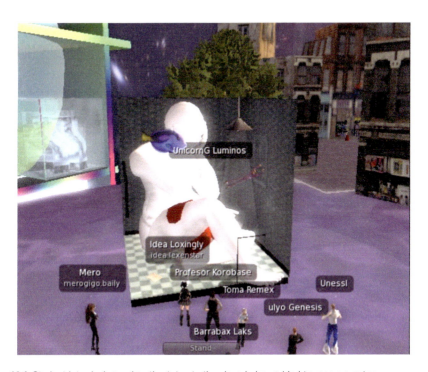

Figure 16.4 Student introducing a gigantic statue to the class in her guided tour as a curator.

grown from being so shy in the beginning to more confident, where she's opened up and is willing to take risks in speaking spontaneously. In fact, Korobase in his posttest also talked about the progress he's witnessed in Barrabax.

We then followed Emelie to the Pyramid installation (Figure 16.5). Emelie's presentation was short. I have noticed that her voice quality hasn't been great, so most of the time we have a hard time understanding her or have to pay very close attention to her speech. After her presentation, she turned our attention to Nikhil, her curator colleague.

Nikhil is such a diligent student, so much so that he did substantial research on the sculpture he's introducing to us: Aphrodite. He even deciphered the root of her name and the birth stories of Aphrodite (also known as Venus Rising). Then he intrigued us with interesting anecdotes about Aphrodite's sacred temple, husband, and famous son, Cupid, as well as her symbolic girdle (see the following chat transcript). It's amazing to see how much time, effort, and commitment each student put into this project; they all accomplished this

LET'S GET OUR HANDS DIRTY

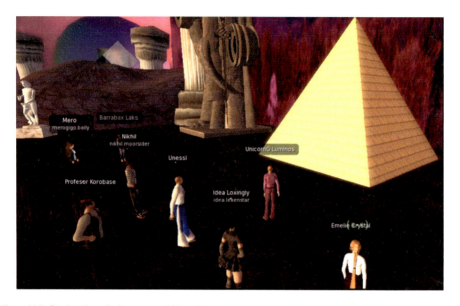

Figure 16.5 Student introducing a pyramid installation to the class in her guided tour as a curator.

task as seasoned curators above and beyond my expectations. Evidently, the immersion, engagement, and motivation afforded and triggered by this SL task is truly palpable.

[2011/06/06 11:25] Nikhil (nikhil.moorsider): Aphrodite
[2011/06/06 11:25] UnicornG Luminos: yes, goddess of love
[2011/06/06 11:25] Nikhil (nikhil.moorsider): Venus
[2011/06/06 11:26] Nikhil (nikhil.moorsider): (aphro="foam"+dite="arisen")
[2011/06/06 11:26] UnicornG Luminos: wow, i like that…go to the root of the words
[2011/06/06 11:26] UnicornG Luminos: it's origin
[2011/06/06 11:26] Nikhil (nikhil.moorsider): Cronus
[2011/06/06 11:26] Nikhil (nikhil.moorsider): Uranus
[2011/06/06 11:27] UnicornG Luminos: that's why Venus was born in the sea where she was surrounded by foams in a shell
[2011/06/06 11:27] Nikhil (nikhil.moorsider): Cyprus
[2011/06/06 11:27] UnicornG Luminos: right
[2011/06/06 11:27] Unessl: interesting
[2011/06/06 11:28] Nikhil (nikhil.moorsider): Cytherean
[2011/06/06 11:28] Nikhil (nikhil.moorsider): Olymous

[2011/06/06 11:28] Nikhil (nikhil.moorsider): Hera
[2011/06/06 11:29] Nikhil (nikhil.moorsider): Hepheastus
[2011/06/06 11:29] Nikhil (nikhil.moorsider): Ares
[2011/06/06 11:29] UnicornG Luminos: her husband
[2011/06/06 11:29] UnicornG Luminos: i c
[2011/06/06 11:30] Nikhil (nikhil.moorsider): Eros
[2011/06/06 11:30] UnicornG Luminos: Cupid = Eros
[2011/06/06 11:30] Nikhil (nikhil.moorsider): cupid
[2011/06/06 11:30] Nikhil (nikhil.moorsider): Hemeros, Pothos(desire), Phobos(fear), Demos, Harmonia and Rhodes
[2011/06/06 11:30] Nikhil (nikhil.moorsider): girdle
[2011/06/06 11:31] UnicornG Luminos: girdle is one of her symbolic tools
[2011/06/06 11:31] Unessl: so informative
[2011/06/06 11:31] Emelie Crystal: very interesting
[2011/06/06 11:31] Barrabax Laks: thanks Nikhil
[2011/06/06 11:31] Unessl: well done
[2011/06/06 11:31] Idea Loxingly (idea.lexenstar): very good^^

Lessons learned:

1. It's my first time delivering this lesson on my own. In my pilot, we went to visit the mind-blowing *Identity Museum*; however, the SIM had disappeared when I teleported there earlier. So I had to modify my lesson to suit the Art theme. To find the next SIM for today's lesson, I did my SL search and finally decided to choose the *Sculpture Gallery* as the site for our gallery walk after comparing it with other SL museums I found. It's exhilarating to see that tasking students to be the curator worked quite well. Many students expressed in their journals that they felt responsible for informing their guided audience about the contents and stories around those sculptures given their role as a real curator. To accomplish this task professionally, they needed to do their homework – researching the background information about the installations they chose to introduce. When a well-planned task is RL oriented and meaningful to the students, it will hit the learning target and stimulate task motivation, engagement, and commitment. Of course, the task wouldn't have worked wonders had it not been supported by the simulated and animated SL features. I wonder if the task could also be delivered seamlessly in RL given the level of cumbersome and costly preparation for a field trip.

2. It was amazing to see how we could all interact with a myriad of unique statues in the gallery whilst listening to the anecdotes delivered by each student curator. Also, following the curators by flying around the gallery was just priceless. Think about this: If we do the same gallery walk with an RL class, we have to travel to the gallery or museum first and then students might get a bit shy when talking to a group of classmates whilst being watched by other visitors at the same time. It's just so much easier to carry out an RL task like this in SL.
3. Korobase got motivated by this project, so much so that he felt that his interest in arts and visiting galleries had been growing. The task also made him want to know more about the subject matter to present it to us (the visitors) as a well-trained curator. This case in point proves that doing meaningful RL tasks in SL can keep students engaged and motivated (or shall I say "hooked"). It also shows that SL has the potential to transfer and extend the content knowledge to RL, which will reciprocally feed back into SL. The learning channel between SL and RL, in this case, is interchangeable.

CHECKPOINT

- Have you ever taken your language students on a field trip? What is your take on conducting a field trip to an art gallery or museum to SL (as illustrated in this lesson) versus doing it in RL? Do you also consider it more labour-intensive for teachers to plan an RL field trip? What are some technical and pedagogical considerations should you choose to carry it out in SL?
- Revisit Checkpoint #2 in Chapter 15. You were asked to discuss the pedagogical aspects underpinning this task with a colleague. Now see if you also can also draw other implications from this task (e.g., task engagement, SLA, etc).
- In this curator project, students worked in pairs (or groups) to choose two sculpture installations and research them before introducing them to the guided visitors (the class). Think about the proficiency levels and dynamics of your class. Would you follow suit or have done it differently? For example, would you ask them to explore SL and find their own gallery/museum instead?
- If you are a researcher, what type of data can you gather from this lesson? How would you analyse them both qualitatively and quantitatively if it was a mixed-methods research design?

YOUR TASK

- In your last task (Chapter 15), you were asked to replicate the same curator task for your class. If you haven't undertaken it yet, please follow your task instructions and give it a go. Record your task delivery and jot down observation notes for task modifications later.
- If you have already done it, great, now move on to the task assessment. See if you can design a rubric (teacher and peer) for each team to receive feedback from you and their classmates.
- Also consider conducting a focus group, survey, or reflection writing with your class to better understand their experience and perspective about this task, and how it translates into their learning.

CHAPTER 17

LESSON 7 (JOBS)

> **OVERVIEW**
>
> Today's class focused on a new topic, *Jobs*. As usual, I first ran the agenda with them by first reminding them of the oral interview (posttest) scheduling and their final task as a SL tour guide to showcase a tourist attraction in their home country. To start the new lesson (*Jobs*), students played the guessing game based on a list of job vocabulary displayed in the Notecards. Each team would compete to earn points by correctly guessing the occupation, described by the other two teams. Afterwards, they were tasked to find a partner to interview each other about their job following the Notecard prompts before reporting it back to the class.

BLOG POST. WEDNESDAY, 8 JUNE 2011

I enjoyed today's class. Despite several students being absent (now I only have nine students who attend the class regularly), we had great fun in today's lesson on jobs. I first went over the agenda for today and next week, which is also our final week. I first checked in with Unessl and Mero who completed the "oral interview" (i.e., posttest) yesterday. Gladly, they both enjoyed the tasks, though they found them a bit challenging as well. After confirming the time with the other students who are scheduled to complete the interview this week, I told them that the travel tour guide will be their final project in that they are required to play the role as a tour guide and locate a SIM that simulates their home country, such as a tourist attraction or any spectacular landmark in their country that they'd like to introduce to us. Their job is to convince us why it's worth visiting (in SL) and hopefully we'll be motivated to actually visit it in RL in the future. See the assignment Notecard in Figure 17.1.

Instead of working in our usual class site, the Rose Garden, I teleported them to *Sky Tables* – a wonderful design that allows students to discuss on different floors in the mid-air so each group won't interrupt other group discussions. I told them that they were going to play a job game today. I first paired them into three teams and gave the Notecard to each of them (see Figure 17.2). I explained that they were working with their partner to come up with a job description for each job title listed on the Notecard. They would tell other teams what each job was about without naming the job title, and the other teams had to guess what the job was. Any team that got the name right would win one point for their own team. Then another team would take turns to describe a new job on their Notecard and other teams had to guess what it was.

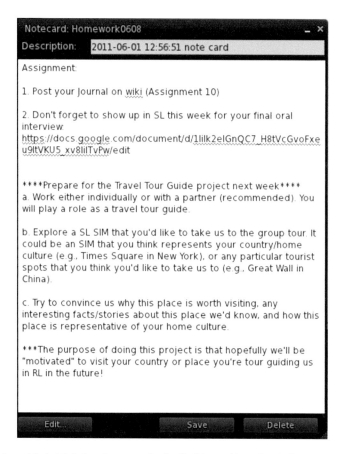

Figure 17.1 Notecard that details how to prepare for the final tour guide project in SL.

After making sure everyone understood the game rules, I sent each team to their designated mid-air floor for group discussion by rezzing the Sky Tables feature. Because Toma was late, I was working with her and guiding her through the game plan. Whilst we were doing so, Mero sent me a teleport request to her floor where she was working with Ulyo. She asked me if both of them should get a different Notecard, which struck me that she might get confused about this task. I explained that this task required Ulyo and her to brainstorm and work out the descriptions for the job titles listed on the same Notecard for other teams to guess. She said it sounded easy and I suggested that she might make the descriptions a bit harder (e.g., longer, more new vocabulary); if she liked, their team could come up with a couple of new job titles should they complete the task earlier.

Figure 17.2 Notecard listing different job titles for student teams to describe for the job guessing game.

After checking in on each team to confirm that they were all done with the discussion, I brought them back to the ground for game competition. I asked them to stay closer to their own team member, whilst reiterating the rules to the game. It was such a blast! Each team took it very seriously and was very engaged in the task because they wanted to earn more points for their team. It's so much fun to see Unessl and Mero compete by verbally "sabotaging" each other in a joking manner (see the following chat transcript excerpt with emphasis in bold). Whilst they were taking turns describing each job title and trying hard to guess the name, I found both Toma and Barrabax were making their descriptions a bit too short so that their classmates had to ask them to describe more about the jobs. After playing the game for several rounds, I, as their gameshow host, announced the winner team, followed by the runners-up who were several points behind.

[2011/06/08 10:42] Unessl: It was really amusing
[2011/06/08 10:44] Idea Loxingly (idea.lexenstar): banker
[2011/06/08 10:44] Unessl: bank clerk
[2011/06/08 10:45] Nikhil (nikhil.moorsider): BRAVO!!!!!!
[2011/06/08 10:45] Mero (merogigo.baily): lawyer
[2011/06/08 10:45] ulyo Genesis: housekeeper

[2011/06/08 10:46] ulyo Genesis: attorney
[2011/06/08 10:46] Idea Loxingly (idea.lexenstar): yes
[2011/06/08 10:47] Unessl: hard worker?
[2011/06/08 10:47] ulyo Genesis: housekeeper
[2011/06/08 10:47] Unessl: slave lol
[2011/06/08 10:47] Idea Loxingly (idea.lexenstar): yep!
[2011/06/08 10:47] Unessl: no cheating pls
[2011/06/08 10:47] Nikhil (nikhil.moorsider): hey are you reading mind Ulyo
[2011/06/08 10:47] Unessl:: -)
[2011/06/08 10:47] Mero (merogigo.baily): shopkeeper
[2011/06/08 10:48] Toma Remex: yes
[2011/06/08 10:48] Barrabax Laks: repeat please toma
[2011/06/08 10:48] Toma Remex: receptions
[2011/06/08 10:49] Unessl: receptionist?
[2011/06/08 10:49] Nikhil (nikhil.moorsider): secretary
[2011/06/08 10:49] ulyo Genesis: yes
[2011/06/08 10:49] Nikhil (nikhil.moorsider): woooooo
[2011/06/08 10:49] Unessl: good job, Nikhil
[2011/06/08 10:50] Barrabax Laks: medical company
[2011/06/08 10:50] ulyo Genesis: insurance agent
[2011/06/08 10:50] Barrabax Laks: ok
[2011/06/08 10:50] Nikhil (nikhil.moorsider): cool…nice job
[2011/06/08 10:50] Unessl: Unicorn, I guess you sent all notecards to Ulyo
[2011/06/08 10:51] ulyo Genesis: no I don't have any
[2011/06/08 10:51] Unessl: just kidding man lol
[2011/06/08 10:51] Toma Remex: designer
[2011/06/08 10:51] Mero (merogigo.baily): computer engineer
[2011/06/08 10:51] Unessl: wow
[2011/06/08 10:51] Unessl: it is not fairrrrrrrrrrrrrr
[2011/06/08 10:52] Mero (merogigo.baily): nurse
[2011/06/08 10:52] Toma Remex: yes
[2011/06/08 10:53] Nikhil (nikhil.moorsider): architector
[2011/06/08 10:53] ulyo Genesis: brick layer
[2011/06/08 10:53] Mero (merogigo.baily): interior designer
[2011/06/08 10:53] Barrabax Laks: home agent
[2011/06/08 10:53] Unessl: wrong
[2011/06/08 10:53] Nikhil (nikhil.moorsider): hmmm

[2011/06/08 10:53] Barrabax Laks: decorating interiors
[2011/06/08 10:53] Unessl: sorry guys this point is ours
[2011/06/08 10:53] Barrabax Laks: jajajaa
[2011/06/08 10:54] Unessl: you won't guess
[2011/06/08 10:54] Nikhil (nikhil.moorsider): civil engineer
[2011/06/08 10:54] Barrabax Laks: architect
[2011/06/08 10:54] Unessl: wrong
[2011/06/08 10:54] UnicornG Luminos: Unessl just spilled the beans
[2011/06/08 10:54] Mero (merogigo.baily): architect
[2011/06/08 10:54] Unessl: yes
[2011/06/08 10:54] UnicornG Luminos: construction
[2011/06/08 10:55] Mero (merogigo.baily): constructor
[2011/06/08 10:55] Unessl: smart Unicorn
[2011/06/08 10:55] Unessl: **the point is ours**
[2011/06/08 10:55] Unessl: **it was construction worker**
[2011/06/08 10:56] Mero (merogigo.baily): **constructor**
[2011/06/08 10:57] **Unessl: Do not try to grasp our points Mero;-)**
[2011/06/08 10:57] **Mero (merogigo.baily): no i want it unessl:)**
[2011/06/08 10:57] **Unessl: come on, let's face it- you lose**
[2011/06/08 10:58] **Mero (merogigo.baily): no u will lose unessl**
[2011/06/08 10:58] **UnicornG Luminos:: pO**
[2011/06/08 10:58] **Unessl:; -)**
[2011/06/08 11:00] UnicornG Luminos: Nikhil, u can also try to step in to give more Information
[2011/06/08 11:00] Mero (merogigo.baily): soldier
[2011/06/08 11:00] Unessl: soldier
[2011/06/08 11:01] Unessl: **oh no Mero**
[2011/06/08 11:01] Unessl: **again you are ahead**
[2011/06/08 11:01] Nikhil (nikhil.moorsider):. +1 for Mero
[2011/06/08 11:01] Unessl: repeat pls
[2011/06/08 11:02] Nikhil (nikhil.moorsider): a person who is having a stick in his hand...
[2011/06/08 11:02] Idea Loxingly (idea.lexenstar): conductor
[2011/06/08 11:02] Barrabax Laks: director
[2011/06/08 11:02] Mero (merogigo.baily): no: (
[2011/06/08 11:03] UnicornG Luminos: key word, 'inside'
[2011/06/08 11:03] Nikhil (nikhil.moorsider): interior designer
[2011/06/08 11:03] Unessl: wow

[2011/06/08 11:03] Idea Loxingly (idea.lexenstar): nice
[2011/06/08 11:03] **Unessl: we are catching you Mero**
[2011/06/08 11:03] Nikhil (nikhil.moorsider): lol last round remained
[2011/06/08 11:03] Unessl: oh no, ha
[2011/06/08 11:04] Barrabax Laks: disaster lol
[2011/06/08 11:04] UnicornG Luminos: good, key word, house
[2011/06/08 11:04] Mero (merogigo.baily): house agent
[2011/06/08 11:05] ulyo Genesis: real estate
[2011/06/08 11:05] ulyo Genesis: real estate agent
[2011/06/08 11:05] Unessl: excellent
[2011/06/08 11:05] Unessl: Mero
[2011/06/08 11:05] Mero (merogigo.baily): **dentist**
[2011/06/08 11:05] Unessl: **dentist**
[2011/06/08 11:06] Unessl: **oh mero your making me crazy**
[2011/06/08 11:06] Barrabax Laks: we are very good
[2011/06/08 11:06] Barrabax Laks: they are bad
[2011/06/08 11:06] Nikhil (nikhil.moorsider): lol. yeah Barrabax
[2011/06/08 11:07] Mero (merogigo.baily): **sorry unessl**
[2011/06/08 11:07] Unessl: **Congratulations mero and ulyo**
[2011/06/08 11:07] Barrabax Laks: **accept defeat with a smile: -)))**
[2011/06/08 11:07] Nikhil (nikhil.moorsider): BRAVO!!!!!!

Because Mero had to leave early, I asked Toma to pair with Ulyo instead for the next task. They were tasked to interview their partner about the job they're currently doing in RL and any interesting aspects related to it. I gave each team their Notecard and sent them off to Sky Tables again. I also flew to each floor to monitor their discussion, ensuring that each team was on task (Figure 17.3). Ulyo and Toma's team finished a bit early, so I IMed them to suggest telling their partner more about the job, such as why it's challenging, interesting, and what their dream job is.

After I brought them back to the ground, we were already running out of class time. So I quickly gave them the assignment Notecard for next week and explained how to complete the final project again. Also, I reminded those who are scheduled to do their oral interview this week to please remember to show up on time. Before we left, a couple of students sent me their completed Notecard worksheets for the task in which they interviewed their partner about the job they're doing. Here is the sample of Barrabax's notes on her interview with her partner, Nikhil (see Figure 17.4).

CHAPTER 17
LESSON 7 (JOBS)

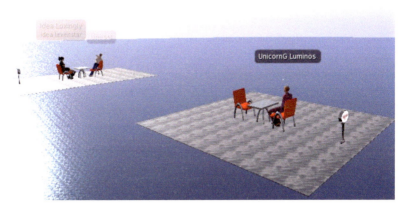

Figure 17.3 My avatar monitoring student pair discussion at the Sky Tables raised on one of the mid-air floors.

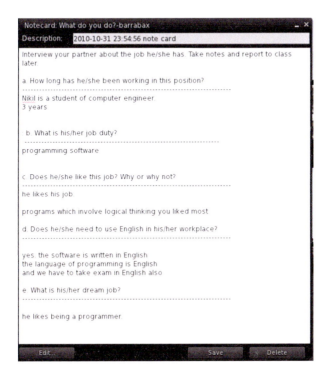

Figure 17.4 Completed notecard worksheet on student pair interview about their partner's current job.

213

Lessons learned:

1. In my view, learning through game play is more effective than conventional rote-drilling because it not only heightens student engagement, but also pushes learners to draw upon their interlanguage resources on the fly. The "positive competitiveness" also adds a fun spin to learning that further stimulates students to produce more language output. In the collaborative gaming discourse, students also find "game-based learning" more goal oriented and meaningful to them because they're competing to secure more points for their team to win the game.

2. Using both voice and text chat modes in SL also facilitates and optimises digital game-based learning. For example, they used voice chat to give out the definition of each job title whilst other teams were typing up the name using text chat. It reinforces the language input/output in dual channels, and it also makes it fair for the host (teacher) to judge which team won the game just because the text chat log would rightfully record the order of answers submitted by any of the teams.

3. Once again, Notecard worksheets really help me as an SL teacher organise my teaching materials and activities. Students at this level still need guided scaffolding to help them stay on task, and a Notecard worksheet does just that (e.g., task instructions). The Notecard function also enables them to input any new information received and ideas exchanged during task interaction. Students might have gotten lost or found it still confusing had I just verbally introduced each task. They still need something more concrete to mediate their thoughts and organise task planning. Indeed, just because it is done online or in SL doesn't mean no structure is needed.

CHECKPOINT

- Why do you think I changed the setting by teleporting them to the Sky Table for group discussion? Is it necessary because they could still discuss in pairs/groups around the class entry site, the Rose Garden? What is the rationale behind this new arrangement?

- Have you done any language games in your class? What is your take on using games for language education and your student reaction to game-based learning? What considerations or concerns would you have when synergising digital game-based learning with SL?
- From the interactionist perspective, the chat log transcript in this lesson sheds light on learner refinement of their language output after being "pushed". For example, I asked a student to "*try to step in to give more information*" about the job title, followed by his reply in text: "*a person who is having a stick in his hand*". If you were conducting a study on CMC or task-based interaction, how would you analyse the language patterns and provide evidence for learner refined output using discourse analysis? Is there any particular SLA model (e.g., negotiation routine, communication strategies) that you would adopt to guide your analysis?

YOUR TASK

- Recreate this job guessing game and pilot it with your students in SL. Depending on the proficiency of your students, you can modify the Notecard worksheet (Figure 17.2) and remember to give each team a different Notecard for them to describe each job tittle. If you are interested in using the Sky Table feature for group discussion, you may also purchase it via SL Marketplace (https://marketplace.secondlife.com/p/Education-Tool-language-learning/790593) and rez (drag) it on any Sandbox ground that allows you to build objects.
- Alternatively, design your own job game to suit the needs and level(s) of your students. Write up a lesson plan for this new game plan and invite a colleague to provide feedback.
- Check in on each team to make sure they are done with defining job titles. Then start the game competition and observe how your students react to their first game-based learning in SL, followed by a focus group or learner journal reflection. If budget allows, give some L$ to the team that won the game, and freebies for the runners-up.

CHAPTER 18

POSTTEST

> ## OVERVIEW
>
> As this virtual class was part of my task-based research, this chapter delineates how the posttest was conducted and evidenced in task-based negotiation among students. Each student pair completed the four communication tasks: *exchanging opinions* ("your opinions about learning English in SL vs. RL"), *jigsaw* ("spot the differences in two pictures"), *information gap* ("follow your partner's instructions to build an object in SL"), and *decision making* ("negotiate with your partner about which gift to buy for a friend's birthday party"). Students' oral outputs were audio/video recorded and screen captured. Research notes were also documented in this chapter.

BLOG POST. TUESDAY, 14 JUNE 2011

This week is the posttest week. I purposefully administered it a week before the final week because I know how unpredictable and cumbersome it will be if I ask them to come back after the course ends. Strategically speaking, it safeguards consistent data collection. To alleviate the negative connotation of a "test", I also indicated that it's the final "oral interview" of completing four tasks rather than taking a posttest.

All in all, I am down to nine students as of now. I've lost around five students due to their RL travel, relocation, and personal business that prevented them from continuing the course. As much as I hate seeing it happen, reality does bite and I just have to "suck it up" with the number of students I have kept for now. In the following, I'll reflect on the feasibility of each task, student task performance, and issues I have noticed in each posttest session this week. They were told to use voice chat only throughout their task completion. There were four tasks for each pair to complete.

- **Task 1: Exchanging opinions** – Your opinions about learning English in SL vs. RL

I asked each pair to share their viewpoints about whether it's better to learn English in SL or RL. They could either agree or disagree with each other, but had to keep the conversation going until I asked them to stop. The purpose for choosing this debatable topic is that I hope to use it as a springboard to spark more conversation because it's quite subjective, which might trigger more negotiated interaction. Their opinions about English learning in these two different environments will also provide a window for me to look into their perceptions about this SL course. This will add another layer of data source within the task itself besides the learning journals, end-of-course survey, and focus group interview.

So far this task has triggered less "negotiation of meaning", surprisingly. Even though students exchanged their opinions about learning English in SL versus RL, they pretty much agreed that SL is more ideal for language learning and has more potential to make English learning fun, interactive, and animated, as well as not following the traditional methods they've been taught in RL. Many students have voiced that they felt they have become more comfortable and less shy when speaking English in SL. Additionally, they have stated that they wouldn't have spent as much time and effort in this SL course as in an RL class where grammar is the main focus and not oral communication. The unique features enabled by SL— such as instantly teleporting to a 3D gallery simulating an RL counterpart, ease of going on multiple field trips in one go, and meeting with friends across cultures— have made SL more suitable for English language learning. The only pair that held different views and debated about their own stance was Unessl and Korobase. Although Unessl also agreed with Korobase on the potential SL can offer for English learning, he also pinpointed the constraints of SL, such as the lack of paralinguistic features when speaking to each other in-world. Interestingly, he further commented that the inhibition of speaking in public with all eyes on the learner, though alleviated in SL, also makes the SL speaking discourse less RL like. Korobase defended by saying that the only disadvantage he has witnessed in SL is the technical glitches, such as the poor voice quality, unstable connection, etc. He backed up his points by using Barrabax's case, witnessing her impressive transformation. He mentioned that Barrabax even told him in Spanish (outside of class) that she initially felt shy and a bit nervous when speaking English in public at the outset of the course. But throughout the course progression, he has witnessed the growing ease and confidence that Barrabax possessed in each of her oral presentations.

Worth noticing is that I found students were more relaxed in this task, as opposed to the second and third ones. They didn't feel pressure to exchange opinions with each other because their partner is the one with whom they've been familiar throughout this course. That said, this task didn't stimulate more negotiation because it didn't require them to reach a common goal, which was the case in task 2 (jigsaw), task 3 (information gap), and task 4 (decision making). Each student in the pair can express their personal opinions without having to reach the consensus. Hence, the opinion exchange task, free from pressing the interlocutor to arrive at the same "decision", doesn't necessarily trigger more negotiation of meaning in the oral discourse.

- **Task 2: Jigsaw** – Spot the differences in two pictures

This task triggered a good deal of negotiation of meaning and use of communication strategies to resolve non(mis)-understandings. Because students already performed a similar task (spot the differences) in their pretest, it's easier to explain to them what this task is about this time around. Each student pair took turns to describe any differences they found in the two pictures in as much detail as possible. Their partner would then use a digital pencil or highlighter to circle those differences. They were also told that there would be six differences for them to spot. The only thing different from the pretest is the two pictures used in this posttest. Rather than being identical as in the pretest, these two posttest pictures were only similar in context, characters, and setting. They were taken as two snapshots whilst I was taking my students to a Berlin bar in the pilot study (Figure 18.1). Additionally, I would like to keep the two tests comparable but not exactly the same to avoid the practice effect. Hence, two ready-made pictures from an RL website (pretest) versus two snapshots of student activities in a Berlin bar in SL (posttest) made the task comparable. The only downside to using not so "identical" pictures in the latter is that students would assume the two images should've been identical like they have experienced in the pretest. But I told

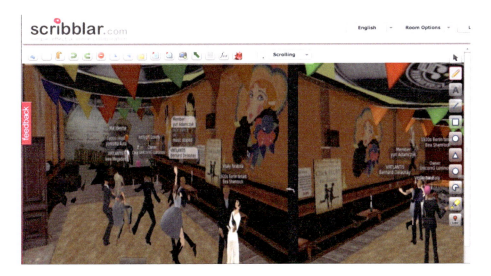

Figure 18.1 Two side-by-side snapshots taken in the Berlin bar in SL for the task of spot-the-differences.

them that it's ok that they're not completely identical as long as they could tell their partner any six differences they could identify in the two pictures. Following TBLT, what really matters is that each pair completes the task by finding those differences together through task interaction and negotiation of meaning.

Because the two pictures are not so identical, they also caused some difficulty in identifying the same differences in both pictures to make their intended meaning understood. The "misunderstanding" or "non-understanding" may sound negative in a normal conversation discourse, but it opens up a viable avenue for students to push more comprehensible output during task interaction. It was evidenced in their use of paraphrasing or communication strategies (e.g., circumlocution or confirmation check) to resolve the communication breakdown. To illustrate, Unessl was trying to tell his partner, Korobase, the first difference he found in one but not in the other picture: "There are two barrels in the left picture, but not in the right one". However, Korobase didn't understand what "barrels" meant, which triggered the hot spot for negotiation of meaning. For Korobase to understand the word, Unessl tried to resolve the non-understanding by describing what a barrel was in much detail: "A barrels is like a container to hold water or wine". Unfortunately, his refined output didn't solve the problem for Korobase, who still raised the red flag by asking him to explain again. As such, Unessl took another strategy to make his description more comprehensible to Korobase. He drew Korobase's attention to the location of the barrels and spoke as slowly and clearly as possible. This strategy finally worked. Korobase finally found it, circled it, and told Unessl that he finally understood what the word barrel meant. It's a perfect example of how a jigsaw task can stimulate more SLA than the opinion exchange task they did earlier.

- **Task 3: Information gap** – Follow your partner's instructions to build an object in SL

This is also another task that triggered a good amount of negotiation of meaning. The task required them to follow their partner's direction to build a 3D object successfully (Figure 18.2). In this task, each student held different pieces of information, which was also a one-way information-gap task. It means that both partners would build two different objects based on the information provided by each other, rather than collectively building the same object. Several considerations were incorporated into the task design to ensure the rigour: (1) The posttest task is an object-building scenario in SL as opposed to following the direction using an RL map; (2) because students are already familiar with the object building (e.g., building a poster), it also strengthened the face validity; (3) it would eliminate the practice effect without having them repeat the same pretest task;

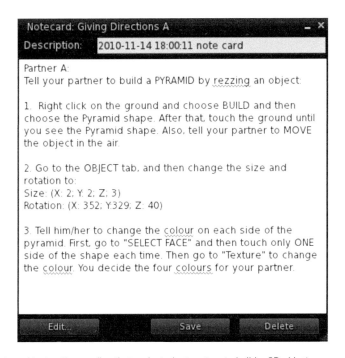

Figure 18.2 Notecard instruction on directing each student partner to build a 3D object.

and (4) although they know how to build, a new building skill (i.e., selecting a face [side] of the shape and adding different colours to each side of the shape) is unfamiliar to them, which would also avoid the practice effect.

This task was quite successful in the way that it kept each pair engaged in building an object by following their partner's instruction. It also provided them with a sense of achievement after creating a new object from scratch. Even though they're familiar with the building feature, the pronunciation of a new shape (e.g., tube versus cube) also caused some misunderstanding, which, however, prompted more negotiation of meaning. For example, Toma told her partner, Barrabax, to build a "tube" but Barrabax misunderstood it as a "cube". So she had to repeat it several times and spoke more slowly, which still didn't get her meaning across, unfortunately. So she used another strategy to explain it, such as "a tube is like a circle but longer". Barrabax didn't get the "longer" part so she just built a ball to show her understanding of a circle. When trying to repeat it several times but still failing to get her meaning across, Toma finally spelled the word "tube" for Barrabax, hoping that she could get it this time. (I'll come back to this part later to provide more examples after listening to the recordings.)

One thing I did regret was that I shouldn't have used text chat to monitor the process of their task completion so frequently. When I saw Toma struggling with explaining the keyword, tube, and it was taking a bit longer on this task, I accidentally spilled the beans by typing up "tube" in public chat rather than using voice chat or IMing Toma to provide further guidance.

The level of student building skills also determined the level of the task difficulty. For example, Korobase was quite skilled in object building so he could follow Unessl's instruction easily. He was also able to direct Unessl to build an object more smoothly than the other pairs. That said, the new building features embedded in this task (i.e., select different faces of the shape to change the colours) also caused difficulty for some students. It also made them not feel confident to give directions after being asked by their partners about where and how to select a face and add a chosen colour. For example, Mero didn't know how to tell her partner to select a face on only one side of the shape, which led to her partner colouring all the faces with only one colour rather than four different colours on each side. To help them complete the task, I had to chime in to demonstrate how to select a face and then change the colour. It might affect the task completion because they did get the assistance from me rather than completing the task all by themselves. It's a dilemma, though, as I couldn't just ignore Mero when she asked me for help. But what I should've done but didn't was to IM Mero to direct her how to do it in private rather than telling her in public whilst her partner was still waiting for her instruction.

- **Task 4: Decision making** – Negotiate with your partner about which gift to buy for a friend's birthday party

Interestingly, I thought this task would also prompt a good amount of negotiation, which, however, didn't appear to be the case as in the previous two tasks. This task was situated in an SL scenario where both paired students would be invited to a classmate's birthday party held in SL. They needed to decide which gift to buy based on two birthday gift advertisements listed on the SL Marketplace. Each of them also had different budget concerns, preferences for choosing an ideal gift, and the time available to meet before returning to their home (Figure 18.3). So they needed to negotiate with each other to reach the consensus. This task was also comparable to that in the pretest in which the scenario of the latter was set in an RL context; that is, they needed to decide at which restaurant to dine based on two authentic RL menus.

Based on my observation, I think that the task conditions could've been more negotiable or challenging to the students. For example, student A only got a tight budget (L$400) and they

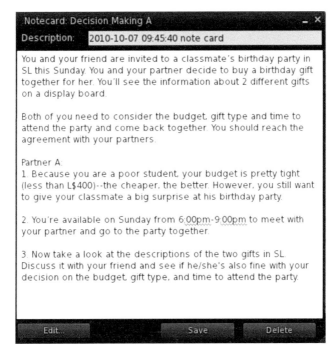

Figure 18.3 Notecard instruction on deciding on which gift to buy for a friend's birthday party held in SL.

had to choose either the gift (birthday party set) at L$5 (Figure 18.4) or the other one (deluxe firework party cake) at L$390. I'd have made the former (L$5) a bit more expensive because it has more perks than the L$390 one, despite its cheaper price. Most students found it "cheap and cheerful" after comparing the descriptions of the two gifts. As such, it left little room for negotiation as it's a no brainer to choose the cheaper one with more perks. I wonder if it would have triggered more negotiation if I had switched the prices for both gifts.

Despite this task requiring them to reach the same decision on which gift to buy and when to meet, students were quite respectful to each other. I'd have thought this task should have prompted more negotiation as the previous two, but they'd compromise with their partner without sticking firmly to their own decision. Unlike this decision-making task, the jigsaw (task 2) or information gap (task 3) didn't require them to express their own opinions to make the same decision. Both tasks were more "convergent" or "closed-ended" as the ultimate target had been made clear to them; that is, spot six differences or build an object instructed by a partner. There was not much leeway for them to express their own decision or to compromise with each other.

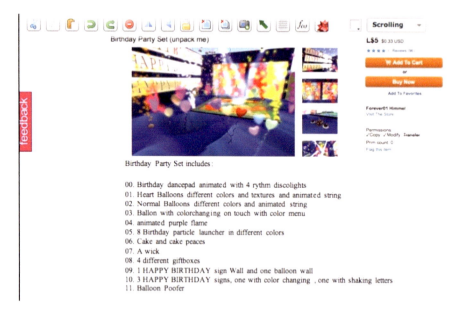

Figure 18.4 Birthday party set (L$5) listed on the SL marketplace for student pairs to decide on buying for their SL friend.

Lessons learned:

1. I found that text chat is a useful communication mode to complement voice-based task interaction when communication breakdown occurs. Students switched to the text chat mode as an alternative to resolve the misunderstanding by spelling out the word or typing up the definitions. Given that voice-based interaction is the main focus of the study, I reminded them to use voice chat only. However, they found it a bit challenging without resorting to the text chat mode as a strategic mechanism to get meaning across. Consequently, this "constraint" "pushed" them to tap into another communication strategy or multimodal resource to resolve communication breakdown via voice chat.

2. Different from the pretest tasks that were contextualised in RL, the task scenarios in the posttest were all set up in SL. The face validity, hence, was strengthened because students by now should've been familiar with all the activities and tasks conducted in SL. Task design that transitioned from RL-based materials and scenarios (pretest) to SL-based ones (posttest) was research sound and practically

feasible as it considered the logical task sequencing and task conditions whilst minimising the practice effect.
3. Compared with the pretest, their task performance this time was better in terms of quality and quantity. Perhaps they felt less nervous after having immersed themselves in SL throughout the course, or perhaps they're already familiar with their partners. Overall, they seemed more comfortable and less inhibited in speaking throughout the task completion. For example, when reflecting on her task experience in both tests, Barrabax, the less proficient student, felt that she became more confident in using English to interact with her partner in the posttest tasks. Because the posttest tasks were new and comparable to the pretest ones, I'd argue that she did exhibit her progress in speaking, evidenced in her improved task performance and gained confidence by the end of the course. However, I need to provide more solid evidence after analysing the quality and quantity of their oral recordings to prove that TBLT in SL does make a difference in learners' SLA. At this stage, I am curious to know how the quality and quantity in their task negotiation and communication strategy use would differ from the pretest to posttest.
4. Generally speaking, the four tasks were effectively designed and executed, except that I could have "intervened" less and the task condition in decision making should have been modified to increase the task complexity. More negotiation of meaning would have been triggered in this case. Well, what is done is done. I could only analyse what I have got this time. When writing up the report, I will make sure to identify limitations before making suggestions for future research.
5. I have been thinking about the issue of "teacher effect", which will be addressed in the limitations section. Folks will argue that the effect that student participants are motivated in class is due mainly to my "passion" or "deliberate commitment" to make each SL session engaging and interesting to them. I have also been quite attentive to their needs or concerns. Not all SL teachers could have the same level of commitment as I have because this free SL course is also research-bearing and integral to my study. These confounding factors might result in student willingness to participate more actively in class, such as the "Hawthorne effect" (participants felt positive about being included in this research study) or the "Halo effect" (they're working harder to please me). Though I don't disagree that my presence as their teacher researcher might have led to these effects, the participant attrition rate in this study proves otherwise; they didn't stay in the

course till the end just because of me or the course. Also, students were quite candid in their journal postings about their attitudes towards or feelings about each SL session and the course. Some also made negative comments about using SL for language learning. Therefore, the counterarguments that I just provided suggest that the researcher bias be alleviated. Truthfully, students were motivated not by my presence, but by the engaging and meaningful task design, immersive simulation afforded by SL, and, above all, were inspired by peer commitment to task performance and the supportive virtual community of practice.

CHECKPOINT

- I purposefully situated pretest tasks in RL-related themes, and posttest tasks in SL-related scenarios. What is the rationale of making this task comparison and design? What are the pros and cons of this research design?
- No research is perfect as we can always find limitations and room for improvement. For example, I identified the flaws in my last task (decision making) where the cheaper gift set (L$5) should have been more expensive given more features included in the set than the other one (L$390). As such, the task complexity was compromised and led to less negotiation of meaning. How would you tackle this constraint in your research design? Would you modify the task and ask your participants to redo it?
- I pinpointed both the Hawthorne effect and Halo effect in my reflection and justified how I considered and addressed them. Look at your own study and try to identify some confounding factors as well. Explain to your colleague how you would minimise these effects.
- In the posttest, both audio and video recordings of student task performance were gathered for data analysis. Additionally, text chat logs were also recorded. Given the nature of multimodality, what type of data analysis tool and approach would you adopt in this posttest? How would you provide evidence for task-based negotiation through triangulation of these different modes?

YOUR TASK

- Although today's blog entry is quite research driven and focused on the posttest, the four tasks are pedagogy oriented and applicable to language teaching. Based on my previous task descriptions and outcomes, first discuss with a colleague each task type (opinion exchange, jigsaw, information gap, decision making) regarding its task complexity, task condition, required SL skills and features, and potential for SLA to take place.
- Then pick any task type that interests you and replicate it in your SL class. Alternatively, adapt it to suit the needs and proficiency levels of your students. If time permits, you may replicate the four tasks and see if similar task performances and outcomes would also take place.
- Remember to audio and video record each task session and take observation notes on what works and what does not during student task interaction. Invite students for a focus group interview to share their thoughts about performing these communicative tasks using SL features, and how each task type pushes them to negotiate meaning with their partner.

CHAPTER 19

LESSON 8 (TRAVEL & FAREWELL PARTY)

OVERVIEW

This is the final lesson of the SL course. Students acted on the role as a tour guide and teleported the class to an SL destination that simulated a famous tourist attraction in their home country. It also served as a summative task to gauge their overall performance throughout this course. We virtually toured around the "world" in one class time, from Alhambra in Spain, to the Nile River in Egypt, Mont Saint-Michel in France, and the Grand Canyon National Park in the United States. The class ended with a touching ceremony during which each student received a 3D certificate customised by me in honouring their completion of the task-based course in SL.

BLOG POST. THURSDAY, 16 JUNE 2011

This is the last lesson before the course comes to an end. Students were assigned a project where they took on the role as a tour guide in SL. They needed to find a SIM in SL that simulates either a tourist spot or famous landmark in their country in RL. After that, they would take us to the SIM they found and convince us that it's worth visiting by informing and entertaining us. The purpose of doing this task is to give each student the chance to promote their home culture to the class. Hopefully we will be motivated by their tour guiding to visit the RL place in the future. This project also served as an exit task to evaluate whether students could apply what they'd learned throughout the whole course. The following is the outline of this summative task.

- Find an appropriate SIM via the Search tool in SL or by word of mouth through your avatar contacts.
- Do further research on the chosen place/tourist attraction on the web.
- Prepare delivering the content information in comprehensible English.
- Plan how to guide the tour professionally as if you were really an RL tour guide.
- Be attentive to your customers' feedback.
- Convince us that the introduced place is worth visiting in RL.

There were three students (Barrabax, Emelie, and Mero) who did their tour guiding on Monday. Originally, other students who were present that day (Ulyo and Unessl) were supposed to tour guide but they privately IMed me that they'd like to wait until Wednesday's session to have more time to prepare for their presentation. It seems that the "positive peer pressure" became the driving force to stimulate students to invest more time and effort in their own presentation.

So Barrabax took the lead to be our first guide, and teleported us to the SIM, *Alhambra*. What pleasantly surprised me was that Alhambra, a magnificent palace built in the 14th century, is actually located in her hometown of Granada in Spain. When asked if this breath-taking SIM looks similar to the real Alhambra in Granada, Barrabax replied that it's pretty similar. In fact, she was also amazed by the resemblance of this virtual palace to the real Alhambra palace in her hometown when doing her SL search for this project. Although Barrabax did a nice job touring us around from place to place and introducing us to the history and anecdotes of Alhambra (Figure 19.1), the serious lagging in this SIM also made avatar movements difficult. I could barely move around or catch up with her when she asked us to follow closely. I had to log off and back in again with hopes of resolving the issue. Nevertheless, the issue of lagging still persisted so I didn't quite fully take advantage of her guided tour as I'd hoped. This also happened to some students, such as Nikhil. After her tour, I asked students to raise some questions for her. It's good to see that Barrabax was very attentive to everyone's needs and tried to address our questions even if she didn't know the answer or words in English sometimes.

Next, Emelie teleported us to another SIM, IDEA. The SIM looked pretty much the same to RL IKEA – the layout, design, furniture, etc. Because Emelie is a student at a university

Figure 19.1 My avatar flying above the Alhambra Palace SIM guided by a student.

Figure 19.2 Student tour guide introducing the SIM that was a replica of IKEA in RL.

in Sweden from which IKEA originates, it makes sense that she also chose this Swedish furniture brand for her tour project. Despite her poor voice quality, which compromised our understanding, she still did her job well by introducing the concept of IKEA and how it was spread all over the world (Figure 19.2). But I sensed that Emelie might get a bit discouraged because she was trying very hard to deliver her speech but that backfired because of the less satisfactory sound quality for which she kept apologising. As such, she didn't talk for too long and finished her tour quickly. I suppose she didn't want to cause too much inconvenience by asking us to listen to her. That said, she still did a decent job answering all the questions we raised about IKEA and used public chat to address them. She also handled the questions pretty well, showing that she's knowledgeable about the IKEA SIM as a professional tour guide. We also had a very productive discussion on whether IKEA could be found in other countries where my students come from. Despite the voice issue, her tour did motivate the whole class to visit the real IKEA close to their home in RL. Interestingly, another student, Unessl, who is also a student in the same school as Emelie, had never been to an IKEA store even though he's in Sweden. He got motivated by Emelie's introduction of IKEA and he said he'd like to visit IKEA in Sweden soon (see the following chat transcript). It's more evidence of how immersive learning amplified by SIM can motivate students to action it in RL.

[2011/06/13 11:01] Emelie Crystal: feel free to sit down behind you:)
[2011/06/13 11:01] Mero (merogigo.baily): i love ikea
[2011/06/13 11:01] UnicornG Luminos: love their furniture design
[2011/06/13 11:02] Mero (merogigo.baily): me too

[2011/06/13 11:03] Unessl: I cannot hear Emelie clearly
[2011/06/13 11:03] Emelie Crystal: i am so sorry
[2011/06/13 11:03] Barrabax Laks: put the mic farther, please
[2011/06/13 11:03] Emelie Crystal: I have tried to fix it but there is nothing I can do
[2011/06/13 11:04] Unessl: ok, carry on pls... sorry for interruption
[2011/06/13 11:05] Emelie Crystal: I am so sorry about the sound
[2011/06/13 11:05] Emelie Crystal: I will type the answers:)
[2011/06/13 11:06] Barrabax Laks: i like this shop very much too
[2011/06/13 11:07] Emelie Crystal: yes in 44 different countries
[2011/06/13 11:07] Barrabax Laks: not in GRanada: -(
[2011/06/13 11:07] Mero (merogigo.baily): but i live in saudi
[2011/06/13 11:07] Mero (merogigo.baily): there is ikea
[2011/06/13 11:08] Emelie Crystal:: (I will tell Ingvar to build one in Egypt lol
[2011/06/13 11:08] Mero (merogigo.baily): thanks emelie
[2011/06/13 11:09] Unessl: I did not understand the relation between IKEA and IDEA. Would you please enlighten this, again?
[2011/06/13 11:09] Emelie Crystal: They didi not have IKEA here because of copyright
[2011/06/13 11:10] Mero (merogigo.baily): i think because they have wonderful ideas
[2011/06/13 11:10] Emelie Crystal: but it is basically the same... the same colours
[2011/06/13 11:10] UnicornG Luminos: logo
[2011/06/13 11:10] Unessl: and you mentioned sth about Sweden, what was that again?
[2011/06/13 11:11] Emelie Crystal: the first one build was in Sweden
[2011/06/13 11:11] Unessl: ok, I see
[2011/06/13 11:11] Emelie Crystal: quite close to my hometown
[2011/06/13 11:11] Emelie Crystal: 1943 was the IKEA started
[2011/06/13 11:12] Barrabax Laks: simple and functional design
[2011/06/13 11:12] Mero (merogigo.baily): yes barrabas
[2011/06/13 11:12] Unessl: Because I am here in Sweden right now, and it is the first time I am hearing the word IDEA
[2011/06/13 11:13] Unessl: we have IKEA here not IDEA
[2011/06/13 11:13] Mero (merogigo.baily): u have to visit it unesssl
[2011/06/13 11:13] ulyo Genesis: Ikea is a wonderful success company
[2011/06/13 11:13] Unessl: thanks for your suggestion Mero
[2011/06/13 11:13] Emelie Crystal::) great:) have some meatballs
[2011/06/13 11:13] Unessl: it is really tempting
[2011/06/13 11:14] Unessl: great job

Figure 19.3 Student tour guide introducing the SIM of Nile River and Egyptian ferrymen to the class.

[2011/06/13 11:14] Emelie Crystal: so sorry for the sound
[2011/06/13 11:14] Unessl: no worries about the voice
[2011/06/13 11:14] Barrabax Laks: dont worry:)

Mero's tour was the highlight of Monday's lesson. Because she's from Egypt, she took us to the SIM of the *Nile River* with a boat ferried by two Egyptian men, dressed as servants working for a Pharaoh (Figure 19.3). Mero was very well-prepared as she talked about why she chose this SIM rather than a typical pyramid (she had done it already in the gallery project). Then she introduced to us how important the Nile River is to Egypt, and what we can do and see and where to stay near Cairo. It's like she's really an Egyptian tour guide who was trying to sell the tour package to all the customers (see the following chat transcript). She was also quite comfortable when speaking and had great confidence in her speech. She later told me that she felt proud to showcase Egypt to the class as its cultural ambassador and enjoyed being a tour guide that day.

[2011/06/13 11:15] Barrabax Laks: ohhhhh
[2011/06/13 11:18] UnicornG Luminos: Nile river
[2011/06/13 11:18] UnicornG Luminos: pls take a picture of me, Nihil: -)
[2011/06/13 11:19] Nikhil (nikhil.moorsider): k
[2011/06/13 11:20] UnicornG Luminos: good promotion of Egypt, Mero!
[2011/06/13 11:20] UnicornG Luminos: Emelie, Barrabax... u can be on board

[2011/06/13 11:21] UnicornG Luminos: Unessl seems to love this boat that he doesn't want to get off it lol
[2011/06/13 11:21] Unessl: ha ha, I hope this can give me a ride
[2011/06/13 11:22] Barrabax Laks: interesting… thanks very much
[2011/06/13 11:23] ulyo Genesis: nice job
[2011/06/13 11:23] Unessl: How much does it cost to go to Egypt?
[2011/06/13 11:23] Unessl: from Sweden?
[2011/06/13 11:23] Emelie Crystal: it is not that expensive
[2011/06/13 11:24] Emelie Crystal: 3700 with hotel
[2011/06/13 11:24] Unessl: so how cheap is the accommodation, then?
[2011/06/13 11:24] Unessl: what about the weather?
[2011/06/13 11:27] Barrabax Laks: diverse
[2011/06/13 11:27] UnicornG Luminos: good word, Barrabax
[2011/06/13 11:27] UnicornG Luminos: haha, desert: -p
[2011/06/13 11:27] UnicornG Luminos: only using camels to travel
[2011/06/13 11:28] Unessl: good question
[2011/06/13 11:28] Mero (merogigo.baily): thanks really:)

The rest of the students did their tour guiding in Wednesday's session. Because Korobase needed to leave early for his RL business, he took the lead and teleported us to the SIM where he usually trains teachers how to use different applications of technology for their SL teaching. He explained to us that he didn't have time to search for a SIM that represents his home country due to his recently added RL commitments. That's why he'd like to take the liberty of introducing his workplace to us. Again, Korobase was born to be a teacher trainer. He walked us through this SIM and demonstrated each facility (paintings, interactive board) and animated objects (using colour chalk to highlight different parts of a horse). As generous as Korobase is always to the class, he gave away the animated horse gift as a token of appreciation for completing the course with his classmates. It's also amazing to see all the artwork displayed by Korobase in his workplace, oozing his multifaceted talent that never ceases to impress us. Finally, he took us to an auditorium and introduced us to some other creative work that he did for training teachers. A lot of students commented that they felt as if they were in a real class because of the RL-like SIM (see the following chat transcript). Again, it proves that SL can augment reality and bring RL to life.

[2011/06/15 10:21] Nikhil (nikhil.moorsider): OK I am ready for class
[2011/06/15 10:22] Unessl: these seats are really comfortable

[2011/06/15 10:22]   UnicornG Luminos:: -)
[2011/06/15 10:22]   UnicornG Luminos: it's like we're in the auditorium: -)
[2011/06/15 10:22]   Unessl: Indeed
[2011/06/15 10:23]   Toma Remex: like real class
[2011/06/15 10:23]   UnicornG Luminos: exactly, Toma and Unessl
[2011/06/15 10:23]   Nikhil (nikhil.moorsider): this is fantastic virtual class room
[2011/06/15 10:26]   Unessl: what is your field of study, then?
[2011/06/15 10:26]   Unessl: what do you do for living?
[2011/06/15 10:27]   Barrabax Laks: your job
[2011/06/15 10:27]   Unessl: ok I see
[2011/06/15 10:28]   Unessl: thanks
[2011/06/15 10:28]   Profesor Korobase: www.artigraf.com
[2011/06/15 10:29]   Unessl: thanks a lot
[2011/06/15 10:29]   Idea Loxingly (idea.lexenstar): ***** AAAPPPLLLAAAUUUSSSSEEE***
[2011/06/15 10:29]   Barrabax Laks: fanstastic
[2011/06/15 10:29]   Nikhil (nikhil.moorsider): BRAVO!!!!!!

Next, Ulyo took us to a very beautiful SIM, *Mont Saint-Michel*, which is a famous scenic spot we can also find in France. As much as I hoped to enjoy the tour, we also encountered a serious lagging issue in this SIM. I found it hard to move around and catch up with Ulyo when he asked us to follow him. Although I asked Barrabax to teleport me back on and off, I still felt a bit behind his tour. Also, Ulyo was so focused on his talk that he forgot to address some questions raised by us. That said, he was very well prepared and took us to as many places as possible in the SIM of Mont Saint-Michel. He also talked about the historical facts and interesting stories about each place throughout his tour guiding. Despite the lagging, all the students were mesmerised by this ethereal setting and praised him for his well-done job as shown in the chat transcript.

[2011/06/15 10:35]   ulyo Genesis: 1434
[2011/06/15 10:36]   Unessl: La porte de la france?
[2011/06/15 10:36]   ulyo Genesis: 1435
[2011/06/15 10:36]   UnicornG Luminos: Ulyo, Unessl was typing a question
[2011/06/15 10:36]   ulyo Genesis: drawbridge
[2011/06/15 10:36]   ulyo Genesis: 1492
[2011/06/15 10:43]   Idea Loxingly (idea.lexenstar): nice for shopping ^^
[2011/06/15 10:50]   ulyo Genesis: Marvel

[2011/06/15 10:51] UnicornG Luminos: it's so spectacular!
[2011/06/15 10:52] UnicornG Luminos: Ulyo, u only have 2 minutes to go
[2011/06/15 10:54] ulyo Genesis: Bruno de Senne ville
[2011/06/15 10:55] UnicornG Luminos: guys, questions??
[2011/06/15 10:55] Nikhil (nikhil.moorsider): fantastic
[2011/06/15 10:55] Emelie Crystal: really interesting well done
[2011/06/15 10:55] Barrabax Laks: is a pretty land, Ulyo
[2011/06/15 10:55] Nikhil (nikhil.moorsider): very well prepared
[2011/06/15 10:55] Unessl: very nice Ulyo
[2011/06/15 10:55] Unessl: where in France?
[2011/06/15 10:56] ulyo Genesis: In the east north of France
[2011/06/15 10:56] ulyo Genesis: Le Mont Saint Michel
[2011/06/15 10:56] Unessl: ok I see
[2011/06/15 10:57] ulyo Genesis: Rouen Caen
[2011/06/15 10:58] Nikhil (nikhil.moorsider): BRAVO!!!!!!
[2011/06/15 10:58] Barrabax Laks: *****APLAAAAAUSOOOOOOOOOOOOS*****
[2011/06/15 10:58] Unessl: Thnaks Ulyo, good job!

Idea and Nikhil's tour was the highlight of today's lesson. They worked together as two professional tour guides who took us to the *Grand Canyon* in SL! It's a perfect example of evidence that students don't need to spend money on expensive travels to experience what the Grand Canyon is like! We could easily teleport there in a second and enjoyed as many facilities in the SIM of the Grand Canyon escorted by our tour guides. Idea originally asked us to join the group CALL so that it would be easier for her to guide us. But Emelie seemed to have trouble configuring the group CALL so we ended up using both the voice chat and public chat as usual. They took turns showing us what we could see in the actual Grand Canyon National Park and why it's worth visiting. We actually accessed (animated) all the facilities in the SIM and had great fun, including skydiving, helicoptering, camping, and seeing rocks falling from the hill, as well as shooting and biking. Student laughter over immersive simulation was propelled by Idea and Nikhil's organised and engaging tour! It was as if they had been doing this job in the National Park for years. I also noticed that Nikhil was more relaxed and confident when he was leading the tour, as opposed to being shy as he sometimes was in the previous sessions. Idea was even more confident and seemed to have genuinely enjoyed her tour guiding with Nikhil. I couldn't be prouder of them both after witnessing the palpable growth in their increasing confidence and oral presentation skills! The following chat transcript says it all.

CHAPTER 19
LESSON 8 (TRAVEL & FAREWELL PARTY)

[2011/06/15 10:59] Emelie Crystal: wow i always wanted to go here
[2011/06/15 11:04] Lisisme Dubrovna: Hello and Welcome to the Grand canyon
[2011/06/15 11:04] ulyo Genesis: click on New group with Unicorn and then click call
[2011/06/15 11:04] Lisisme Dubrovna: WE hope you will join our Group also.
[2011/06/15 11:04] Barrabax Laks: We are a group of English students
[2011/06/15 11:04] Lisisme Dubrovna: wonderful, there is much to see and do here
[2011/06/15 11:07] ~JD~ MTF Shooting Gallery 1.0: Nikhil Moorsider prepare for game…
[2011/06/15 11:07] ~JD~ MTF Flintlock Shooting Gallery Toy 1.15: Detaching… no JD MTF Shooting Gallery was detected
[2011/06/15 11:08] Unessl: nice shot
[2011/06/15 11:08] ulyo Genesis: i would like to try
[2011/06/15 11:08] ~JD~ MTF Shooting Gallery 1.0: TOTAL TARGETS: 24
[2011/06/15 11:08] ~JD~ MTF Shooting Gallery 1.0: TOTAL HITS: 0
[2011/06/15 11:09] UnicornG Luminos: wow, first nation people
[2011/06/15 11:09] UnicornG Luminos: they got their totem poles
[2011/06/15 11:10] Idea Loxingly: https://grandcanyonguru.com/grand-canyon-destinations
[2011/06/15 11:12] My Tip Jar: Thank you for the donation, Barrabax Laks!
[2011/06/15 11:12] Emelie Crystal: amazing
[2011/06/15 11:12] UnicornG Luminos: gracias!!
[2011/06/15 11:12] Barrabax Laks::)
[2011/06/15 11:13] SEmotion Pleasure 01: UnicornG Luminos, say '/1 Hide' to hide me, or '/1 Show' to make me show. Or just right-click and sit on me to use me.
[2011/06/15 11:14] UnicornG Luminos: colorado river
[2011/06/15 11:15] Helicopter C700 COLA Gun V6.4 test: Click me for Menu
[2011/06/15 11:15] Barrabax Laks: i dont want to dieeeee
[2011/06/15 11:15] Emelie Crystal::)
[2011/06/15 11:15] Barrabax Laks: help helppp
[2011/06/15 11:16] Unessl: I do not like to fly
[2011/06/15 11:16] Helicopter C700 COLA Gun V6.4 test: Click me for Menu
[2011/06/15 11:16] Barrabax Laks: jajajaja
[2011/06/15 11:16] Unessl: ha ha
[2011/06/15 11:16] UnicornG Luminos: JUmP!!
[2011/06/15 11:16] Idea Loxingly (idea.lexenstar): click stand to helicopter
[2011/06/15 11:16] UnicornG Luminos: whew
[2011/06/15 11:16] Barrabax Laks: I do not trust unicorn
[2011/06/15 11:16] Unessl: control tower do not let Unicorn to take off lol

[2011/06/15 11:16] Unessl: ha ha
[2011/06/15 11:16] UnicornG Luminos: u're bad, Unessl
[2011/06/15 11:18] UnicornG Luminos: i'd like to do a spa
[2011/06/15 11:18] UnicornG Luminos: so relaxing
[2011/06/15 11:19] Barrabax Laks: i want to duck
[2011/06/15 11:19] Terra Skydiving Pod 2.0 (temp): Altitude set to 3000 meters.
[2011/06/15 11:19] Terra Skydiving Pod 2.0 (temp): Altitude set to 206 meters.
[2011/06/15 11:19] Terra Skydiving Pod 2.0 (temp): Launch!
[2011/06/15 11:19] Barrabax Laks: are brave eh?
[2011/06/15 11:19] Terra Skydiving Pod 2.0 (temp): Get ready...
[2011/06/15 11:20] Terra Skydiving Pod 2.0 (temp): 3...
[2011/06/15 11:20] Terra Skydiving Pod 2.0 (temp): 2...
[2011/06/15 11:20] Terra Skydiving Pod 2.0 (temp): 1...
[2011/06/15 11:20] Terra Skydiving Pod 2.0 (temp): GO! GO! GO!
[2011/06/15 11:20] Emelie Crystal: wow
[2011/06/15 11:20] UnicornG Luminos: skydiving
[2011/06/15 11:20] UnicornG Luminos: are we going to die
[2011/06/15 11:20] UnicornG Luminos: no parachute?
[2011/06/15 11:21] UnicornG Luminos: so much fun
[2011/06/15 11:22] UnicornG Luminos: indeed, it's so extraordinary
[2011/06/15 11:22] Conover's Cannonball 0.1: Please wait, adjusting cannonball...
[2011/06/15 11:22] Conover's Cannonball 0.1: 5...
[2011/06/15 11:22] Conover's Cannonball 0.1: 4...
[2011/06/15 11:22] Conover's Cannonball 0.1: 3...
[2011/06/15 11:22] Conover's Cannonball 0.1: 2...
[2011/06/15 11:22] Conover's Cannonball 0.1: 1...
[2011/06/15 11:22] Conover's Cannonball 0.1: 0...
[2011/06/15 11:22] Conover's Cannonball 0.1: BOOOOOM!!!!
[2011/06/15 11:24] Barrabax Laks: i am aliveee
[2011/06/15 11:24] UnicornG Luminos: yes, national park
[2011/06/15 11:26] Sportboat 230 Wake V1.2 blue test: Speed: 2
[2011/06/15 11:26] Sportboat 230 Wake V1.2 blue test: Click me for Menu
[2011/06/15 11:27] Sportboat 230 Wake V1.2 blue test: Speed 1
[2011/06/15 11:27] Idea Loxingly (idea.lexenstar): http://maps.secondlife.com/secondlife/Grand%20Canyon/85/243/23
[2011/06/15 11:29] Barrabax Laks: a fun place

[2011/06/15 11:30] Unessl: you are killing us here
[2011/06/15 11:30] Barrabax Laks: jajaja
[2011/06/15 11:30] Toma Remex: haha
[2011/06/15 11:31] Unessl: I guess I lost my memory due to the stones hit my head
[2011/06/15 11:31] Barrabax Laks: *****APLAAAAAUSOOOOOOOOOOOOS*****
[2011/06/15 11:31] ulyo Genesis: I landmarked it
[2011/06/15 11:32] Unessl: it was very nice

Because Toma is from Saudi Arabia, she took us to the *Arabian Empire*, a SIM that is the replica of Arabic culture, buildings, and customs. She took us from one place to another in the SIM and talked about what each place actually represents in the Arabian world. However, she stayed in each place for a pretty short time and spoke a bit too fast so I had to ask her to repeat herself sometimes. Nevertheless, all the class seemed impressed by this exotic and breath-taking SIM in SL (see the following chat transcript). She later told me that she thought it was hard to find a SIM that represented her Arabic culture in SL, but was pleasantly surprised that she was able to locate one and to introduce her home culture to the class.

[2011/06/15 11:33] Barrabax Laks: beautiful placeee
[2011/06/15 11:34] *TRADITIONAL BISHT gray: Right click and Choose 'Pay'
[2011/06/15 11:37] Barrabax Laks: the camel looks bad Unicorn
[2011/06/15 11:37] UnicornG Luminos: ha
[2011/06/15 11:37] AMOONRA (semsem.nexen): stop
[2011/06/15 11:37] AMOONRA (semsem.nexen): who r u ppl
[2011/06/15 11:37] Barrabax Laks: no have money
[2011/06/15 11:38] AMOONRA (semsem.nexen)::)
[2011/06/15 11:38] Toma Remex: sorry we r english class people
[2011/06/15 11:38] UnicornG Luminos: Toma, pls continue
[2011/06/15 11:38] AMOONRA (semsem.nexen): ~','','Oh.kay.kay.kay',',''~
[2011/06/15 11:39] UnicornG Luminos: is this a house?
[2011/06/15 11:39] Barrabax Laks: a tent
[2011/06/15 11:40] holy (qutsal.alex): shouts: seninkilerde gelir birazdan makya-jƒ±nƒ± tazele
[2011/06/15 11:40] URA Kombat: shouts: Fulya Fang has been defeated by semsem Nexen
[2011/06/15 11:41] UnicornG Luminos: what kind of game, Toma
[2011/06/15 11:41] Barrabax Laks: a combat sim

239

[2011/06/15 11:43] Idea Loxingly (idea.lexenstar): nice; -)
[2011/06/15 11:45] UnicornG Luminos: is it a typical Arabic house
[2011/06/15 11:45] UnicornG Luminos: i mean the interior design
[2011/06/15 11:45] Barrabax Laks: the tiles is similar to the wall ¬¥s Alhambra
[2011/06/15 11:45] UnicornG Luminos: right, B
[2011/06/15 11:46] UnicornG Luminos: Toma, u have 2 minutes to go
[2011/06/15 11:46] Barrabax Laks: in the arab house there aren't a lot of furniture
[2011/06/15 11:46] UnicornG Luminos: i c…wow, u know a lot of abrabic stuff
[2011/06/15 11:46] Barrabax Laks: ajajaja
[2011/06/15 11:47] prision cell: Sorry Idea Lexenstar, this door is locked
[2011/06/15 11:47] UnicornG Luminos: what's the canal again
[2011/06/15 11:48] UnicornG Luminos: can u type it
[2011/06/15 11:48] Barrabax Laks: carries the water
[2011/06/15 11:48] UnicornG Luminos: ya, some description here
[2011/06/15 11:49] UnicornG Luminos: on the wall
[2011/06/15 11:49] UnicornG Luminos: i think we're running out of the time
[2011/06/15 11:49] UnicornG Luminos: any question for Toma?
[2011/06/15 11:50] UnicornG Luminos: good question
[2011/06/15 11:50] ulyo Genesis: wonderful job
[2011/06/15 11:50] Idea Loxingly (idea.lexenstar): so interesting
[2011/06/15 11:50] UnicornG Luminos: what's the name of this place
[2011/06/15 11:50] Barrabax Laks: arabian empire
[2011/06/15 11:50] UnicornG Luminos: is it similar to what we can see in Saudi Arabia?
[2011/06/15 11:51] Unessl: ok I see. thank you so much
[2011/06/15 11:52] UnicornG Luminos: exotic
[2011/06/15 11:52] Barrabax Laks: thanks:))
[2011/06/15 11:52] Toma Remex::)

Unessl was the last tour guide of the today. He had a hard time finding a SIM that represented Iranian culture. Even though I suggested he reach out to some Iranian groups in SL or use different keywords (tourist sites in Iran) through the SL search, he still couldn't find a SIM. Eventually, he found one that displayed all kinds of Persian carpets. From his tour guiding, we could tell that he was very well prepared to introduce to us the origin, history, anecdotes, weaving style, textures, and patterns of Persian carpets. While quite informative in content delivery, it sounded a bit scripted, as if Unessl was just reading from his notes. However, he still delivered it professionally and handled the questions raised by us very well.

To wrap up today's lesson, I gave each one of them their personalised certificate to acknowledge their participation, commitment, and performance throughout the whole 10-session SL course (Figure 19.4). It was quite emotional because we couldn't believe that time really flew so fast and that it was our last session. They all expressed their gratitude but felt sad about the end of the course. I thanked them for being there with me till the end and told them that we are more than just teacher and students, but partners in crime given a supportive virtual community we have built in-world. I encouraged them to keep in touch with each other and continue practising English and having fun in SL. Although all good things

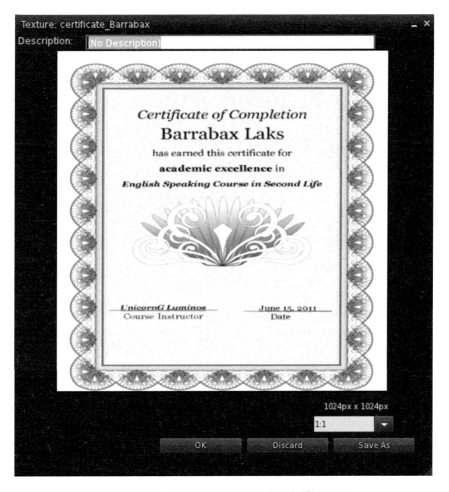

Figure 19.4 Digital certificate awarded to students who completed the full SL course.

must come to an end, our SL friendship remains. I think we've all learned a lot from and were inspired by each other. The ending is just another way to start a new beginning: our SL paths will cross again soon!

Finally, my dissertation research would not have been made possible without the following student participants who graciously devoted their time and effort to my official SL study, and above all, took a leap of faith with me. For that, I will always be indebted to y'all (Figure 19.5)!

Figure 19.5 Collage of all the student avatars who participated in the SL course.

Lessons learned:

1. TBLT has proven to be a beneficial teaching approach, especially when it's implemented in SL. When being "tasked", students find their own voice and develop a sense of autonomy and responsibility for their own learning. They sense that they need to speak and work like professionals in the assigned task to deliver accurate and useful information to their audience. Specifically, TBLT will be strengthened if enacted in a subject domain that is meaningful, engaging, authentic, and collaborative. For example, the final task that required them to take on the leading role as a local tour guide epitomised TBLT. Not only did the task itself resonate with the student participants (i.e., finding a SIM that enabled them to promote their home culture to the class), but it allowed them to see the personalised connection between doing an authentic task in SL and the potential of actually promoting the tourist site and home culture to foreigners visiting their country in RL. Additionally, a unique feature in SL, augmented reality and immersive simulation, makes performing the task even more RL like, thus leading to their heightened motivation and engagement. Who would have thought that we could travel to the Grand Canyon for shooting, camping, skydiving, or to the Nile River for boarding a boat ferried by ancient Egyptian ferryman?! The truth is: all of this could happen by simply teleporting there in a second without having to spend even a penny on traveling. I wonder if we could have done it had the same lesson been carried out in an RL class.
2. Even though students were well prepared for their final task as tour guides, some seemed to have followed the script too closely. I'd have reminded them in advance not to read from the notes but speak spontaneously as if talking to their clients in RL. I'd also have drawn their attention to the fact that one of the duties of being a tour guide is to engage and entertain their customers without sounding too scripted.
3. Acknowledging student achievement in and commitment to the course is a perfect way to take a bow. I'm glad that I did it this time, thanks to the valuable suggestion of Valery, a student in my pilot study. My students seemed quite delighted to receive the certificate as a token of appreciation for their capstone of completing this task-based, SL course.
4. I initially had planned to conduct a focus group interview with the class in the final session. However, the time constraint made it challenging to execute it. The backup plan would be to select three to four students with different levels of English proficiency, time spent in SL, and experiences with language learning in SL. The rationale behind this purposeful sampling is "maximum variation" – enhancing

transferability through sampling a heterogeneous makeup of interviewees with diverse backgrounds and experiences. Following this train of thought, I would have chosen Unessl – who only comes to SL for the course, Korobase – who is highly motivated to learn in SL, and Barrabax – who is less proficient comparing with her counterparts. I might include two more students, such as Mero (another motivated student with an advanced English proficiency) and Emelie (who didn't seem to spend extra time in SL outside the assigned tasks). I'd like to probe more into their attitudes toward and beliefs about doing those task-based projects in SL. For example, did they find those tasks conducive to language learning (or not)? How would they compare doing authentic tasks in SL with RL? How did they perceive using avatars for language learning in a 3D MUVE, as opposed to other Web 2.0 tools, such as Skype or Blackboard? How did they compare the sense of avatar identity in SL with learner identity in a conventional class setting?

5. I felt so touched when meeting Nikhil in SL today. He went, "… btw I have got confidence in RL too…I can speak better than earlier. This is what I feel when I joined college 5 days before today and talked with my friends [in English]". I couldn't be happier to see his actual progress and skill transfer from SL to RL! I rest my case here.

CHECKPOINT

- Imagine you are doing the same tour guiding project with your students in a F2F class setting. Can you identify the benefits and challenges in carrying it out in RL? For example, will there be sufficient resources or inevitable constraints in your planning and student performing the task? How will the task outcomes connect the learning aspects, such as SLA, intercultural competence, etc?
- By the same token, what is your take on conducting this tour guiding project in SL? Would you have done it differently if you were me? For example, would you also ask students to explore SL on their own and find a SIM that is a replica of a famous scenic spot in their home country? What are the technological, pedagogical, and research considerations in your planning and student task performance?

- In my fourth lesson learned, I was planning to use maximum variation as a purposeful sampling strategy to increase transferability of the findings. Have you adopted or considered this sampling approach in your research study? What are other qualitative research approaches you have considered including to ensure the rigour (trustworthiness) in your research design? Share your experience and thoughts with a colleague.

YOUR TASK

- Replicate this final lesson with your class. Depending on the proficiency levels, SL skills, and demographic backgrounds of your students, you may modify the lesson plan by exploring in-world tourist sites first and landmarking a number of SIMs that represent various tourist spots in student home countries before giving them to your students. You may also demonstrate first how to be an SL tour guide to promote tourism for a target country so that students can follow suit. Alternatively, you may invite a colleague or SL contacts to try out this tour guiding project if you haven't got your own SL or F2F class yet.
- Create a digital certificate and customise it so that every student can have their avatar name on it. You can find some free certificate makers available online or simply use Microsoft Office Word to create one (choose one from the "New from Template" under "File"). Once you are happy with the design, upload it to your Inventory Folder. Award it to your students after their task completion.
- Remember to take observation notes and record the session(s) of student task performance. Invite them to discuss with you their first SL tour guiding experience at the end of the project or in the next class. They can also post their learning reflection if it is part of the class assignment.

PART III

WEAVE IT ALL TOGETHER

Chapter 20: Snapshots of my Second Life research   248

Chapter 21: Second Life resources for teaching and research   262

CHAPTER 20

SNAPSHOTS OF MY SECOND LIFE RESEARCH

OVERVIEW

Drawing upon the rich data gleaned from the virtual course and subsequent SL projects, this chapter sketches out the research outputs published in high impact, refereed journals. It demonstrates to readers, particularly novice researchers, how we can teach and research in SL concurrently, flourishing in multiple empirical articles. Rather than reprinting those articles in exhaustive length, this chapter annotates each publication by highlighting its research design and take-away lessons for research and practical implications. Those keen on reading the full text can refer to the original sources provided in this chapter.

Before presenting a curation of my published articles related to SL research and teaching, I would like to give my readers some background information about how these publications reached fruition. Who would have thought a single PhD research project could lead to a great number of publication outlets? For my fellow researchers, we are fully aware that the nature of a full-blown, data-rich research project desires a wide range of outlets to disseminate different aspects of the findings. Given the depth and scope of my PhD study, I wouldn't be able to report all the findings in only one capacity. There were so many interesting and thought-provoking (at least to me) results drawn from the study that I would love to share with other educators and researchers in Applied Linguistics, Teaching English to Speakers of Other Languages (TESOL), Educational Technology, and Language Education. Consequently, I carefully and strategically re-orchestrated my dissertation, parsing the parts that I deemed significant enough to stand alone as a compelling single case. My intention was to tell different stories that could resonate with readers of diverse interests and needs, whilst standing firm on my home base.

Years later, I undertook another grant project on innovative scholarship of learning teaching (iSoLT), under the auspices of Curtin's Teaching Excellence Development Grant (TEDF). Working with my colleagues, I established an SL professional development program to train an English as a second language (ESL) teacher to become a capable SL teacher so she could further help her underachieving, disengaged students retain the passion for learning English. I observed her online teaching in each SL class, documenting the challenges she encountered, strategies she utilised, and reflections she shared with me as her mentor. This project enabled me to report on her journey as an SL novice, and teacher identity shift from a classroom-based teacher to a capable SL educator. Her story was just too unique and inspiring not to be told.

In the following, I present each publication chronologically and thematically, along with a commentary on my current view and reflection on the study. I hope readers will find this guided reading accessible and insightful.

RESEARCH SNAPSHOT 1

Chen, J. C. (2016a). EFL learners' strategy use during task-based interaction in Second Life. *Australasian Journal of Educational Technology*, *32*(3), 1–17. https://doi.org/10.14742/ajet.2306

"Motivated by theoretical and pedagogical concerns that the link between second language (L2) learners' second language acquisition (SLA) and language use in 3D multi-user virtual environments (MUVEs) is still not fully connected in current SLA literature, this study examined the patterns of English as a foreign language (EFL) learners' employment of communication strategies during task-based interaction in Second Life (SL). Nine adult EFL learners worldwide were recruited, and they used their avatars to negotiate meaning with peers in interactional tasks via voice chat in SL. Results reveal that confirmation checks, clarification requests, and comprehension checks were the most frequently used strategies. Other types of strategy use were also discovered, such as a request for help, self-correction, and topic shift – accompanied by a metacognitive strategy and spell-out-the-word that had not been previously documented in task-based research in 3D MUVEs. This study demonstrated that SL could offer an optimal venue for EFL learners' language acquisition to take place and prompt their cognitive processing during task-based interaction. Additionally, 3D multimodal resources afforded by SL provide additional visual support for EFL students' input acquisition and output modifications. A call for more research on voice-based task interaction in 3D MUVEs is also needed" (p. 1).

Commentary

This is my first published SL research article. ☺ I demonstrated how EFL learners used a wide variety of communication strategies to negotiate meaning and resolve breakdowns during task interaction. I found the notion of interaction hypothesis (input, interaction, output) really useful as it helped me develop a coding scheme for discourse analysis of recorded oral samples. Of course, no interaction would have been triggered, and discourse samples gathered, had my students not fully engaged in the four communication tasks: *opinion exchange, information gap, jigsaw and decision making.* I still recall watching them performing each dyad task with their partners, and how exciting it was to really test the hypothesis and see them being "pushed" to use different strategies to negotiate meaning when communication breakdown occurred. More important, using discourse analysis allowed me to generate different types of communication strategy use and see clearly which type weighed more than the others (e.g., confirmation checks > topic shift). It was also reassuring to witness the multimodality, simulated immersion, and spontaneous communication all played out in SL! Did I also mention that my students genuinely had fun without realising that they were using English for meaningful and authentic purposes?

RESEARCH SNAPSHOT 2

Chen, J. C. (2016b). The crossroads of English language learners, task-based instruction, and 3D multi-user virtual learning in Second Life. *Computers & Education, 102,* 152–171. https://doi.org/10.1016/j.compedu.2016.08.004

"English as a foreign language (EFL) learners' task-based practices in 3D multi-user virtual environments are a dynamic avenue that has attracted research attention in current second language acquisition literature. This study explores EFL adult learners' perceptions and language practices in a 10-session, task-based course in Second Life (SL). A full-blown task-based syllabus that capitalised on meaningful real-life tasks was designed and documented in this study. Employing the grounded theory approach and triangulating multiple qualitative data sources, two core themes emerged: factors that influence SL learning experience and effects of task-based instruction on language learning in SL. SL was evidenced as a viable learning environment due to its conspicuous features, immersive and virtual reality, sense of tele- and co-presence. This study implicates that 1) 3D multimodal resources in SL provide EFL learners with visual and linguistic support and facilitate language teaching and learning; and 2) tasks that draw upon SL features, accommodate learners' cultural/world knowledge, and simulate real-life scenarios, can optimise learners' virtual learning experiences" (p. 152).

Commentary

Not trying to be overdramatic, I was extremely ecstatic about having this qualitative study accepted in *Computers & Education* (C&E), one of the top-ranking journals in Educational Technology. Although I was fully aware of its preferable orientation to quantitative, large-scale studies, I decided to aim high just because I wholeheartedly believed this study had the potential to reach a wider readership. My intuition was right as it has been read 2,223 times (ResearchGate) and cited 164 times worldwide (Google Scholar) at the time of writing. In my humble opinion, what makes this heartfelt article appealing to the readers (besides C&E's high-impact and wide readership) is that it tells a compelling story by transporting readers to the virtual class in SL as if they were with those EFL learners every step of the way. Following the ethos of qualitative research loyally, I detailed richly what was going on in this task-based, SL-enabled class, illustrated by vivid task examples, recorded verbatim in student task engagement, and multiple data sources (interviews, surveys, journals, observation notes). Because of these triangulated data, I was able to weave it all together to show that incorporation of task design in a 3D MUVE could make a difference in EFL learners' language acquisition, motivation, and experience. I also highlighted the importance of respecting learners' cultural knowledge and worldviews, and task alignment with real-world tasks as these key elements would make learning more authentic, engaging, and fun. If you have a spare moment, I recommend reading it as I know you would adore it as much as I do.

RESEARCH SNAPSHOT 3

Chen, J. C. (2018). The interplay of tasks, strategies and negotiations in Second Life. *Computer Assisted Language Learning*, *31*(8), 960–986. https://doi.org/10.1080/09588221.2018.1466810

"Driven by interactionist theory and operationalised by task-based interaction, this study aims to investigate EFL learners' task-based negotiation in Second Life (SL), a 3D multiuser virtual environment (MUVE). A group of adult EFL learners with diverse cultural/linguistic backgrounds in L1 participated in this task-based virtual class. Learners used avatars to interact with peers in communication tasks via voice chat. Discourse samples were collected through their oral production to examine their language patterns during negotiated interaction. A framework of negotiation of meaning was employed to code and analyze the transcribed data. Two types of negotiation routine were identified: single-layered trigger-resolution sequence and multi-layered trigger-resolution sequence. Specifically, the interrelationship among task types, negotiation and strategy use was also established in the study: jigsaw task prompted the most instances of negotiation and strategy use, followed by information-gap and decision-making tasks, whereas opinion-exchange task triggered the least. This study suggests that two-way directed tasks with convergent, obligatory, single-outcome conditions will stimulate more cognitive and linguistic processes of negotiation involving interactional modifications-leading to more complex and lengthy negotiation routine. It is concluded that SL as a 3D MUVE is conducive to theoretically-driven, pedagogically-sound, task-based research in language acquisition" (p. 960).

Commentary

This is the sequel of my first SL research article (Chen, 2016a; see above). Recall that the first article focused on the type of communication strategy and the extent to which each strategy type was utilised by my EFL learners. In this article, I shifted my focus to negotiation of meaning during their task interaction. Using Varonis and Gass's (1985) model for analysing the patterns of negotiation of meaning (Triggers, Indicators, Responses, Reactions to Responses) really helped me code the recorded oral discourse samples. I was able to see clearly which type of communication task (*opinion exchange, information gap, jigsaw, and decision making*) stimulated more task-based negotiation, regarding the turns involving negotiation, strategy use, and their interrelationship across tasks. By presenting the associated discourse samples in task negotiation, I provided solid evidence of demonstrating the different levels of negotiation, from only one single-layered sequence (e.g., 4 turns) to a multi-layered one (e.g., 22 turns) before a breakdown was resolved. I really enjoyed coding, analysing, and interpreting the evidence-based data as the process proved how task-based research could be realised and done rigorously in the 3D virtual world, advancing research in second language acquisition (SLA) and computer-assisted language learning (CALL).

RESEARCH SNAPSHOT 4

Chen, J. C. (2020a). The effects of pre-task planning on EFL learners' oral performance in a 3D multi-user virtual environment. *ReCALL, 32*(3), 232–249. https://doi.org/10.1017/S0958344020000026

"Prior research on pre-task planning examines its effects on the quality of second language (L2) learners' planned output. Planning mitigates the cognitive overload placed upon L2 learners' oral performance, thus improving language production. Despite the pedagogical benefits, studies on pre-task planning on L2 learners' oral output are conducted mostly in a lab or class setting. Whether or not similar effects of pre-task planning can be evidenced in three-dimensional (3D) multiuser virtual environments (MUVEs), such as Second Life (SL), is still less explored. Hence, this study investigates whether pre-task planning could enhance the quality and quantity of English as a foreign language (EFL) learners' task-oriented, voice-based outcomes in SL. Nine EFL learners worldwide participated in this 10-session virtual class. Data were collected through students' oral presentations in performing real-life simulated tasks related to their home cultures and interests. Yuan and Ellis's (2003) framework of T-units measures was adopted to analyze their linguistic performance measured by complexity and accuracy. Results indicated that EFL learners showed statistically significant improvement on grammatical complexity on the levels of syntactic complexity and variety (but not on lexical variety) and on linguistic accuracy across all measured levels (error-free clauses/T-units/verb forms). It is suggested that pre-task planning can be seeded in task-based instruction either in a classroom-based or 3D MUVE setting to optimise the quality of learners' linguistic performance. Tasks that are real-world oriented and targeting learners' cultural repertoires and world knowledge also positively impact their virtual learning experiences. These significant implications add new research and pedagogical dimensions to the field of computer-assisted language learning" (p. 232).

Commentary

I have to admit that it is probably one of the most "hardcore", heavily quantitative SLA studies I have ever undertaken. Though trained as a mixed methods researcher, I still find the statistical procedures and analyses quite taxing. That said, I appreciate the whole experience and the fact that I was able to show the link between pre-task planning and its effect on EFL learners' oral output in SL. As most pre-task planning research was conducted in a physical class, this study carved out the 3D path as a viable venue for connecting SLA research to the virtual world. I adopted Yuan and Ellis's (2003) T-unit framework to code and analyse the complexity and accuracy of students' task-based performance as evidenced in the recorded oral discourse samples. It was reassuring to learn that student language outputs did progress qualitatively (the complexity, variety, and accuracy in grammar and sentence structures) and quantitatively (improvement in oral production). As they all participated voluntarily, I was pleasantly surprised that they were fully committed to planning for and completing all the assigned tasks without coercion. If the tasks were boring or not engaging to them, I don't think they would be so engaged and invest their time and effort in this SL class along with their real-life commitments. Seeing their peers deliver each task professionally further motivated them to do as well as their counterparts, if not better. I am pleased that this study contributes to the body of knowledge in how pre-task planning can also be operationalised in the 3D virtual world.

RESEARCH SNAPSHOT 5

Chen, J. C. (2021). The interplay of avatar identities, self-efficacy, and language practices. *Australian Review of Applied Linguistics*, *44*(1), 65–81. https://doi.org/10.1075/aral.19032.che

"This study intends to examine English as a foreign language (EFL) learners' attitudes toward practicing English in Second Life (SL) and to unpack the effects of avatar identities on EFL learners' sense of self-efficacy and language practices. Nine EFL learners worldwide participated in a task-based course in SL, using avatars to carry out SL-related tasks whilst interacting with peers and the teacher via voice chat. Qualitative data were triangulated from multiple sources: learner reflective journals, a post-course survey, and semi-structured interviews. Three major themes emerged: (1) the effects of masked identity on learning, (2) the impact of telepresence and copresence on learning, and (3) the perceived attitudes toward avatar affinity. Findings implicate that the avatar form renders masked identities to safeguard learners' self-efficacy and empower their language practices. It also opens up a research avenue on the impact of avatar identities on language learning and teaching in 3D virtual environments" (p. 65).

Commentary

This is a short and sweet article to wrap up my PhD research. As part of the rich qualitative dataset, I chose to focus on an interesting aspect of avatar identity because previous research had made some positive claims about the benefits of language learning through this virtual dummy. I was curious to know whether the positive impact that avatar identity could have on learners' development of self-efficacy and language use could also be evidenced in my study. I was not disappointed. I witnessed that my students enjoyed changing their avatar appearances and outfits (that might or might not resemble their real-life self) and built a special bond with their avatar presence that represented how they would like to be perceived in front of us. Despite speaking through a virtual dummy, it was still them after all. Some of them (old-timers) even went to great lengths to buy customised clothing for their avatars just because they were not satisfied with the freebie styles. Because they could use their avatar form as a shield, those who tended to be shy in the beginning of class or even in real life gradually gained more confidence in speaking English spontaneously without worrying much about losing face when making grammatical mistakes. When asked whether they thought they could transfer the growing confidence and risk taking in speaking English to real-life situations, a majority believed that they would be able to carry the avatar effect over. In fact, some of them commented that they had felt less shy and willing to take risks in using English in public or class. Nothing could make a teacher happier than seeing the empowerment of learner self-efficacy and improved oral proficiency shine through real practice.

RESEARCH SNAPSHOT 6

Chen, J. C., & Kent, S. (2020). Task engagement, learner motivation and avatar identities of struggling English language learners in the 3D virtual world. *System*, *88*, 102168. https://doi.org/10.1016/j.system.2019.102168

"This study investigated at-risk ESL learners' task performance and attitudes towards a 3D approach of improving their English spoken and written communication skills in Second Life (SL). It documented how these SL "newbies," who had not previously experienced 3D virtual learning, carried out SL-enabled, real-life oriented and interactive tasks. Qualitative data were triangulated from students' weekly blog entries, reflective essay writing and a focus group interview, followed by a thematic analysis approach. Despite the technical glitches impeding the flow of virtual class management and causing communication breakdown, students overall held positive perceptions of the task-based design implemented in SL. Unique SL affordances were found to maximise task execution and engagement, thus fostering more authentic and crosscultural communication, building confidence, boosting motivation, and empowering learners via avatar anonymity. The game factor also transformed a conventional English class into a fun virtual learning playground. Such findings not only highlight pedagogical suggestions for curriculum design and language program improvement, but also implicate both challenges and possibilities of conducting research and teaching at-risk language learners in a 3D sphere" (p. 1).

Commentary

This is the first study borne out by the TEDF grant and my maiden attempt to lead a collaborative project in SL. Drawing upon my specialisation in TBLT and skills in 3D virtual teaching, I met and brainstormed with an ESL teacher (whom you will know more about later) to develop a fully online English Support Program (ESP) in SL. The main reason for revamping the ESP was that students in the program tended to "shut down"' in class as they found the syllabus too grammar-driven, topics too academic-subject heavy, and activities too writing-oriented. Therefore, our goal was to co-design a task-based, SL-enabled syllabus that was needs-based, communication-driven, and game-oriented with hopes to rekindle their passion for English learning whilst enhancing their oral communication skills. Note that none of the students had experience with SL before this experiment, let alone that they were assessed as "at risk" given their lower-level English proficiency that failed to meet the academic entry requirements. So the stakes were quite high and we were also unsure about whether this new take on the original ESP would work for this student cohort. Thank goodness, it worked! Students really enjoyed doing those tasks that were gamified (e.g., helping each other to get out of a 3D Maze), authentic (e.g., interviewing an SL resident), and related to real-life scenarios (e.g., taking a field trip to an art gallery). Not only did the gathered data indicate students' heightened engagement and investment in task completion, the teacher also witnessed the change when some students who were initially reticent in class started to speak more in SL. Despite the technical and administrative challenges encountered in this pilot, we all felt that the end result was rewarding and this innovative syllabus was worth replicating in the program.

RESEARCH SNAPSHOT 7

Chen, J. C. (2020b). Restorying a "newbie" teacher's 3D virtual teaching trajectory, resilience, and professional development through action research: A narrative case study. *TESOL Quarterly, 54*(2), 375–403. https://doi.org/10.1002/tesq.550

"Unique affordances of 3D multi-user virtual environments (e.g., immersive simulation, avatar tele/copresence) have attracted language teachers and researchers to explore the effects of Second Life (SL) on learners' language outcomes and perceptions. Research on such a synergy of language education and virtual learning has suggested learners' heightened motivation, improved communication skills, boosted confidence, and developed avatar identity. Nevertheless, the target population in prior research was predominately language learners; teachers' professional development and beliefs in 3D virtual teaching are relatively under-researched. Motivated by action research, this case study explores how an ESL teacher switched her role from an experienced classroom-based teacher to an SL "newbie" teacher, thus reconstructing her teacher identity and fostering professional growth. Coinciding with narrative inquiry, her verbatim account was documented in her critical reflections in blogging, shadowed and interviewed by the researcher as her mentor. Her story epitomises an online teacher's resilience in striving to equip herself with a new skill set and new understandings of online teaching vis-à-vis challenges encountered, strategies employed, and lessons learned through critical reflections in dialogue blogging. These aspects open a new avenue for research and pedagogy in virtual teacher training and professional development through action research in the 3D virtual environment" (p. 375).

Commentary

This study holds a special place in my heart: I was able to mentor the ESL instructor (see Research Snapshot 6) to transition into virtual teaching from scratch. Whilst a demanding task for me as a researcher and her as an SL newbie, I had fond memories of training her to grasp SL skills, from knowing all the basics (e.g., teleporting, changing avatar appearances) to upskilling all things considered in VR teaching (e.g., sending group chats and notecards, building 3D posters for presentation). Without building these needed skills, teaching in SL would be a moot point. What really moved me was that she trusted me as her mentor, allowed me to shadow her in each SL lesson, and invested her valuable time in keeping a reflection journal for us to debrief on her challenges, strategies, and a-ha moments in SL. Through the approach of narrative inquiry, I was able to "restory" her maiden teaching in SL and transport readers to her SL class and how she rose to the occasion from a classroom teacher to a capable online educator. Her story was so fascinating that I believed it would also inspire many fellow teachers who would like to embark on this SL journey. The truth is, she now can not only teach any mode of class, but also deliver professional development for her colleagues in the same program and beyond. I am deeply grateful to *TESOL Quarterly* for providing me with the space to share her story with a wider readership.

CHECKPOINT

- Consider your current teaching/research context. Which research snapshot do you think will motivate you to follow suit? Why?
- For teachers:

    What challenges do you consider in adopting a task-based syllabus in SL? Why? Do you think teaching in SL will benefit both your professional development and student learning outcomes? How?

- For researchers:

    What challenges do you consider in conducting task-based research in SL? Why? Compare and contrast the research methods, findings, and implications in all the snapshot articles. Discuss your new understandings with your colleagues. How are they different?

YOUR TASK

- Pick any snapshot that interests you and read the full article. Feel welcome to read all the snapshot articles if you are an overachiever. ☺
- For teachers:

    Choose one or two tasks from the syllabus in either snapshot 2 or 6 and see if you can adopt it in your language class conducted in SL. If time permits, you may try out the full-blown syllabus. Keep a teaching journal to reflect on what works and what does not, and how you would improve it next time.

- For researchers:

    Choose one or two snapshot studies that relate to a research context that you are keen to investigate. Replicate the same task-based syllabus and research design and see how they translate into real practice. Document and reflect on your observations in your researcher journal before sharing it with your supervisor or colleagues.

REFERENCES

Chen, J. C. (2016a). EFL learners' strategy use during task-based interaction in second Life. *Australian Journal of Education al Technology*, *32*(3), 1–17. https://doi.org/10.14742/ajet.2306

Chen, J. C. (2016b). The crossroads of English language learners, task-based instruction, and 3D multi-user virtual learning in Second Life. *Computers & Education*, *102*, 152–171. https://doi.org/10.1016/j.compedu.2016.08.004

Chen, J. C. (2018). The interplay of tasks, strategies and negotiations in Second Life. *Computer Assisted Language Learning*, *31*(8), 960–986. https://doi.org/10.1080/09588221.2018.1466810

Chen, J. C. (2020a). The effects of pre-task planning on EFL learners' oral performance in a 3D multi-user virtual environment. *ReCALL*, *32*(3), 232–249. https://doi.org/10.1017/S0958344020000026

Chen, J. C. (2020b). Restorying a "newbie" teacher's 3D virtual teaching trajectory, resilience and professional development through action research: A narrative case study. *TESOL Quarterly*, *54*(2), 375–403. https://doi.org/10.1002/tesq.550

Chen, J. C. (2021). The interplay of avatar identities, self-efficacy and language practices. *Australian Review of Applied Linguistics*, *44*(1), 65–81. https://doi.org/10.1075/aral.19032.che

Chen, J. C., & Kent, S. (2020). Task engagement, learner motivation and avatar identity of struggling English language learners in the 3D virtual world. *System*, *88*, 102168. https://doi.org/10.1016/j.system.2019.102168

Varonis, E. M., & Gass, S. (1985). Non-native/non-native conversations: A model for negotiation of meaning. *Applied linguistics*, *6*(1), 71–90. https://doi.org/10.1093/applin/6.1.71

Yuan, F., & Ellis, R. (2003). The effects of pre-task planning and on-line planning on fluency, complexity and accuracy in L2 monologic oral production. *Applied Linguistics*, *24*(1), 1–27. https://doi.org/10.1093/applin/24.1.1

CHAPTER 21

SECOND LIFE RESOURCES FOR TEACHING AND RESEARCH

OVERVIEW

This final chapter outlines a useful list of hands-on, in-world resources for like-minded readers who consider conducting teaching/research in SL. It summarises the characteristics of each source along with its SL locations (SLurls) for ease of accessing those sites. For example, you will know where to find freebies and save them in the avatar outfit inventory, or how to rez different 3D scenarios (e.g., a cinema) to immerse students in real-life tasks. Teacher researchers who like to start task-based research in SL will also be introduced to some key players in the field and where to find in-world conferences to attend or present at. I conclude with my final thoughts on the overall experience of task-based research and teaching in SL and its future directions.

When I was a newbie teacher, I appreciated having a "cheat sheet" that could highlight and summarise all things considered in teaching and research in SL. This chapter does just that. I have curated a list of useful, free SL resources to give every newbie teacher researcher a jumpstart (Table 21.1—21.5). Note that the list is comprehensive but definitely not exhaustive as I only handpick the resources closely related to language teachers and researchers in our field. You may use this cheat sheet as your home base before getting ready to explore other SL resources and adding them to the list on your own. For now, this sheet will come in handy, especially when you need some fast, discerningly curated information (e.g., a language exchange island or SL researchers).

Concluding, I share my final thoughts on the overall 3D virtual teaching and research experience. I candidly pinpoint the dos and don'ts for SL newbie teacher researchers, such as issues of recruiting student participants, dealing with gatekeeping and ethics, expecting the unexpected (technical malfunctions), improvising lesson plans on the go, honing SL technical and teaching skills, and documenting systematic and consistent data. I hope both teachers and researchers will find your battery charging spot in this coda.

Table 21.1 SL basics and wikis

Source	Weblink	Annotation
Second Life Quickstart	https://community.secondlife.com/knowledgebase/english/second-life-quickstart-r373/#Section__7	This is the go-to place for all SL newbies. As the title rightly suggests, the page provides a step-by-step, reader-friendly guide to help you grasp all the basic skills that you need to function in-world. You will find concrete visual examples that illustrate how to use the SL features from scratch, such as walking, flying, using voice chat, and finding nearby people and friends.
New Resident Island	http://maps.secondlife.com/secondlife/Laws't%20Paradise/219/33/23	As the name entails, this island is particularly for newbies who just joined SL and like to get some more information and tips about how to function better in-world. You will appreciate the generous help and mentorship provided by SL volunteers or old-timers. If they are not around, you can also interact with those tutorials in the most relaxing atmosphere.
Freebie Spots	https://secondlife.com/destinations/howto/freebies	You can never have too many freebies. ☺ Nothing is sweeter than getting free giveaways as a newbie. I found four freebie sites in SL where you can select a wide variety of avatar clothing and appearances, accessories, furniture for your home, and more. In fact, I am pleasantly surprised that "Free Galaxy" still stays strong as many freebie spots that I landmarked a decade ago don't exist anymore. So go and grab a freebie whilst it's still there.
Help Island Public	http://maps.secondlife.com/secondlife/Help%20Island%20Public/128/128/26	This is the island for both new and regular residents alike to learn basic or advanced SL skills such as building, scripting, etc. There are a wide variety of tutorial and demo areas available for residents to brush up on their SL skills. Even better, there is a freebie store for you to pick out goodies for your avatar.
Destination Guide	https://secondlife.com/destinations/	I find this guide really informative and hands-on as it categories all things considered in SL and helps you navigate the boundless destinations in SL and where to find them such as art galleries, virtual campuses, resorts, and even LGBTQ+ friendly spots for the rainbow community.
Events Calendar	https://secondlife.com/events/	You can find any current or upcoming events using the SL Events Calendar, including free language classes, Jazz clubs, DJ concerts, games, and dances, to name a few.
Second Life Knowledge Base	https://community.secondlife.com/knowledgebase/english/	This SL wiki has so much to offer and is contributed to by all the community members, particularly those old-timers who have become SL gurus and can offer newbies their valuable know-how. You can find any information related to SL, ranging from how to make avatar friends and partners (yes, you got it right) or own your first home, to more sensitive topics like dealing with harassment in-world. Reading articles in Knowledge Base is open to anyone; however, you need to use your created SL account name to sign in the SL wiki to ask or reply to the posts in the Forum.

(Continued)

CHAPTER 21
SECOND LIFE RESOURCES FOR TEACHING AND RESEARCH

Table 21.1 SL basics and wikis *(Continued)*

Source	Weblink	Annotation
Second Life Education	https://wiki.secondlife.com/wiki/Second_Life_Education	This wiki page is exclusively for teacher educators who are interested in finding information or using SL for teaching. It provides teaching tips to help teachers get started and points you to useful resources such as educational campuses in SL, SL glossary, and virtual museums. It also showcases some success stories that demonstrate how universities and institutions utilise SL to facilitate teaching and enhance learning, leading to optimal outcomes. You will also get your questions about education answered in the FAQs page, ranging from cost and billing to object building and platform stability.

Table 21.2 Conference and social networking

Source	Weblink	Annotation
Virtual World Best Practices in Education (VWBPE)	https://www.vwbpe.org/	VWBPE is the most long-standing, reputed conference devoted to education in the 3D virtual world. It is held in SL every year (SL time [SLT]) and encourages everyone to present at this friendly and supportive virtual conference. It welcomes both teacher practitioners and seasoned researchers alike to share their current projects, as well as everyone who likes to be inspired or just wants to know more about teaching and learning in the virtual world. Because it promotes collaboration and deeper discussion in the virtual community, VWBPE has attracted around 2,000 educators over 90 countries around the world, and hosted over 200 virtual presentations. Similar to face-to-face (F2F) conferences, they also invite keynote speakers, organise the program book, and recruit volunteers to support the annual conference. I presented my pilot study in this SL conference and received valuable feedback from the attendees. This year marks their 15th anniversary.
SLanguages Symposium	https://www.facebook.com/groups/slanguages/	SLanguages used to hold an annual symposium in SL for language educators to discuss, share, and collaborate on projects in the 3D environments. Whilst it has been replaced by VLanguages (see later), their Facebook group is still active and keeps updating the recent or upcoming events, conferences, and workshops related to language teaching and learning in VR, such as VWBPE.
VLanguages	http://vlanguages.pbworks.com	Language educators will rejoice at this wiki, which builds a tight-knit virtual community to bring together like-minded teachers, researchers, administrators, and instructional designers interested in how to use VR applications to enhance language teaching and learning. A lot of food for thought and resources are generously shared in this wiki.

(Continued)

265

Table 21.2 Conference and social networking (Continued)

Source	Weblink	Annotation
OpenSimulator Community Conference	https://conference.opensimulator.org/about-oscc/	Whilst this annual conference focuses on OpenSimulator (another 3D VR platform), it is open to any type of presentations, keynotes, and social events including but not limited to SL.
Virtual Worlds Education Round Table (VWER)	https://vwer.info/	VWER is another friendly and inclusive forum that has brought like-minded educators in-world since 2008. They meet every Thursday at 12 noon (SLT) and welcome members to discuss thought-provoking issues related to education in VR (e.g., what is metaverse?) and exchange information that is of great interest to educators (e.g., Horizon Report or how to use Holodecks in teaching). They also open the forum to any topic or even hold social gathering in SL to bring members closer.
Second Life for Educators	https://www.facebook.com/groups/sledfire/	This Facebook group provides a space for educators to exchange information on events, teaching resources, training opportunities, freebies, etc., in SL. This is a public group so everyone who is interested in SL or VR can join immediately. Have a good one.
VR & Augmented Reality (AR) Educators	https://www.facebook.com/groups/virtualpioneers	This is also a public group for educators interested in using VR and AR for educational purposes. They also hold different events for members to experiment with new ways of 3D teaching, mentored by seasoned educators.
The Federal Consortium for Virtual Worlds (FCVW)	https://www.facebook.com/groups/FederalConsortiumVW	Whilst this group aims to "improve government collaboration through the use of virtual worlds", members often share best practices, hands-on resources, and upcoming events and conferences held in SL.
Electronic Village Online (EVO)	https://www.facebook.com/groups/electronicvillageonline	Since 2000, EVO has offered free professional development workshops that last for 5 weeks. All the workshops are conducted by volunteers who are seasoned teacher trainers or language educators in VR. Although EVO is geared toward English for speakers of other languages (ESOL) teachers, educators teaching other languages are also welcome to participate in a wide variety of hands-on workshops to upskill their online teaching skills. For example, the most recent one was focused on VR, including how to build in SL and OpenSim.
SIG Virtual Worlds & Serious Games of EuroCALL & CALICO	https://www.facebook.com/groups/SIGvw.gamesEuroCALL/about	This is the final Facebook group that I would like to introduce to the readers. Different from the previous groups, it is particularly targeting language educators and researchers. All the shared posts are VR, AR, or extended reality (XR) related and interest members in the fields of CALL and digital game-based learning. You will also find useful information regarding CALL conferences, in-world events, virtual tours, and call for proposals.

CHAPTER 21
SECOND LIFE RESOURCES FOR TEACHING AND RESEARCH

Table 21.3 Language teaching islands & demonstrations

Source	Weblink	Annotation
VIRTLANTIS	http://maps.secondlife.com/secondlife/EduNation%20III/112/197/2390	VIRTLANTIS is an SL place that I hold dear to my heart. It is a free, virtual island open to all language teachers who like to volunteer offering different language classes, and learners who like to practise any language, be it English, French, German, Chinese, etc. In fact, I attended my first Spanish class there and it was also my home base for my virtual class. Be sure to try their Holodeck feature to rez different role-play scenarios for your class. There is also a Sandbox for you and students to build objects. You can contact Kip Boahn (aka Kip Yellowjackets) if you want to access more resources, offer classes, recruit students, or seek collaboration. It is now located in EduNation Island III (see later).
EduNation Islands (I & III)	http://maps.secondlife.com/secondlife/EduNation/102/190/23	Co-owned by Randall Sadler (aka Randall Renoir) and Heike Philp (aka Gwen Gwasi), EduNation Islands are a nonprofit that offers language educators rich resources and spaces to experiment with their VR language teaching in SL. It is commendable that the islands are maintained by a group of educators who are dedicated to VR teaching and invest their time (even money) to keep the islands active in SL. Whether you are looking for a Sandbox to practice building objects, rezzing Holodeck scenarios for role-plays, seeking telecollaboration opportunities with other educators, or simply exploring simulations in-world, EduNation Islands covers it all. Make sure you landmark them for quicker teleporting.
NTNU Language Island	http://maps.secondlife.com/secondlife/NTNU%20Language%20Island/144/47/23	As part of the technology-enhanced language learning (TELL) laboratory projects housed at the National Taiwan Normal University (NTNU), this SL island provides situated immersive learning opportunities for anyone interested in learning Mandarin Chinese, or local Taiwanese elementary school students learning English. For example, learners can simulate real-life tasks in different scenarios built in the island, ranging from shopping in a supermarket or dining at a restaurant or night market.
Chinese Island	http://maps.secondlife.com/secondlife/Monash%20University%202/201/176/26	This is another virtual island dedicated to Chinese language teaching and learning. It is housed by the Chinese Studies Program at Monash University, Australia. Whilst the island is designed for teaching staff and students at Monash, it is also accessible to the public. All the in-world facilities, learning materials, and activities are developed following the principles of technology-enhanced TBLT. If you are interested in some concrete lesson plans and virtual resources used in the Chinese Island, feel welcome to contact the project lead, Scott Grant (Scott. Grant@monash.edu).

(Continued)

Table 21.3 Language teaching islands & demonstrations *(Continued)*

Source	Weblink	Annotation
International Regions	https://secondlife.com/destinations/international	I purposefully single out this resource in case you miss it on the Destination Guide. Whilst all the in-world spots are not designed with language teaching and learning in mind, the authentic culture vibes and real-world embodiments that appeal to both native speakers and language learners alike have great potential for language education. All the international regions allow avatar visitors to be immersed in the target culture and local attractions whilst making friends with people speaking the target language as a lingua franca. You will be surprised to find many language spots built in SL, ranging from Japanese, French, Spanish, and Italian to less commonly taught languages such as Turkish, Polish, and Norwegian.
Start Living English as a Second Language (SLESL)	http://slesl.net/index.html	English language teachers who are just starting to explore teaching in SL will find materials and sample lesson videos shared in this website particularly useful and informative. The developer, Barbara McQueen (aka Barbara Novelli), also has her own YouTube channel to demonstrate those sample lessons in SL: https://www.youtube.com/watch?v=IB1W8oHS-W4. Happy watching.
Cypris Chat	http://maps.secondlife.com/secondlife/Mallo/194/139/22	Similar to VIRTLANTIS, Cypris Chat is a nonprofit SL community for anyone who likes to practice, learn, and teach English. It is located in the Cypris Village in-world and offers free lessons, events, discussions, resources, and fun activities for English language learners and teacher volunteers. Some of my former students were also recruited from Cypris Chat and I am so pleased to know that they are still active in-world even after over a decade and keep providing free and fun English learning opportunities.

Table 21.4 Academic publishing

Journal	Weblink	Annotation
Language Learning & Technology	https://www.lltjournal.org/	The first half of the publishing outlets are flagship journals in the field of computer-assisted language learning (CALL) that connect applied linguistics and language education to learning technologies. They welcome studies related to VR, AR, or mixed reality (MR), and I personally have published in some of them (e.g., *ReCALL*, *System*, and *CALL*). The second half of the journals focus exclusively on VR-related studies across disciplines, such as education, health sciences, arts, business and media. You will find a lot of novel studies framed by research-sound theories (e.g., digital game-based learning) or using cutting-edge VR/AR/MR tools (e.g., metaverse headsets or tracking technologies). For researchers who like to aim high and publish in Q1 journals, I am pleased to add that most CALL-related journals on the list are Q1, Scopus, or SSCI indexed (e.g., *Language Learning & Technology* or *System*). *Virtual Reality* (https://www.springer.com/journal/10055) is also a high-impact, Q1 journal. So make sure you read their aims and scope as well as submission guidelines before choosing one for which your study is a good fit.
Computer-Assisted Language Learning	https://www.tandfonline.com/action/journalInformation?show=aimsScope&journalCode=ncal20	
ReCALL	https://www.cambridge.org/core/journals/recall	
CALICO Journal	https://journals.equinoxpub.com/CALICO	
System	https://www.journals.elsevier.com/system	
CALL-EJ	http://callej.org/	
The Journal of Teaching English with Technology	https://tewtjournal.org/	
International Journal of Computer-Assisted Language Learning and Teaching	https://www.igi-global.com/journal/international-journal-computer-assisted-language/41023	
Virtual Reality	https://www.springer.com/journal/10055	
Journal of Virtual Worlds Research	https://jvwr.net/	
Journal of Virtual Studies	https://jovs.urockcliffe.press/	
International Journal of Virtual Reality	https://ijvr.eu/	
International Journal of Virtual and Augmented Reality	https://www.igi-global.com/journal/international-journal-virtual-augmented-reality/145080	

Table 21.5 SL researchers and specialists

Researcher	Title	Profile
Randall Sadler (aka Randall Renoir in SL)	Associate Professor of Linguistics at the University of Illinois at Urbana-Champaign and Director of the Illinois ESL and TESL Programs, USA. Co-owner of the EduNation Islands in SL.	https://linguistics.illinois.edu/directory/profile/rsadler
Mark Peterson	Associate Professor of Foreign Language Acquisition & Education and Founder of the Peterson Lab at Kyoto University, Japan.	https://petersonlab.weebly.com/
Jessamine Cooke-Plagwitz	Associate Professor of German & Applied Linguistics, Coordinator of Foreign Language Instructional Technology Graduate Certificate Program, and Director of Undergraduate Studies at Northern Illinois University, US.	https://www.niu.edu/clas/world-languages/about/directory/cooke-plagwitz.shtml

(Continued)

Table 21.5 SL researchers and specialists *(Continued)*

Researcher	Title	Profile
Yu-Ju Lan	Distinguished Professor in the Department of Chinese as a Second Language at National Taiwan Normal University (NTNU) and Principle Investigator of the NTNU TELL Lab, Taiwan.	http://tell.tcsl.ntnu.edu.tw/index.php?inter=people&did=39
Scott Grant	Lecturer of Chinese Studies and Member of Monash Data Futures Institute at Monash University, Australia.	https://research.monash.edu/en/persons/scott-grant
Mats Deutschmann	Professor in English at the School of Humanities, Education and Social Sciences, Örebro University, Sweden.	https://www.oru.se/english/employee/mats_deutschmann
Judith Ann Molka-Danielsen	Professor in Informatics and Information Sciences, Department of Informatics, Molde University College, Norway.	https://www.himolde.no/personer/log/vit/molka/index.html
Kristi Jauregi Ondarra	Associate Professor of Language and Education, Utrecht Institute of Linguistics, Utrecht University, Netherlands.	https://www.uu.nl/staff/mkjauregiondarra/Profile
Silvia Canto	Assistant Professor of Spanish, Institute for Cultural Inquiry, Utrecht University, Netherlands.	https://www.uu.nl/staff/SCanto
Luisa Panichi	EFL Lecturer in the Centro Linguistico, Università di Pisa, Italy. Coordinator of the EU-funded AVALON project.	https://people.unipi.it/luisa_panichi/
Susanna Nocchi	Lecturer in Italian and CALL, School of Languages Law and Social Science, Technological University Dublin, Ireland. Section editor of the *Journal of Virtual Studies*.	https://www.tudublin.ie/explore/schools-and-disciplines/business-law-and-languages/languages-law-social-sciences/people/academic-staff/languages/susan-nanocchi.html
Vance Stevens	Founder of Learing2gether.net, Section Editor of On the Internet of TESL-EJ (2002-2021), and Coordinator of TESOL/CALL-IS Electronic Village Online (EVO).	https://learning2gether.net
Heike Philp (aka Gwen Gwasi)	CEO of Let's Talk Online SPRL, Immersive Language Education Specialist, Teacher Trainer of the EU-funded Projects (LANCELOT, AVALON, CAMELOT, GUINEVERE), and Co-owner of EduNation Islands in SL.	http://www.letstalkonline.com/
Barbara McQueen (aka Barbara Novelli)	Course Developer of Higher Education Consulting and SLESL.net	https://www.linkedin.com/in/barbara-mcqueen-409a2320/
Karelia Kondor (aka Karelia Kondor)	Teacher and Manager in a UK Secondary School. Avid Language Learner (Italian, German, French) in SL and Owner of All London & MFLResouces in EduNation I (http://maps.secondlife.com/secondlife/EduNation/208/52/23).	https://kareliakondor.wordpress.com/ https://www.youtube.com/watch?v=mdkz59vfn3g

FINAL TWO CENTS (MAYBE MORE)

Although other metaverse environments via AR or XR can also create a fully immersive 3D experience, VR headsets (e.g., Oculus Quest or HTC Vive) are required and generally pricey (except for Google Cardboard). Unless your institution can afford purchasing those headsets for every single student, I personally would favour gadgets that are "cheap and cheerful", or even better, free of charge. Maybe it is just me but I also find wearing those VR headsets sometimes makes me feel dizzy or even nauseous. Compared with its AR/XR counterparts, SL still does the job creating a sense of immersive tele-/co-presence without users spending a fortune. From the standpoint of sustainability, it is relatively more affordable and accessible to all the educational stakeholders. By using a regular desktop, laptop, or even a mobile phone, we can build 3D learning experiences for our students. I also prefer a more sophisticated, aesthetic feel of avatar presence in SL that looks more like a "human" than the robot-like avatars generated by some metaverse software. Your personalised avatar is still virtually representing who you are and how you would like to be perceived by others. In my case, I still care as much about my virtual self-image and the way my avatar dresses as my true self in the real world. It is all about self-/virtual identity after all.

When it comes to teaching in SL, anything can happen. Sometimes an avatar stranger might accidentally teleport or walk to your class site unless it is a private location only accessible to the registered members. This realness also makes SL resemble RL – expecting the unexpected. Noteworthy is that teachers should also do their "lesson planning" before the virtual class by navigating and exploring in-world to find out some useful sites for field trips, Sandbox for object building, and Holodecks for changing RL scenarios for student role-play. You are advised to landmark those good sites you found to teleport the class more efficiently. That said, some SL locations that you already landmarked might disappear when you want to visit again, partly because the island owner might decide to stop paying for SL land fees. Please don't feel deflated; this is how it goes in SL. Just move on to discover other replacements and you might be surprised by the newfound locations. Equally important is to first contact the land owners about your intention to access their facilities for research or teaching purposes. You need to pass their gatekeeping; otherwise, you may not be able to access the island or be restricted to limited resources. That said, if budget permits, you might consider purchasing some useful 3D items to create fun and interactive activities. Recall the 3D Maze I introduced in Chapter 2 when exemplifying a task-based syllabus that the ESL teacher and I co-designed? 3D items like this can be reused for your future classes and they are usually not too expensive, either.

I can't stress enough how crucial it is to first get ethical approval from your institution and consent from your student participants (in class or/and SL) should you decide to conduct research with them. Some may argue that the avatar handle names already anonymise real-life identity, making it unlikely for researchers to reveal it. Hence, participant confidentiality is ensured. I beg to differ: Remember that we are still dealing with "human subjects" even though we can only see and interact with them through their avatar form. All the information they are sharing and digital data they left in-world still belong to them as "informants". The rule of thumb is to inform your SL participants at the outset that their participation is completely voluntary without coercion, what is expected of them, and what benefits and risks are involved. This is the same code of conduct we researchers abide by when dealing with participants in F2F settings. Please refer to Chapter 5 again to see how I gathered informed consent from my participants before I started the pretest. Nowadays, some institutions might approve of using an online survey format for participants to tick off the box and type in their avatar name in lieu of a paper format. Please consult with your Institutional Review Board (IRB).

In a similar vein, recruiting student participants can be quite tricky sometimes. Of course, it would be convenient if you already have your own class in real life. Then you can incorporate SL in your lesson planning and may even start with just one lesson rather than a full-blown syllabus that takes the whole semester to complete. If you have a cross-cultural or telecollaborative project in mind that requires a partner school or class in another country, it is vital to arrange and sort out the logistics with the partner teacher beforehand. You can reach out to language teachers in-world or contact SL researchers who may be interested in collaborating with you (see Table 21.5 SL researchers and specialists from the list in this chapter). On the other end of spectrum is recruiting participants at random by sending out the project information through SL groups that you have joined, similar to what I did for my study (i.e., convenience and snowball sampling). However, sorting out the class time that can accommodate everyone's time difference is no easy task. You may use Doodle or a quick survey to gather their time/date preferences and go with the majority vote. It is challenging but still manageable (see Chapter 4), and teaching a student cohort with culturally/linguistically diverse backgrounds is just priceless.

After going through the tutorials in SL and this book, you may co-teach with a like-minded colleague of yours or reach out to one in VIRTLANTIS – if you are still not confident about teaching in SL by yourself. It is what I did in my pilot study. Having a colleague teaching side by side with you can definitely bolster your confidence level, honing your SL teaching techniques. Along with following my task-based syllabus in this book, you may bounce off ideas with colleagues on task design that are more tailored to the learning interests and needs of your students. Be bold and creative; also remember to consider SL features and how they can optimise real-life task simulation and heighten learner engagement and motivation.

Have I mentioned the feeling of exhilaration coursing through your veins when seeing students have so much fun doing your tasks and immersing themselves in SL without worrying about grammar or making mistakes? Have I also mentioned the excitement of seeing them engaged in simulating real-life tasks in SL whilst using the language spontaneously? You will soon find your own proud teacher moment for always challenging yourself by going above and beyond. When you are ready to share some of your best practices, research findings, or even pitfalls in your maiden teaching in SL, I highly recommend presenting them in in-world conferences, such as the *Virtual World Best Practices in Education* held in SL every year. You will get valuable feedback from and be inspired by seasoned SL educators around the world. I have learned so much from in-world workshops or conference presentations because there is always something new or inspiring that I can take away.

My final thought is to keep a reflection journal as you go. In hindsight, my personal blogging benefited me tremendously as a teacher researcher. I still remember jotting down quick observation notes in each SL session and fleshed them out as soon as I exited SL, just because my memory was still fresh and could serve me well. Blogging allowed me to critically reflect on my lesson delivery, zooming on my strengths and weaknesses in tandem with student reactions to the tasks undertaken in SL. I was able to have a deep, honest dialogue with myself, picking myself up when feeling deflated, or patting myself on the back when lessons went smoothly as planned. It was as therapeutic as I could get and carried me throughout the ups and downs in my SL journey. Those teaching episodes and reflections later became a useful audit trail, providing solid evidence of consistent data collection and researcher reflexivity. For my fellow teachers, you can take a step further and create a class blog for your students to reflect on their learning progress and task-based performance after each SL session as part of the assignments (e.g., learner journal). This allows you to build rapport and dialogue with your students beyond the class walls. Similarly, my fellow researchers can tap into this blogging space as another data source. Along with using screen capture software (e.g., Camtasia) to record each virtual session, I find it useful to take snapshots of any in-world activities that surprise or interest you, and save them into your SL inventory. Of course, public chats, group chats, or IMs that you send to the class can be automatically recorded as transcripts for you. Integral to digital data mining, these are all important data sources that you can gather and triangulate with other types of data, such as focus group interviews or surveys.

> **FINAL CHECKPOINT**
>
> - After reading through my final two cents, what struck you as something that you haven't considered in teaching or research in SL? Do you agree or disagree with these suggestions?
> - What are the pros and cons of having your own class and conducting the SL sessions in a physical lab versus recruiting student participants in-world and teaching remotely?
> - Do you think keeping a teaching journal (or blog) really makes a difference in improving the quality of your teaching? If you are a teacher trainer or supervisor, what can you benefit from having student teachers keep an SL teaching log? Will you also dialogue with them by commenting on their journal entries?

CODA

There are many VR platforms that also can create situated and immersive experiences for teaching and learning besides SL. Indeed, your 3D journey does not just end in SL. On the contrary, your teaching and research practices in SL will serve as a test drive that equips you well to try out other similar platforms, such as OpenSim. Later on, you may take a step further to experiment with AR, MR, or XR for educational purposes. Having said that, I truly appreciate having this opportunity to be your SL tour guide and hopefully you have enjoyed your 3D ride with me. If you run into me in-world, feel free to say hi or IM me (aka UnicornG Luminos) as I am keen to know more about your SL experience after reading this book and giving it your own shot. Who knows, we may even collaborate on some interesting research or teaching projects in-world. To wrap up this monograph, I went back to my very first blog post (03/10/2010) when I just started experimenting with SL for my pilot study. It conjures up many fond memories and sits rightly at the ethos of the book. I can't think of a better way to end our journey than bringing us back to how we started – teaching and researching in SL as a newbie:

> Another note I'd like to add here is what drove me to the SL world. Don't get me wrong. I am not a game player, AT ALL. Playing online games is definitely not my thing. Never in a million years did I think I'd officially become a MMORPG player. But when I first heard of SL back in early 2008, I was like, "WOW, it's so awesome! I wonder how English language learners can also benefit from this 3D virtual world. Maybe it could be a new fertile ground for my dissertation research?" So I pushed myself to become a MMORPG player and get my hands really dirty with SL. I have to be perfectly honest that I was totally terrified and frustrated the first time entering this overwhelming 3D world. The learning curve of SL was far steeper than I had expected. Too much to learn and practice, much less get a hang of it. So I was intimidated by it a bit, wondering if I could really carry out my project in SL. Nevertheless, seeing the potential that SL can offer brought me back to this virtual sphere again. I tried to attend several SL workshops offered by Sloan-C Consortium to hone my SL skills and conquer my fear. After the training in several workshops and thanks to the new Viewer 2 version that has made SL more user-friendly, I finally felt a bit more comfortable being an SL resident and started to see the possibility of me conducting my research study in SL. I can still vividly remember how exhilarating it was when I built my first object in SL (or in SL term, "to rez"). Everything seems possible in SL, depending on how far you can release your imagination and creativity. Oh, forgot to mention, my avatar in SL is a female because I wanted to see how wearing a different gender skin feels like and I can always switch back to a male avatar role at my disposal.
>
> (UnicornG Luminos, Blog Post, 03/10/2010)

YOUR FINAL TASK

- Bookmark a virtual conference held in SL from the list of Conference and Social Networking (see Table 21.2) and try to attend or present at their conference next year. From the same list, join at least one Facebook group (e.g., VWER) and start making your first post and participating in their regular events.

- For researchers:

    Start your (first) research project in SL and aim for publishing your findings in one of the recommended journals from the Academic Publishing list (see Table 21.4). Make sure you read the scope and submission guidelines before deciding on the most suitable outlet for your study. Also consider reaching out to an SL researcher from the list (see Table 21.5) and seeking advice or collaboration opportunities.

- For teachers:

    It's time to hit the ground running. If you have completed your previous task in Chapter 20, great, then start exploring some of the Language Teaching Islands from the list (see Table 21.3) and designing your next syllabus so it can capitalise on those virtual resources (e.g., Holodeck or Sandbox) and facilitate the task delivery. You may also consider consulting an SL specialist from the list (see Table 21.5) and seeking telecollaboration opportunities. They might connect you to other like-minded teachers who are keen to co-teach a language course with you. This may turn into an action research project. Have fun!

- If you can, please add one additional source to each category on the list. That is how you expand on it and make it your own "SL cheat sheet".

INDEX

Note: - Page number in *italics* for figure and **bold** for table.

3D display board *109*
3D menu booklet *128*
3D multi-user virtual environments (MUVEs) 4, 6, 7, 250–251, 253–254, 258
3D multi-user virtual learning 251–252
3D objects 15, 39, 44, 53, 76–78, 99, 220–221
3D painting 200
3D simulation 11, 14
3D virtual teaching 27, 258–260, 263
3D virtual world 4, 8, 16, 152; English language learners in 257–258; multiplayer gaming environments 11; technology-mediated TBLT in 40

action research 258–260
affordance 4, 8, 12–13, 15, 27, 39, 45, 257, 258
Altberg, E. xvii, xx
Applied Linguistics 249
arts 189–195, 197–205
augmented reality (AR) 6, 11, 12, 243, 271; *see also* extended reality (XR); mixed reality (MR); virtual reality (VR)
Australasian Journal of Educational Technology 250
Australian Review of Applied Linguistics 256
authentic: communication 15, 29, 43, 257; interaction 73; language 35, 40; real-life tasks 14; stimulate 31; target-language speaking environments 15; target task samples 34; task interaction 34
avatar 10–11, 17–18; anonymity 257; appearances and outfits 69–71, *70–71*, 177, *178*; expressiveness 53; identities 17–18, 256–258; learner 15; movements 230; non-binary 54; socialise 13; updating profile *65*; using IM function 60, *60*; walk/run/fly *58*
"Avatar" (movie) 17

basic account 10
blog/blogging: arts 189–195, 197–205; charade activity 147–153, *148*; chat transcript 121–133; digital poster 147–153; greetings 99–105; guessing name 147–153; holiday/festival poster 147–166; jobs 207–215; learning reflection 121–133; music 169–175; oral presentations 113–118; posttest 217–227; pretest 91–96, *92*; role-play activity 101–102, 135–145, *140*, *141*; show-and-tell presentations 107–111, *109*; SL teaching 85–88, *86*; sports 177–187; technical issues 155–166; text chat 135–145; travel and farewell party 229–245

camera controls 58, *59*
Cameron, J. 17
charade activity 147–153, *148*
chat log 73, 126, 131, 135, 158–159, 163, 173, 183, 186, 191–192, 194, 215; *see also* text chat
cheat sheet 263
Clarke, J. 17
class wiki 103, *103*
cognitive interactionist theory 37
collaborative: gaming discourse 213; interactions with peers 17; perks 16; problem-solving 40, 44; task 7, 39, 43
communication: authentic 15, 29, 43, 257; breakdown 31, 36, 220, 224, 251, 257; cross-cultural 189; multimodal 27, 40; strategies 31–33, 36, 40, 94, 164, 215, 219–220, 224, 250–251, 253; tasks 32, 254
computer-assisted language learning (CALL) 254
computer-mediated communication (CMC) environment 12–13
Computers & Education (C&E) 251–252
convergent (closed) tasks 32, 33, 40, 223, 253
Cooke-Plagwitz, J. 17
copresence 18, 40, 44, 165, 256, 258
corrective feedback 31, 36, 39
creativity 11, 13, 44, 187, 275

279

cross-cultural communication 189; *see also* communication
cultural heritage 47, 107, *115*
culturally and linguistically diverse (CaLD) 15, 44, 111

decision making 93, 217–218, 222–223, 225, 251, 253–254
Dede, C. 7, 17
DeMers, M. 12
digital certificate *241*
digital divide 3, 5, 6, 19n1
digital game-based learning (DGBL) 4, 6–9, 213; *see also* game-based learning
digital game design 7
digital mania 5
digital natives 5–6, 11, 16–17
digital poster 102, *109*, *115*, 147, *148*, *151*, 156, *156*, *179*, 191; *see also* blog/blogging
digital technologies 7–8
divergent (open) tasks 32–33
Doughty, C. 38–39
Duff, P. 32

Educational Technology 249
Ellis, R. 29–30, 33–34, 36–37, 254–255
English as a foreign language (EFL) 6, 108, 250, 251, 256; *see also* language
English as second language (ESL) 42, 249; *see also* language
English language learners 251–252
English Support Program (ESP) 258
experiential learners 4
extended reality (XR) 12, 271, 274; *see also* augmented reality (AR); mixed reality (MR); virtual reality (VR)

focus on form(s) 36, **37**, 38, 108
focus on meaning 30
foreign language education 14
Fortnite 6
freebies **46**, 71, 81, *143*, 215, 263, **264**, 266
fun 8, 16–17, 42–44, 126, 142, 152, 194, 218, 257, 271, 273

game-based learning 213; *see also* digital game-based learning (DGBL)
gamification 7, 9
Ganem-Gutierrez, G. A. 18
gap 30; *see also* information gap
Gass, S. 253
Gee, J. P. 7–8
Generation Alpha 4–6
Generation Y 4
Generation Z 4–6
Global Kids 12
González-Lloret, M. 39–40, 42
Google Docs 87, *87*, 88, 89, 197
greetings 99–105
griefers 16, 74, 128
Guidebook 56, 67

Halo effect 225
Hawthorne effect 225
Holodecks 16, 76–77, *77*, 135, 140, *140*, 145, 271
home culture 44, 103, 229, 239, 243, 254
Horizon Report: 2009 K-12 Edition 11–12, 20n7

ice-breaking activity 100–101, *101*
identity 10, 17–18, 70, 271; *see also under* avatar
immersion 15, 40, 104, 126, 169, 186, 202
immersive learning 183, 200, 231
immersive mediated interaction 6
immersive simulation 14, 17, 236, 243
Imprudence Viewer 96
independent-goal tasks 32; *see also* divergent (open) tasks
information-age mindset 5
information gap 32, 40, 93, 220
innovation and scholarship of learning and teaching (iSoLT) 249
input 16, 181–182; elaborate and rich 39; language 186, 213; multimodal 16; refine 31; simple **38**; in target languages 15
instant messages (IM) 58–60, *60*, 101
Institutional Review Board (IRB) 272
interactive tasks 31–33

International Virtual Collaboration Space
  project 12
interplay of avatar identities 256–257
interplay of tasks 253–254
in-world 13, 15–16, 54, 56, *138*; activities 273; conferences 273; landmark *63*; location 10–11; media 62; object 60, 77; region 11; walk/run/fly 57; workshops 273

jigsaw 32, 40, 93, 217, 219–220, 223, 251

Kluge, S. 16

landmarking 62, *63*
language: authentic 35, 40; input 186, 213; output 43, 152, 200; teachers 5–6; *see also* English as a foreign language (EFL); English as second language (ESL); second language (L2)
language education 3, 5, 6, 8, 14–19, 249; foreign 14; knowledge co-construction/reconstruction in 39; online 39; Second Life (SL) in 14–18; TBLT in 28
learner internal syllabus 44
learner motivation 257–258
learning by doing 7, 38–39, 43
learning styles 5–6, 8, 19n2
lesson planning 271, 272
Linden dollars 10, 13, 54, 172
Linden Lab 9–10, 13–14, 17, 53–54
Long, M. 28, 32, 34–35, 38–39, 42
Lost Ark 6

massively multiplayer online role-playing games (MMORPGs) 6, 8, 11
Mayrath, M. 16
metaverse 11, **266**, **269**, 271
mixed reality (MR) 12; *see also* augmented reality (AR); extended reality (XR); virtual reality (VR)
modify output 31
Moffat, D. C. 16
multi-layered trigger-resolution sequence 253–254
multimodal: 3D 16, 250, 252; communication 27, 40; features 44; features of SL 15; input 16; input enhancement **45–46**; MUVE 14; output reinforcement 16; ways of delivering curricula 5
music 169–175

needs analysis 34–36, 40, **41**, 48
negotiation 93
negotiation of meaning 30–33, 35, 37, 43–44, 218–221, 253
non-binary avatar 54
non-linguistic repertoire 44, 46
non-verbal gestures 10
Notecards 72, *72*, *94*, 94–95, *95*, *100*, 101, *102*
notecard worksheet 72, *116*, *149*, *181*, *190*, *214*
Nunan, D. 28, 35

object building 16, **46**, 47, 53, 77–82, *79*, *80*
old-school teaching 5
one-way information gap (open-oriented) 32, 220; *see also* divergent (open) tasks; independent-goal tasks
one-way tasks 32–33
online language education 39
OpenSim **266**, 274
opinion exchange task 33, 93, 217, 251
oral presentations 113–118
Ortega, L. 39, 42
output: L2 learners' planned 254; language 27, 43, 152, 200; modify 31; multimodal 16; refine 33

Pacific Time Zone (PST) 89n1
Peterson, M. 40
Petrakou, A. 16
Pica, T. 32
positive competitiveness 213
positive peer pressure 230
PowerPoint (PPT) presentation 114
premium account 10
Prensky, M. 3, 5
pre-task planning 254–255
pretest 91–96, *92*

281

primitive objects (prims) 10
private text chat 60; see also text chat
problem-solving 5, 7, 27, 31, 33, 39–40, 43–44
public chat 14, 121, 122, 123, 127, 135, 136, 147, 151, 158, 173, 181, 186, 190, 222, 231, 236
public text chat 10, 59, 109

real-life (RL) tasks 3, 7–8, 10, 13–14, 18, 39–40, 43, 45, 47, 95, 132, 200, 251, 273
real-world relevance 43
ReCALL 254
refine input 31
refine output 33; see also output
resident 10–11; see also Second Life (SL resident)
rez 76–77, 81–82, 145, 189, 215, 263, **267**, 275
Riley, L. 16
role-play activity 16, 109, 135–145, *140*, 145, *141*, 145, 271

Sandbox 78, 81, 102, 108, 113, 155, 215
second language (L2) 250
second language acquisition (SLA) 8, 28, 181, 250, 254
Second Life (SL) xvii; 3D multi-user virtual learning in 251–252; academic publishing **269**; account registration and installation 54–56, *55*; advanced skills 67–82; advantages of 13; basics and wikis **264**–**265**; basic skills 57–67; blog post 85–88, *86*; camera controls 58, *59*; changing avatar appearances and outfits 69–71, *70*, *71*; changing environment setting 65, *66*; changing profile 63–64, *65*; conference and social networking **265**–**266**; controlling in-world media 62, *63*; conversation logs and transcripts 73; defined 9–11; features and logistics 53–82; group setup 73–76, *74*, *75*, *76*, *77*; Holodecks 76–77, *77*; importance of 11–14; instant message (IM) 58–60, *60*; interacting with objects 60–60, *61*; landmarking 62, *63*; in language education 14–19; language teaching

and learning in 3–19; language teaching islands **267**–**268**; lesson plans 44, 99, 272; log into 56; newbie 53, 54, 56, 70, 91–92, 257, 259, 263, 275; Notecards 72, *72*; object building 77–82, *79*, *80*; researchers and specialists **269**–**270**; research snapshot 249–261; resident 10–11, 15, 17, 27, 47, 56, 70, 127, 275; resources for teaching and research 263–276; snapshot 62–63, *64*; strategies and negotiations in 253–254; task-based interaction in 250–251; task-based language teaching (TBLT) 27–48; teaching 85–88, *86*; technology-mediated TBLT in 38–42; Teen 10; teleporting 67–69, *68*, *69*; text chat 58–60, *59*, *60*; voice chat 58–60, *61*; walk/run/fly 57–58, *57*–*58*; Welcome Island 56, *56*
Second Life Time (SLT) 87, 89n1, 155
Second Life Viewer 54, *55*
shared-goal tasks 32
show-and-tell presentations 102, 107–111, *109*, 113, 114, 177; see also blog/blogging
simple input **38**
SIMs (simulators) 15
simulation: 3D simulation 11, 14; gaming 7; immersive 14, 17, 236, 243; of RL tasks 40, 200, 273
single-layered trigger-resolution sequence 253–254
situated learning 6
Skehan, P. 29–30
Sky Sculpture Gallery 189, 191, 197
SL-enabled, task-based syllabus **45**–**46**, 45–48
SL features 43, *56*, 273; salient 40; simulated and animated 203; teleporting 67, *68*
SL locations (SLurls) 69, *69*, 136, 263
spontaneous 15–16, 29, 32–34, 36–37, 45, 67, 142, 201
sports 177–187
Starry Starry Night 189–190, *190*

task(s): collaborative 7, 39, 43; communication 32, 254; convergent (closed) 32; defined 28–31; design 30–32, 36–37, **38**, 40, 42–47, 63, 86, 113, 220, 224, 226, 273; divergent

(open) 32; engagement 44, 257–258; independent-goal 32; of information gap 93; interactive 31–33; interplay of 253–254; one-way 32; open-oriented 32; operationalising 42–48; principles 43–44; selection 44–45; sequencing 225; shared-goal 32; SL-enabled, syllabus **45–46**, 45–48; type 31
task-based instruction 251–252
task-based interaction 35, 41, 43, 215, 250–251
task-based language teaching (TBLT) 27–48, 135, 220; methodological principles of 39; overview 27; task-based syllabus design **37**; technology-mediated 38–42
task-based syllabus 27, 33–37, **38**, 40, 43, **45–46**, 45–47, 251, 271
Teaching English to Speakers of Other Languages (TESOL) 249
Teaching Excellence Development Grant (TEDF) 249
teaching in 3D virtual environments 4
technical glitches 16, 53, 107, 155, 218, 257
Teen Second Life 10
teleport/teleporting 10–11, 67–69, *68, 69*, 123, 197, 271
telepresence 18–19, 256
TESOL Quarterly 258–260
text chat: blog/blogging 135–145; log 126, 135–136; private *60*; public 10, *59*, 109; Second Life (SL) 58–60, *59, 60*

Trinder, K. R. 16
two-way information gap (closed-oriented) 32, 40; *see also* convergent (closed) tasks; shared-goal tasks

Varonis, E. M. 253
VIRTLANTIS 86, 88, 91, 135, 140, 155, **267**, 272
virtual field trips 13, 44, 132, 135, *170*
virtual identity 10, 17–18, 70, 271; *see also* avatar
virtual language learning 189
virtual reality (VR) 11, 12, 252, 271, 274
voice breaking up 93
voice chat 10, 12–13, 58–60, *61*, 135, 152, 183, 222, 236

Welcome Island 54, *56*, 56–57, 70
What Video Games Have to Teach Us About Learning and Literacy (Gee) 7
Willis, D. 34
Willis, J. 28, 34
world (background) knowledge 31, 34, 44, 169, 252, 255
World of Warcraft (WoW) 6, 11

Yuan, F. 254–255

zone of proximal development (ZPD) 104, 192